AF575947

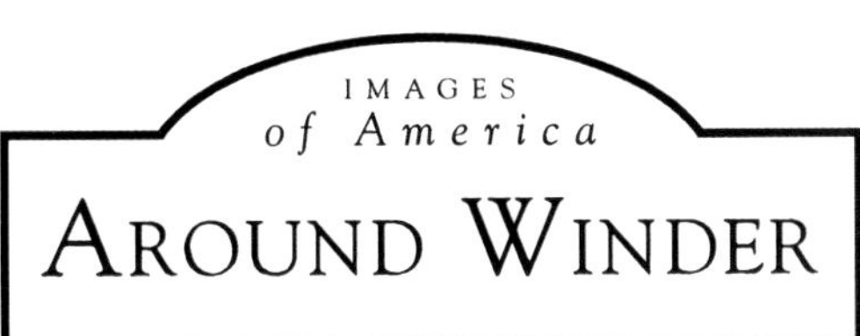
IMAGES
of America
AROUND WINDER

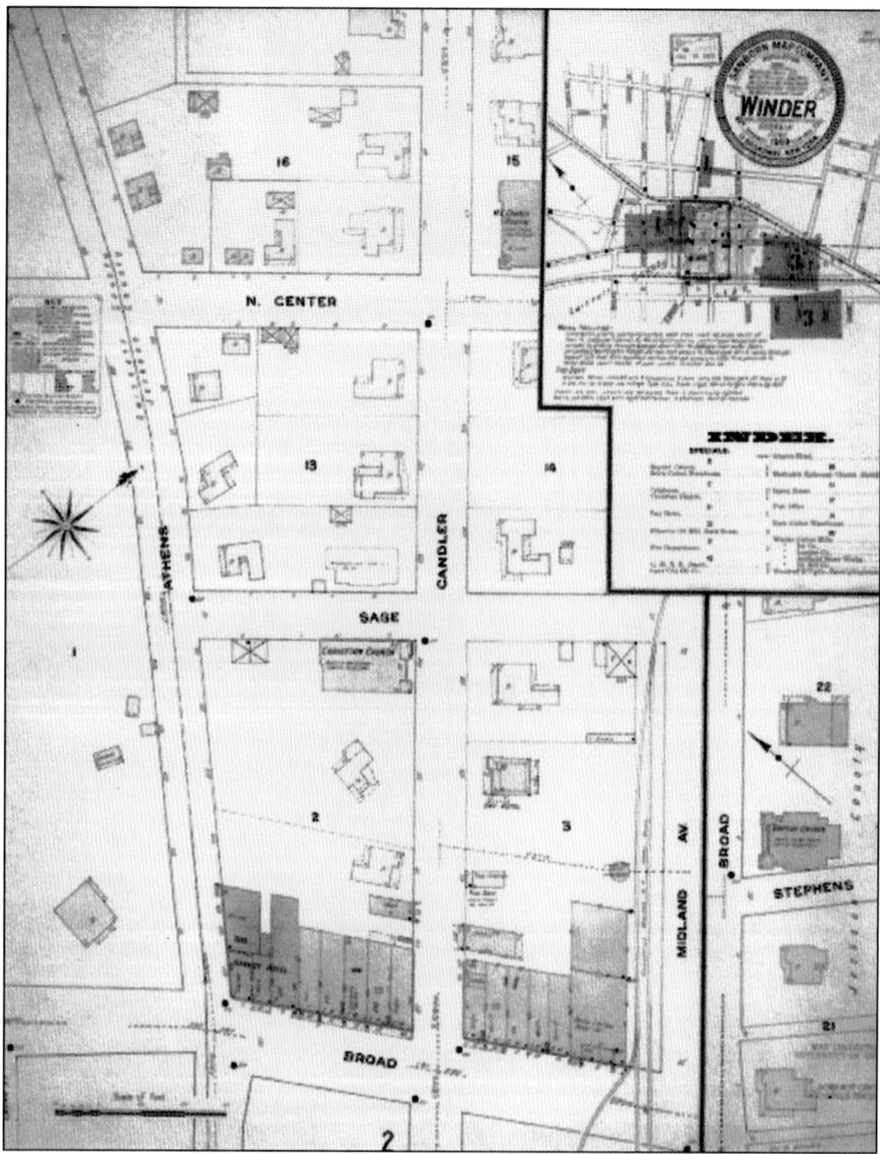

Located at the intersection of Walton, Gwinnett, and Jackson Counties, Jug Tavern (now known as Winder, Georgia) got its name from the double log cabin that served as a rest stop for travelers between the Blue Ridge Mountains to the north and the Georgia coast to the east. Barely three decades separated Winder, Georgia, from its earlier life as a travelers' rest at Capt. Garland Reynolds's Jug Tavern. The tavern had achieved fame for the unusual practice of drinking whiskey from a pottery jug thrown over one's shoulder. The practice was a departure from the traditional beverages served in glassware in other roadside taverns. (Barrow Preservation Society image.)

On the Cover: Celebration is a big part of life in the northeast Georgia town of Winder. For over a century, marching bands and decorated floats have processed along Broad Street past the buildings that beckon to visitors. This c. 1949 National Guard parade is one of many that have thrilled Winder residents. Parades in Winder have feted Little League seasons, the Fourth of July, the Armed Forces, and, of course, Christmas. (Courtesy of Evelyn Arnold.)

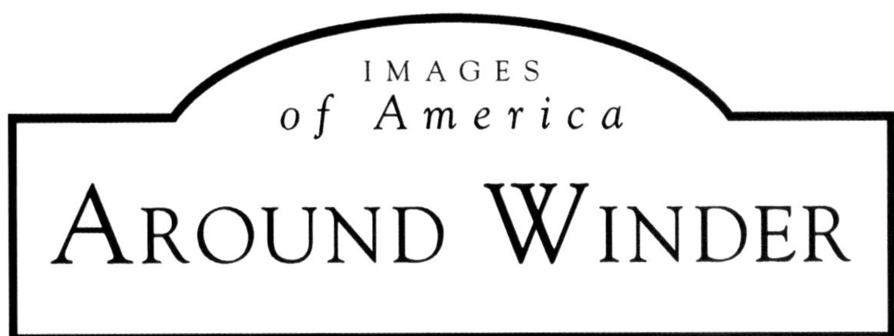

Barrow Preservation Society, Inc.

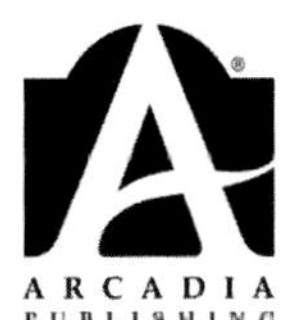

ISBN 978-0-7385-9409-5

Published by Arcadia Publishing
Charleston, South Carolina

Printed in the United States of America

Library of Congress Control Number: 2012933857

For all general information, please contact Arcadia Publishing:
Telephone 843-853-2070
Fax 843-853-0044
E-mail sales@arcadiapublishing.com
For customer service and orders:
Toll-Free 1-888-313-2665

Visit us on the Internet at www.arcadiapublishing.com

To the people who have believed in Winder, the strength of community spirit, and the importance of presenting our best face to the world through the buildings our lives have inspired. Their vision and commitment to the community created a city here in northeast Georgia.

Contents

Acknowledgments

Without members of some of Winder's oldest families taking part in this project, *Around Winder* would not have been possible. Many thanks to Joe Bowen; Bill Summerour; John C. Jackson; Caroline Robinson Stallings; Frances Shumake; Evelyn Arnold; Bob Hill; Kay Eddleman; photographer Pierson Stell, whose years of service chronicled on film the Winder we all remember and enjoy today; the Barrow County Historical Society, for providing support throughout the production of *Around Winder*; and the people of Winder who have so willingly shared their love of their hometown so the Barrow Preservation Society can present this peek into the heritage of our northeast Georgia home.

This book could not have happened without the dedication of the members of Barrow Preservation Society, an organization formed in 2009 to focus on the architecture of Barrow County and its cities, including Winder. Many thanks to those members who continue to see value in our old buildings and the important role they play in defining our city's future, as well as its past: Paul Brown, Amber Eskew, Gwen Hill, Jannie Jennings, Helen Person, Patricia Stallings, and Kathy White; past board members Troy Hensley, Brian Ray, and Mace Strickland, who continue to support Barrow Preservation Society; our online partners who no longer live here, but whose hearts pump red Georgia clay; and the many local folks who have supported our efforts during Barrow Preservation's short existence.

Our heartfelt appreciation to our original editor Elizabeth Bray, who guided us through the proposal and early phases of creation for this book, and her successor, Liz Gurley, who seamlessly stepped into the editorial role—encouraging, supporting, and hand-holding to ensure this book lived up to Arcadia's standards of excellence in publishing. Thank you both for all you have done for us.

And, finally, thank you to our families for their support and patience as we strive to establish Barrow Preservation Society, Inc., as the foundation for a strong future for the preservation of the history of Winder and Barrow County. We love you all and we promise to try to be home for supper at least three nights next week.

—Helen Arnold Person, founding chair

INTRODUCTION

If you did not grow up in Winder, Georgia, you might look at the images presented within these pages and wonder: What makes this place special?

Around Winder offers a look at some of the people, places, and events that continue to make Winder a special place. Likewise, we offer a look at some of the missing pieces that helped define the city, its foundation, and its reputation as "a stem-winder" of a town as early as 1920.

The buildings we call "home," as well as those from which we operated the family business, tell the story of our hometown. Winder is not unlike many towns dotting the face of America: the city bears testimony to the evolution of American society and architecture. The modest commercial architecture of Winder's traditional downtown business district is bookended by its Queen Anne–style railroad depot and survivors of its proud North Broad Street residential corridor. Populated with Queen Anne homes dripping with gingerbread and ornamental details, Winder's residential districts offer a chance to walk through the history of American architecture. From the Queen Annes and Arts and Crafts homes to Early Tudor Revival and National Railroad cottages, the houses blanketing the 1905 Wood Lawn Heights development and Park and Georgia Avenue neighborhoods are silent witnesses to the settling of this northeast Georgia community.

When towns like Winder were planted, residents walked to town from nearby neighborhoods. Country dwellers rode in horse-drawn carriages or wagons to conduct business at the bank or dry goods store, or to see the doctor. Parking of their conveyances was usually done in the middle of the wide boulevards or on a side street more conducive to the length of the vehicle. Business district parking lots were not necessary until automobiles became a staple throughout America in the mid-20th century.

The advent of the suburban shopping center in post–World War II America ushered in the independence of the American housewife/second-income earner and the flight of city dwellers to the country. By the end of the 20th century, it was not uncommon for households to have more cars than licensed drivers. With the 21st century well underway, the current cost of petroleum is causing suburbanites to rethink their daily commutes, making loft living and in-town neighborhoods take on renewed appeal.

In 2012, many residents who have lived in Winder all or most of their lives remember a time when Winder was the self-proclaimed Work Clothes Capital of the World. With 10 manufacturing plants churning out clothing worn by people all over the world, Winder, the seat for Barrow County in northeast Georgia, was a bustling mini-metropolis. The term "self-sufficient" was nothing if not a description of the people of Winder. Booming agriculture, world-class manufacturing, and dynamic transportation systems—with great proximity to arteries connecting our town to the north, south, east, and west—all pointed to an even brighter future for this scrappy community.

The mid-20th century brought with it global change that Winder was not able to escape. Textile manufacturers began to find new, inexpensive locations outside of the United States. New technology and the appeal of larger cities enticed young people looking for a different way of life than working on the family farm. With the kids gone, the family farms became liabilities; farmers made more money selling their acreage for real estate developments like residential subdivisions and shopping centers. The railroad that brought so much promise early in Winder's history became a transportation relic as improved road systems allowed greater accessibility for trucks than railcars.

The sign at the construction site says it all: "Pardon Our Progress." A once-proud building that was home to a local institution has been reduced to a ruin surrounded by a chain-link fence to keep curious kids from investigating. When the remnants are cleared, construction will commence on the new parking lot.

A recurring dilemma in cities across America is whether to rehabilitate a crumbling derelict that once was the local bank or demolish it to make way for a shiny new three-story big-box tenant; Winder is no different. The 1914 First Baptist Church—a stately, urban, Gothic Revival church—was demolished for fear no developer would want the church building, and now a vacant lot sits in its once sacred place. The dust has barely cleared from the demolition of the Granite Hotel—the last locally quarried, locally constructed granite hotel in the state of Georgia. Its site will soon be home to a dozen parking spaces and a park occupying a prime real estate corner in the downtown commercial district.

Photographs of the former facades of our town tell the stories of good people who wanted to contribute to their community. The buildings they constructed created the rhythm of the street, the ups and downs of single- to three-story buildings, the variety of simple to ornate decoration, and the architectural symphony that underscores everything that happens there. As we lose parts of our physical appearance, the rhythm and melody of our streets become disrupted. Like a puzzle with missing pieces, the character of our built heritage is incomplete. Deferred maintenance causes small repairs to become major rehabilitations too costly for owners to tackle. Creative solutions, with diversified funding sources and forward-thinking business plans, can propel the physical past into new life as an economic engine for Winder. New jobs and new uses can be packaged in the familiar envelopes that offer Winder residents and guests a sense of place that is hard to reconstruct.

As Winder and communities like her look to the future, how do we keep the familiar faces of the past while creating new spaces for the future? Though the voices of our earliest residents have been stilled, the spirit they left in the buildings they created can offer inspiration for a new beginning. Come and join the members of Barrow Preservation Society as we take a tour *Around Winder.*

One

Becoming Winder

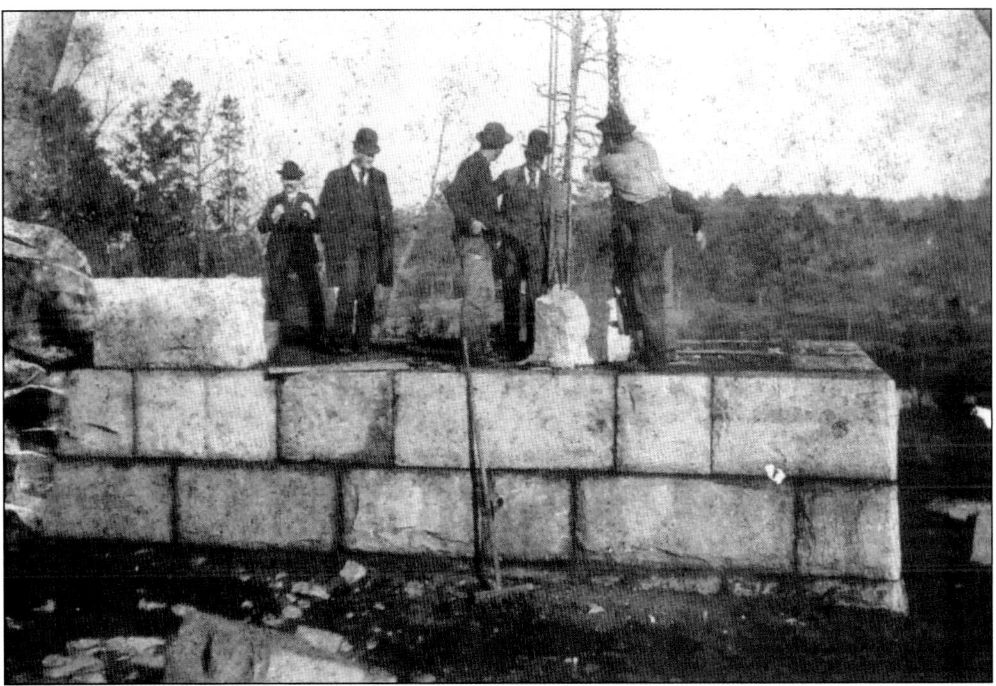

The Flat Rock quarry, located about a mile south of downtown, yielded granite block used to construct several commercial, social, and residential buildings in the community now known as Winder. Flat Rock stone is part of the vast Elberton granite outcropping that sweeps through northeast Georgia and into neighboring states. This early photograph of Flat Rock owner and stonemason Charles Madison (C.M.) Ferguson (center) with a group of unidentified civic leaders is believed to be from the laying of the foundation for the 1899 Granite Hotel. The hotel stood at the downtown corner of Broad and Athens Streets on the site of the old Jug Tavern, from which the city took its previous name. (Courtesy of Bill Summerour.)

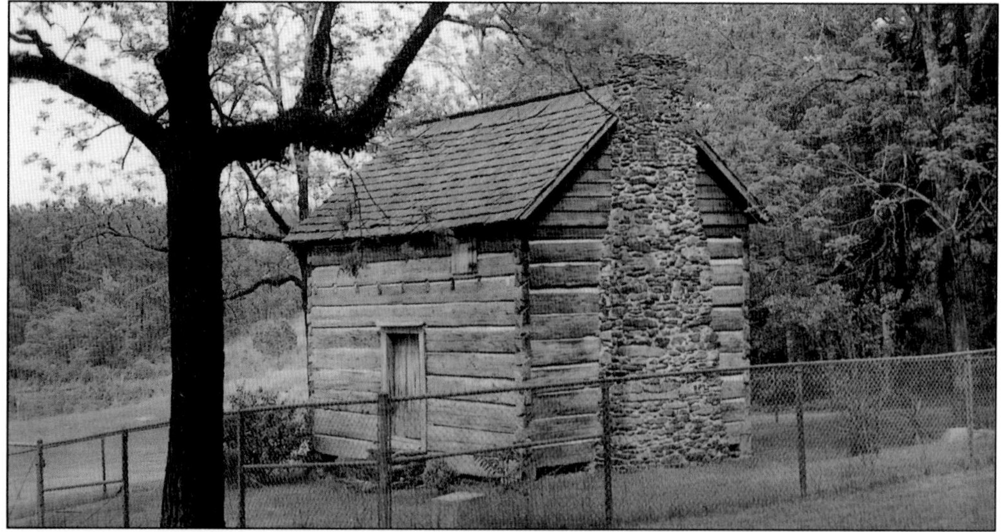

The block house known as Barrow County's oldest extant building stands at the heart of the state park that bears its name. Fort Yargo, constructed in 1792, served as a fortification against aggressive action from Native Americans living in the area. The fort was restored in 1927 by local businessmen with support from the Sunbury Chapter of the Daughters of the American Revolution. (Courtesy of Joe Bowen.)

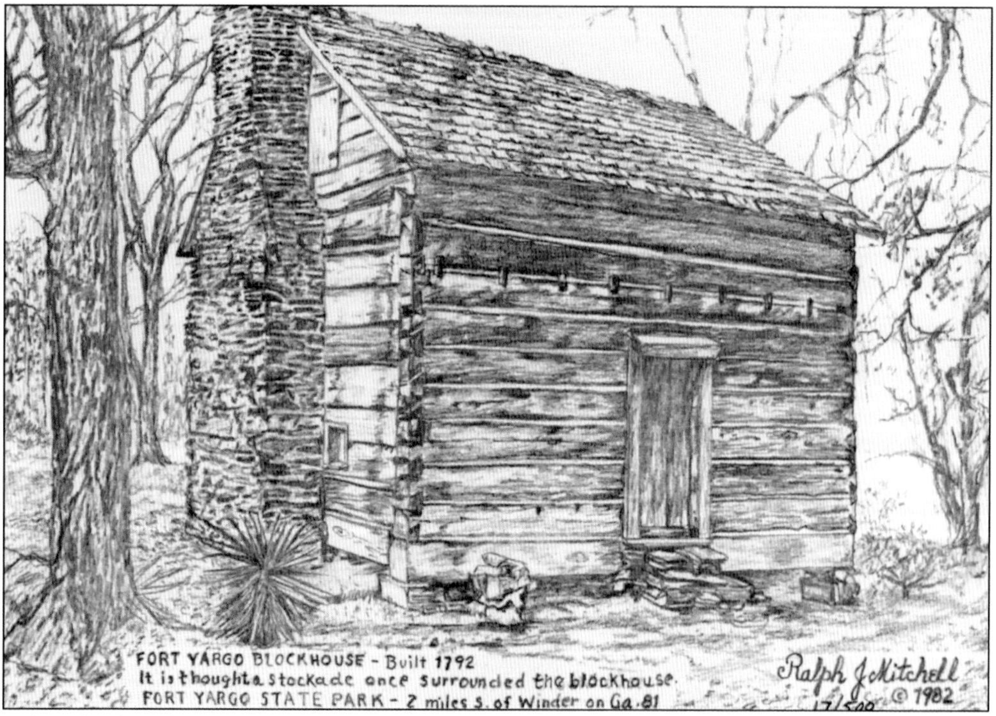

Believed to have been encircled by a stockade, Fort Yargo has inspired many local legends associated with the Creek village of Snodon, which was located approximately three miles from the fort. The 1983 book *Beadland to Barrow*, created and published by the Barrow County Historical Society, shared stories of the Creek Indians who inhabited Talasee Colony, Pea Ridge, and the village of Snodon, which gave birth to the town that would become Winder. (Courtesy of Joe Bowen.)

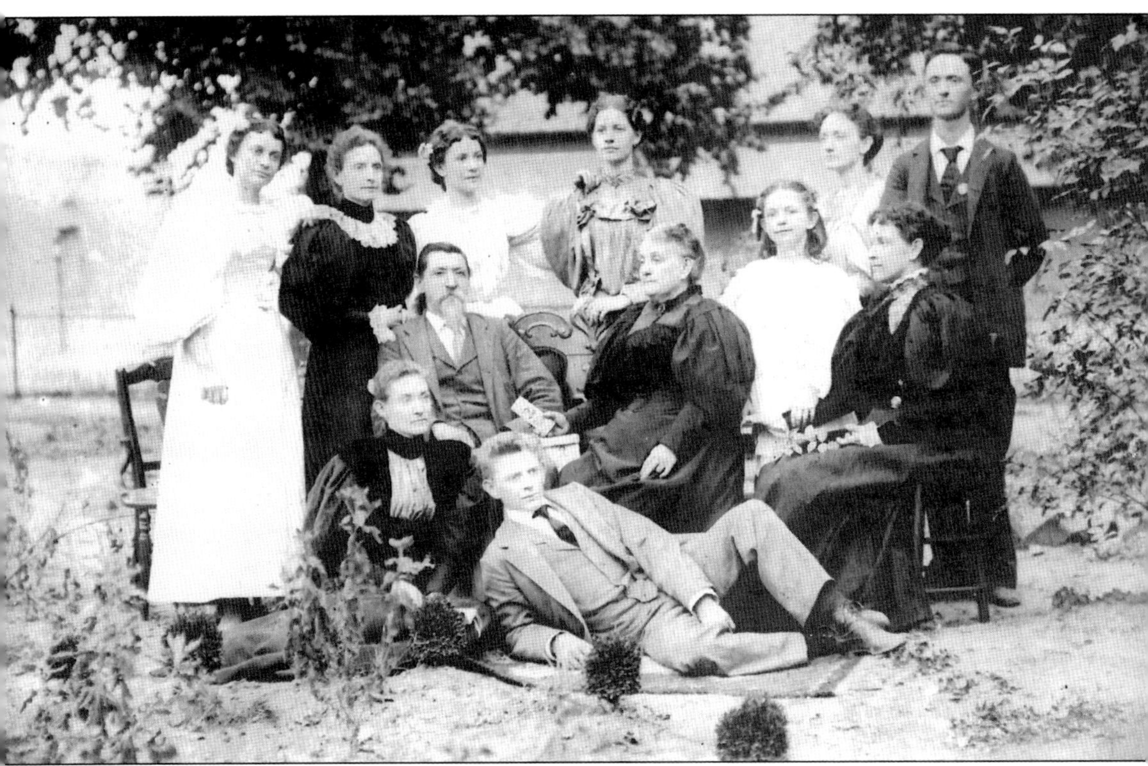

Wiley Harrison Bush, his wife, Laura, and five of their eventual 12 children came to Jug Tavern from Oglethorpe County by way of Cut Off (present-day Fort Yargo) in Walton County. The Bush family lived on the corner of Hog Mountain Road across from the site of the tavern for which the community was named. The Jug Tavern had achieved fame due to its owner's unusual practice of hanging an earthenware jug from a rope to let travelers know his establishment was open. This 1900 photograph was taken on the lawn of the Bushes' stately, two-story, frame house; the 1899 Granite Hotel is visible in the background. When the County of Barrow was created by order of the Georgia General Assembly on July 7, 1914, Bush moved his house to make room for the new courthouse. (Courtesy of Bill Summerour.)

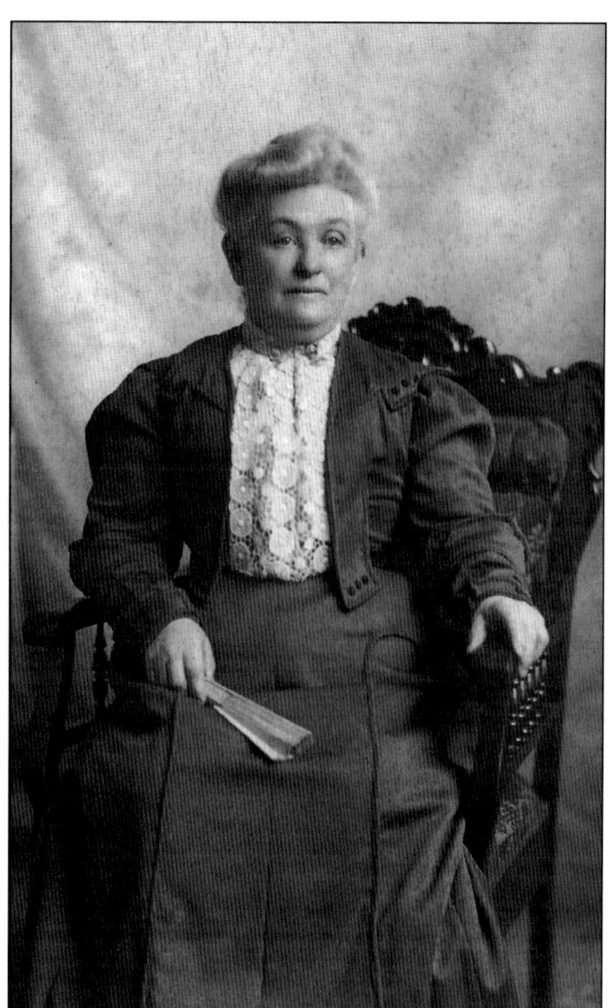

Born Laura Emiline Latimer on May 4, 1842, in Oglethorpe County, Georgia, she married Wiley Harrison Bush on March 7, 1861, at her family's home. Nine years and five children later, the Bush family moved to the community of Jug Tavern. Laura Bush served as a supportive partner to her husband as he and other residents organized the community into a city. (Courtesy of John C. Jackson.)

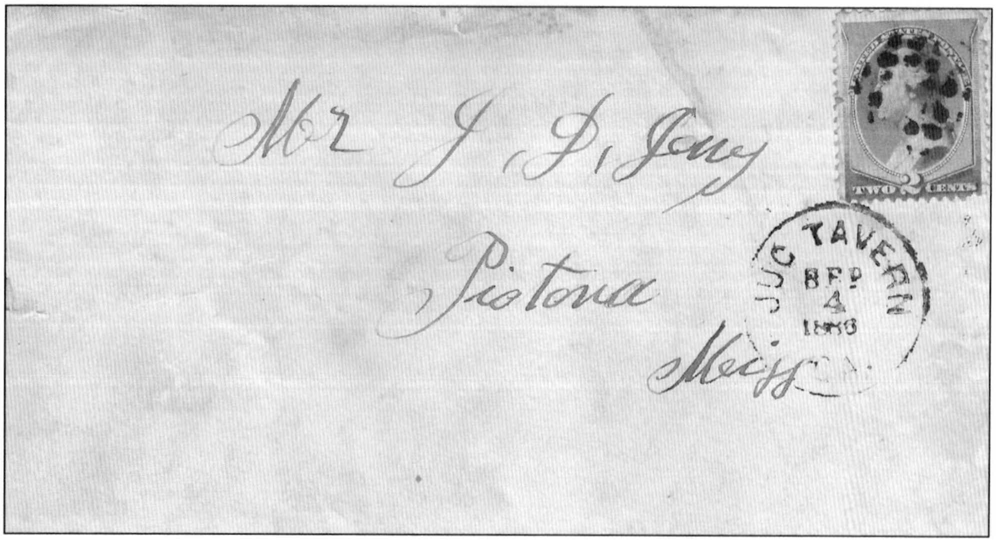

By 1876, even the US Postal Service could not ignore the rapid growth in Jug Tavern. On June 22 of that year, the *Daily Constitution*, an Atlanta newspaper, posted a piece from the *Gainesville Southron* (1875–1885) that said "a new post route in Jug Tavern in Walton County is needed." This letter to Mr. Jones is postmarked September 4, 1886. Additionally, new railroad routes from Seaboard Air Line and Gainesville Midland Railroads were spawning growth in manufacturing and shipping for Jug Tavern. (Courtesy of Joe Bowen.)

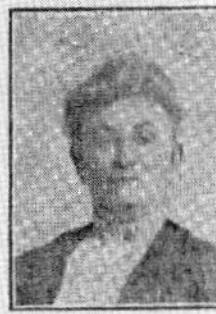

MRS. BUSH'S SPECIFIC

The Greatest Burn Cure on Earth

Cures Burns, Scalds, Spasmodic Croup, Erysipelas, Poison Oak, Chilblains, Skin Eruptions.

This Specific has relieved more suffering than any other known remedy. It will positively remove pain from BURNS and SCALDS immediately. It's worth its weight in gold if properly used. Never leaves a scar.

DIRECTIONS FOR BURNS—Cover burn with medicine, lay on same a cloth thoroughly greased with mutton suet or tallow; this prevents cloths from sticking.

Dress two or three times daily, change cloth next to burn often.

Third or fourth day sponge burn with warm castile soap suds water, dry lightly with clean cloth.

ERYSIPELAS, POISON OAK, CHILBAINS, same treatment as a burn, leaving off tallow cloth.

EARACHE—Warm medeline, drop two or three drops in ear; place small piece of cotton to exclude air.

CROUP—One half teaspoonful for child up to six months old. One teaspoonful to year old. Then increase according to age.

TESTIMONIALS:

Atlanta, Ga., Feb. 6, 1909.

Mrs. W. H. Bush
Winder, Ga.

Dear Madam:—I have used your medicine in my family in two cases of severe burns and relief was afforded instantaneously. We alway keep it in our hourse. It is a valuable remedy.

PHILIP COOK,
Secretary of State of Ga.

Athens, Ga., Feb. 20, 1909.

I have used for years Mrs. Bush's Specfic for burns and can say unhesitatingly it is one of the best that I have ever tried. I feel that it should be in every home ready for emergency. It is not only cooling to the burn but is very healing.

M. RUTHERFORD,
Ex-Principal Lucy Cobb Institute.

Mrs. Bush, Winder, Ga.—I have had occasion to use your valued Specific twice in my family—both times for severe burns. It's effect was immediate, remarkable.

I recommend it unhesitatingly as a most excellent remedy for burns. Every family ought to keep it on hand.

C. P. WILCOX,
Prof. of Modern Languages,
University of Georgia.

Atlanta, Ga., Feb. 22, 1909.

Mrs. W. H. Bush,
Winder, Ga.

Dear Mrs Bush: My father and mother considered your Specific for burns as being the best in existence. I remember on one occasion mother was scalded by the bursting of a hot water bottle and suffered intense agony until your Specific was rubbed over her feet and inside of five minutes the pain had entirely left her. It is indeed a pleasure to give this testimonial.

Yours very truly,
JOSEPH M. BROWN,
Governor of Georgia.

Jefferson, Ga., Feb. 9th, 1914.

I take great pleasure in commending to everybody who may have need of a remedy for burns, Mrs. Bush's Specific. I have tried it and know what it will do. My daughter, who was badly burned, has no scar left and is perfectly well as a result of the use of Mrs. Bush's Specific.

Respectfully,
WILLIAM DUNBAR,
Pastor First M. E. Church, S.,
Jefferson, Ga.

While her husband, Wiley, was busy acquiring prime acreage in Jug Tavern and spearheading the building of a city, Laura Bush became famous in her own right. As the developer, inventor, manufacturer, and distributor of Mrs. Bush's Specific patent medicine, she received widespread admiration and respect for her product. A mother of 12, she had discovered remedies for the inevitable mishaps that befall youngsters. Mrs. Bush's Specific received accolades from medical professionals, prominent politicians, and regular people grateful for a product that was actually as good as it claimed. (Both courtesy of Joe Bowen.)

WINDER, GA.

I can recommend Mrs. Bush's Specific and certify that the physicians in this territory use nothing else for burns. In fact, we are hardly ever called upon to treat a burn as this preparation has done such wonders in so many cases its merit makes its reputation. I visited the plant when in operation and can truthfully say that it is no fake preparation.

Respectfully,
S. T. ROSS, M. D.

Atlanta, Ga., March 30, 1896.

Mrs. W. H. Bush:—Some months ago one of my children was badly scalded on one of his legs I procured a bottle of your remedy for Scalds and Burns and applied same as directed. It acted like a charm and the leg healed up without a scar and my son never complained of any pain after application was made.

R. U. HARDEMAN,
Treasurer of Georgia.

Atlanta, Ga., July 19, 1909.

I have known and prescribed Mrs. Bush's Specific for a number of years and regard the preparation without equal when it is used as it to the general public as a safe and it to tse general public as a safe and reliable preparation and no home should be without it.

M. C. MARTIN,
City Physician.

Atlanta, Ga., Dec. 17, 1909.

This is to certify that on June 14, 1907, in a gasoline explosion near No. 4 Engine House, Atlanta, I was badly burned. My face was solidly burned on the entire surface and my leg and hand was terribly rousted, all of the skin peeling off and even my finger nails slipped out. A physician was called but his remedies did not seem to do me any good. A brother Fireman recommended to me Mrs. Bush's Specific. I used this remedy with the most satisfactory result. The application of the splendid remedy cured me completely. I therewith pleasure, recommend in the strongest possible way, the use of Mrs. Bush's Specific to all who have the misfortune to suffer from burns or scalds.

R. H. PRESSLER,
Second Asst. Chief, Atlanta Fire Dept.

Atlanta, Ga.

Mrs. Bush, Winder, Ga.

I send you enclosed $5 for which I wish you to ship me another $5 box of your medicine. I have recently had some experience with it and it acted admirably. I desire to keep a supply on hand.

JOSEPH E. BROWN.

This is to certify that about two years ago one of my little boys was badly burned on his back and after using two or three bottles of Mrs. Bush's Specific for burns, it was entirely cured leaving no scar whatever.

M. T. JOHNSON, M. D.
Prof. of Electric Medicine and Surgery, Lawrenceville, Ga.

Manufactured by

MRS. BUSH'S BURNS SPECIFIC

WINDER, GEORGIA

For Sale by All Druggists and Stores

COTTON OPTION NOTE.—No 14

Use this Note for Port Royal Acid Phosphate.

HAMMOND, HULL & CO., SAVANNAH, GA.

STATE OF GEORGIA, Jackson County. } Jug Tavern Ga., April 23, 1887.

$131 25/

On or before the 1st day of Nov next, I promise to pay to **HAMMOND, HULL & CO.**, or order, One Hundred Thirty One and 25/100 Dollars, for value received, with interest from maturity (if not promptly paid) at the rate of eight per cent per annum, from first proceeds of sales or pickings of my Cotton crop of this present year. In event of suit hereon, or, if placed in hands of an Attorney for collection after due, I agree to pay ten per cent. for Attorneys fees and all other Costs and expenses of collection. And in consideration of the credit hereby given me, I (the maker, security and endorser of this note) do hereby expressly waive and renounce for myself and family, all the rights and benefits which I or they may now or hereafter have under or by virtue of any Homestead or Exemption law or laws now or hereafter to be of force in the State of Georgia, whether State or Federal, so far as this debt is concerned; and I hereby authorize and empower the said **HAMMOND, HULL & CO.**, or their representative, for me, in my name to file any plea or objection in any Court of Law or Equity in this State against the setting apart of any of my property (either real or personal) for the benefit of myself or any of my family, so long as this obligation shall remain unpaid.

This obligation is given by me for 35 *bags* 7000 *lbs. of commercial fertilizer known as*

PORT ROYAL ACID PHOSPHATE,

valued at this date, at .... *Dollars,*

and bought by me from **HAMMOND, HULL & CO,** for the purpose of aiding me in making a crop upon my plantation in Jackson County, Ga., during the present season, with the privilege of paying the same in Cotton, on the basis of 15 cents per pound for Middlings or above said grade, 14½ cents per pound for Low Middlings, 13 cents per pound for Good Ordinary, and 12 cents per pound for Ordinary Cotton; grade to be determined by **HAMMOND, HULL & CO.**, or their Agent, and Cotton to be delivered free of expense to them or their representative, well ginned and packed in merchantable bales (of not less than 400 pounds each) on cars at nearest railroad depot or river landing, if so delivered prior to maturity of this obligation; otherwise the privilege of paying in Cotton to cease, and this obligation to become due and payable in United States current funds only.

And I further declare that I have never heretofore failed or refused to pay in full for any fertilizer bought by me, and make this declaration part of the consideration for the credit herein accorded me, and that I buy this fertilizer for my own use, or to be used on land cultivated for me.

And Whereas, The Laws of the State of Georgia provide that no Commercial Fertilizers shall be offered for sale or distribution in this State, except such as come up to a certain standard of *Chemical Analysis*, and that the Commissioner of Agriculture shall have all Commercial Fertilizers offered for sale or distribution in this State properly *inspected and analyzed*, and the seller of the Fertilizer for which this Note is given, having fully complied with all the requirements of the laws of this State as evidenced by the *Manufacturers guaranteed Analysis branded on each and every bag and the Inspector's Tag attached thereto*, failure to benefit crops or any other failure of consideration, partial or total, shall not be pleaded by me in any action at law or equity under this contract; and, it is understood and agreed, that I purchase said Fertilizer for which this Note is given without any [illegible]rranty whatever on the part of the sellers, save only that the analysis is true and correct as branded upon each bag and does not fall below the Standard required by the [illegible] the State of Georgia, and accept the Analysis of our State Chemist appointed by the Commissioner of Agriculture for this purpose, as a full, complete and final test of the [illegible]ts of said Fertilizer.

And to further secure the payment of the debt hereby created, and of all costs of collection, including ten per cent. upon the principal and interest for attorney's fees, which I have agreed to pay, in the event said debt is placed in a lawyer's hands for collection, I hereby *mortgage* to the said **HAMMOND, HULL & CO.**, the following named property owned by me and free from any and all encumbrances whatever, viz:

....

....

....

and authorize and empower said **HAMMOND, HULL & CO.**, or their attorney in case of default in payment, to take possession of the above described property, or any part thereof, and sell the same at public or private sale, without notice to me and out of the proceeds to pay the expenses of such sale, and the debt, costs, expenses and fees aforesaid; the surplus, if any, to be refunded to me.

In Witness Whereof, I have hereto set my hand and seal the day and year first above written.

Signed, Sealed and delivered in the presence of

[SEAL.]

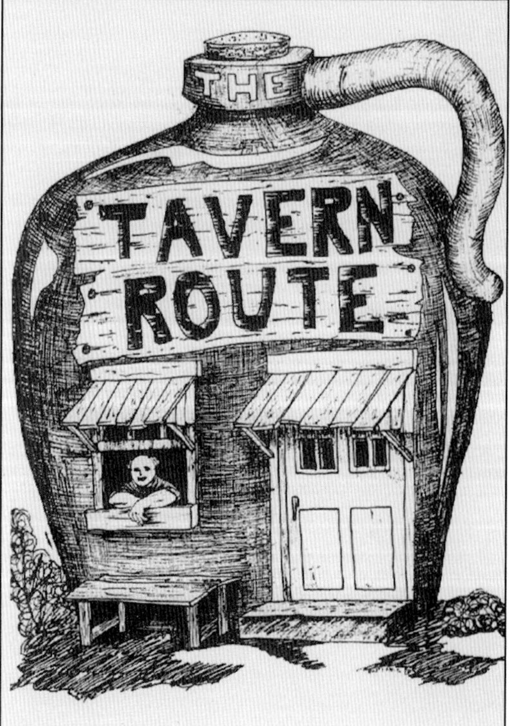

Jug Tavern continued to grow, with agriculture as its chief economic engine. In 1887, Alexander A. Hill purchased 7,000 pounds of Port Royal Acid Phosphate for use on his Jug Tavern farm. This note for the purchase price of $131.25 gave Hill six months to plant, grow, harvest and sell his crop to pay Hammond, Hull & Co. of Savannah, Georgia, for the fertilizer. (Courtesy of Bob Hill.)

With Wiley Bush and others working together, a formal governmental structure was established in 1885, with N.J. Kelly as Jug Tavern's first mayor. Manufacturing, retail, banking, and other commercial concerns were rapidly opening and Jug Tavern began to be recognized as an up-and-coming community. The "Tavern Route" was established with the introduction of the Seaboard Air Line and Gainesville Midland Railroads connecting Jug Tavern with major cities on the Eastern Seaboard. The Tavern Route helped put the city on the map. (Courtesy of Bob Hill.)

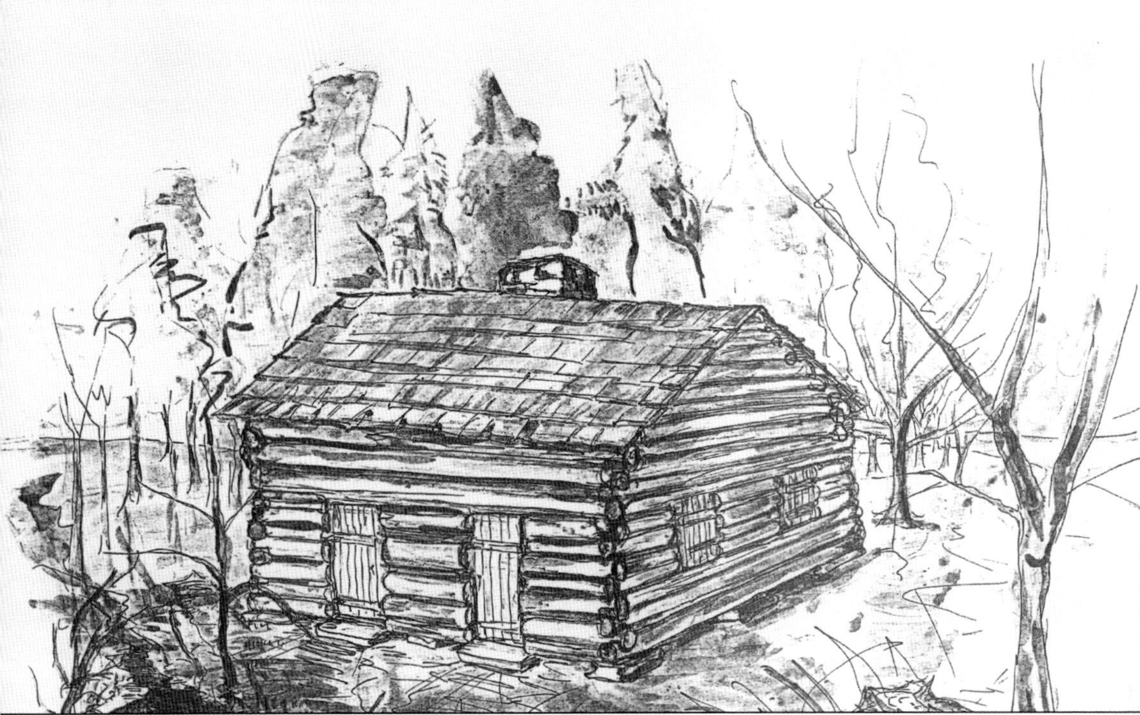

The Concord Methodist Episcopal Church, established in 1836, was the area's first formal religious congregation. In 1986, local artist Pat Landress captured the image of the first log church on Hog Mountain Road, located west of the Jug Tavern, with this pen-and-ink drawing based on descriptions from the church's archives. (Courtesy of Winder First United Methodist Church History Committee.)

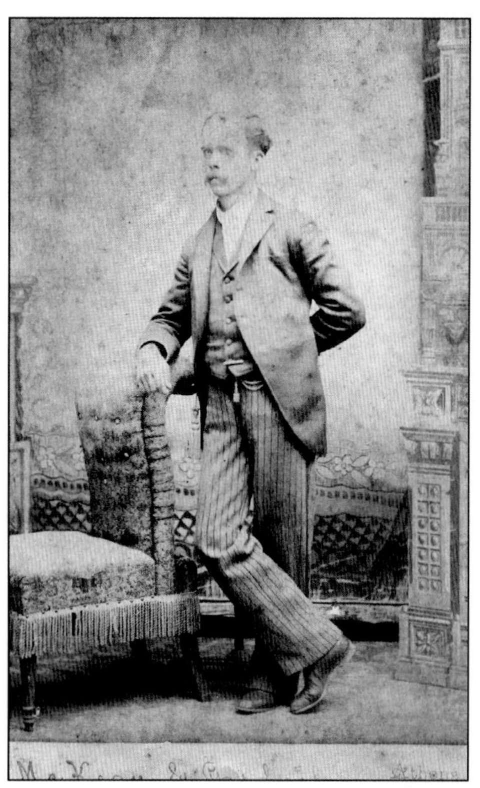

This elegant portrait of Charles Madison Ferguson portrays the man who operated the Flat Rock Quarry, served as chief builder and general contractor for the construction of masonry buildings in Winder, and provided mortuary services for the people of Jug Tavern and Winder. Ferguson was the son-in-law of town founder Wiley Harrison Bush. He was married to the Bushes' third-oldest daughter, Frances Beulah. (Courtesy of Bill Summerour.)

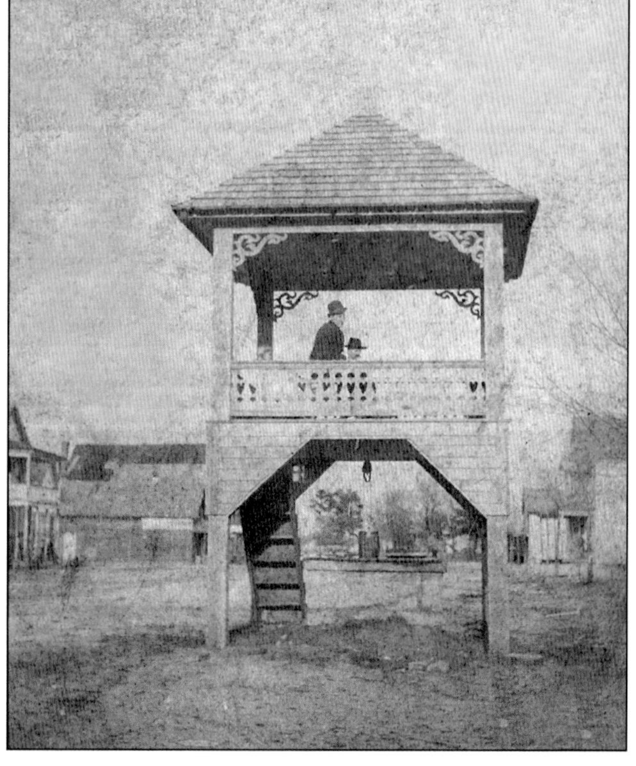

A tributary of the Mulberry River, which begins northwest of town, runs beneath the city of Winder. This bandstand, with the well located underneath, was built in the middle of Broad Street near its intersection with Hog Mountain Road. The bandstand was demolished in the early 20th century. (Courtesy of Bill Summerour.)

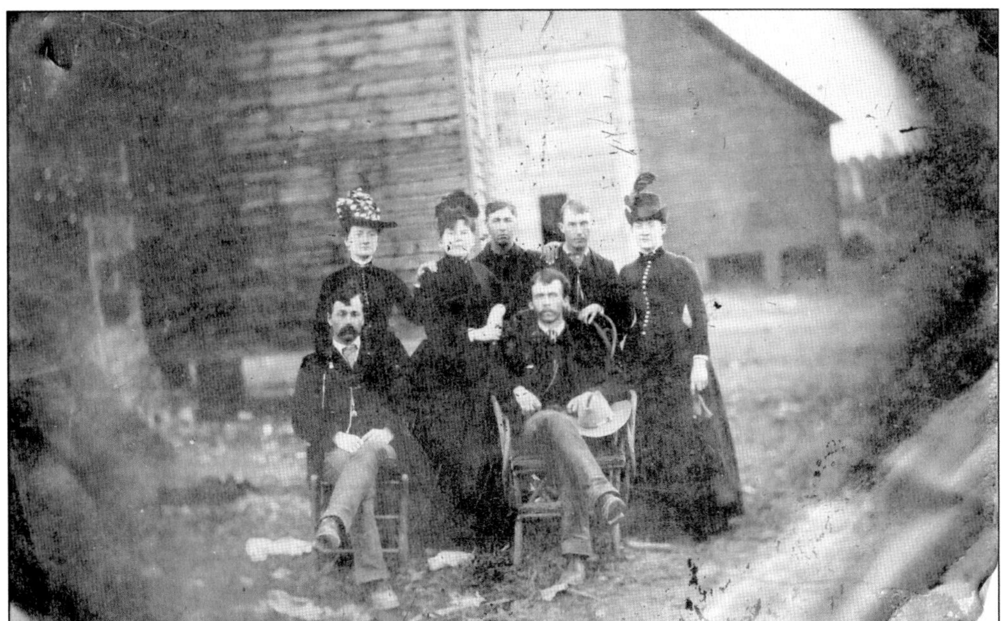

Simple wood-frame buildings were considered temporary structures by the builders of Winder. This photograph of Charles Madison Ferguson (seated); his wife, Frances (Fannie) Bush Ferguson (arm resting on chair); and other members of the extended Bush family depicts early Jug Tavern–Winder high society. Elegant clothing, primitive earthen streets, and rough wood buildings present the juxtaposition of dreams and realities in new cities working to catch up with the local gentry. (Courtesy of Bill Summerour.)

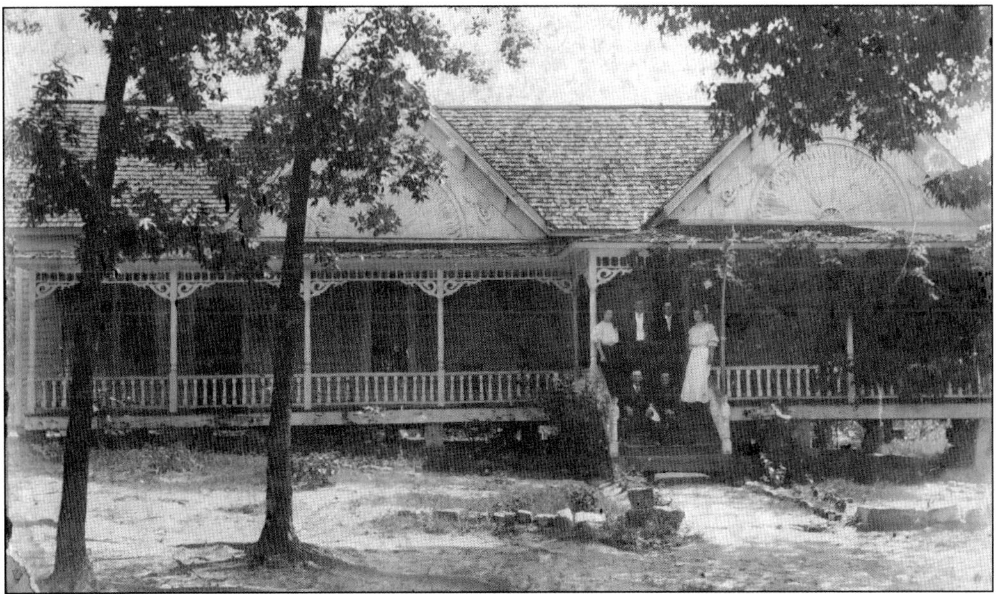

This house on Hog Mountain Road contains the Queen Anne features that typified the homes of many of Jug Tavern's earliest residents. Despite beliefs that the Jug Tavern community was devoid of many residents, the truth is that the community was populated but, as of the mid-19th century, had not created a formalized government. Wiley Bush was the catalyst the community needed to step into the future. (Courtesy of Bob Hill.)

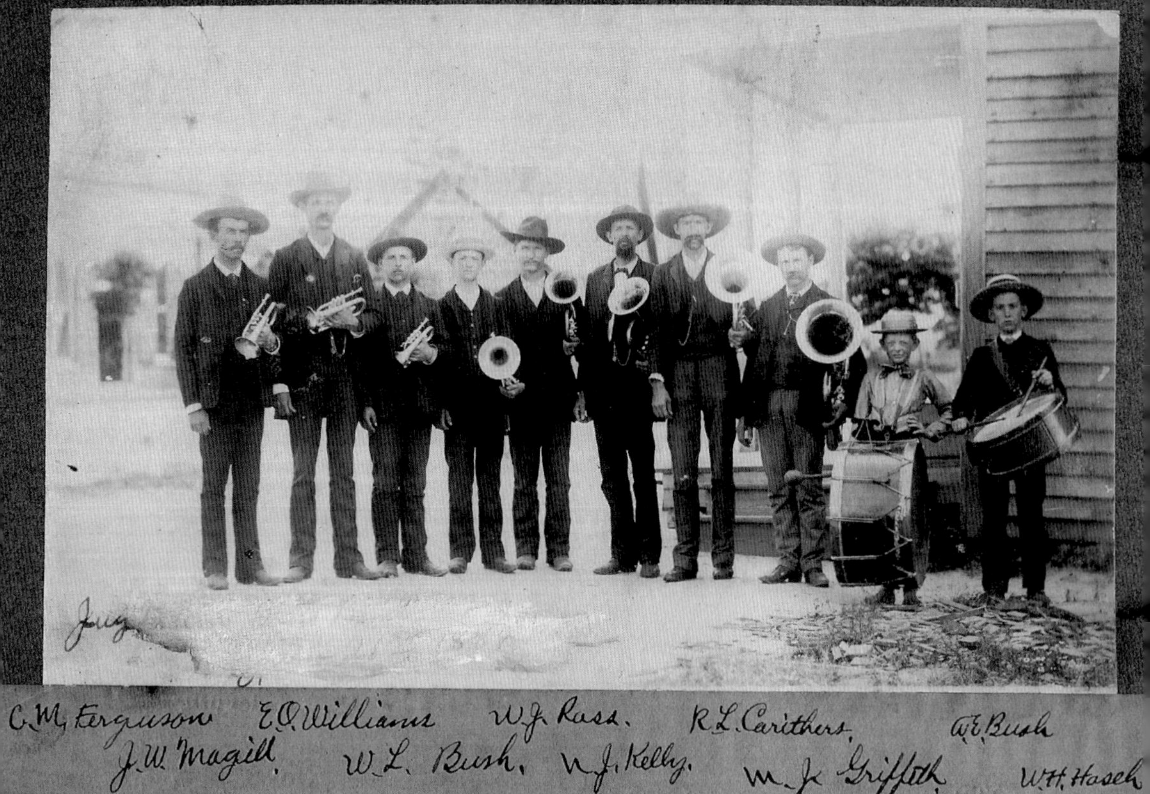

Celebration was in order for everything from parties and weddings to visits by dignitaries. Like many communities of the time, Jug Tavern had a brass band. This 1889 photograph features many of Jug Tavern's leading citizens. From left to right, the members are: Charles Madison Ferguson, J.W. Magill, E.O. Williams, W.L. Bush, W.J. Ross, N.J. Kelly, R.L. Carithers, M.J. Griffeth, A.E. Bush, and W.H. Hosch. Kelly was Jug Tavern's first mayor. (Courtesy of Bill Summerour.)

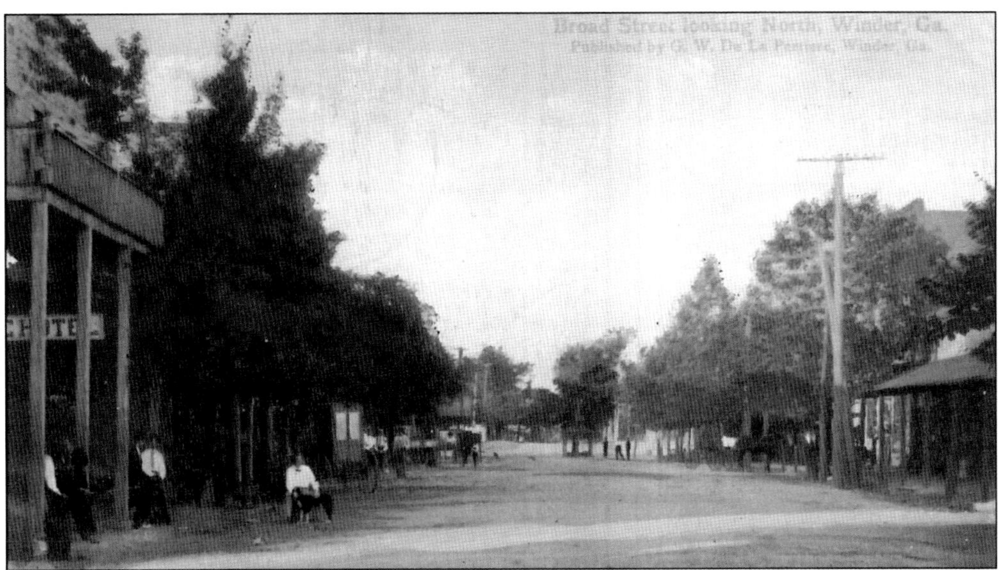

Though the community's name was colorful, city fathers believed a tribute to the railroad manager would serve the additional role of elevating the community's image as a more sophisticated place to live, do business, and raise a family. In 1893, the town of Jug Tavern was officially renamed Winder in honor of John H. Winder of Seaboard Air Line Railroad. Winder had been instrumental in routing the railroad through Jug Tavern. This 1906 postcard shows Broad Street, a collection of granite, brick, and wood-framed commercial buildings indicating its pattern of growth. (Courtesy of Joe Bowen.)

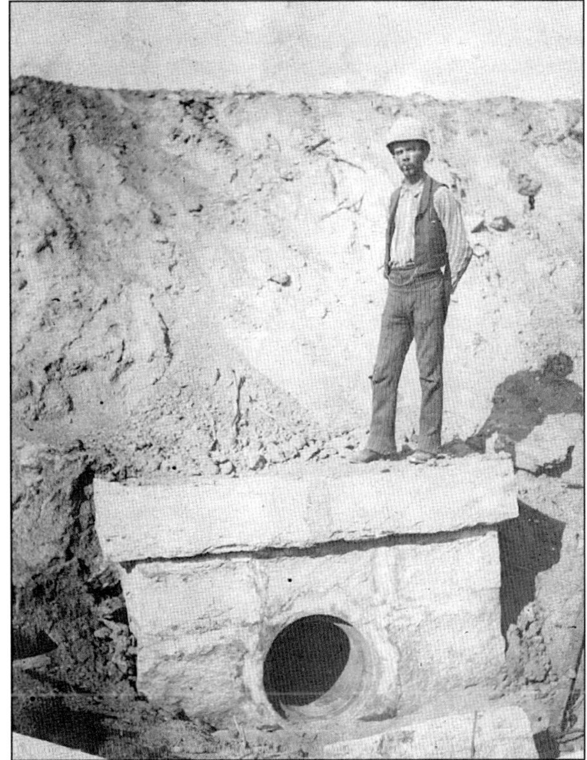

Charles Madison Ferguson was photographed at Flat Rock Quarry, around town, and at several construction sites where he served in a supervisory capacity. A granite mason, Ferguson was the chief builder for Winder's premier lodging facility, the Granite Hotel, built in 1899. The hotel served as a gathering place, event center, restaurant, and temporary home for visitors and new residents who arrived by rail and other public transportation. (Courtesy of Bill Summerour.)

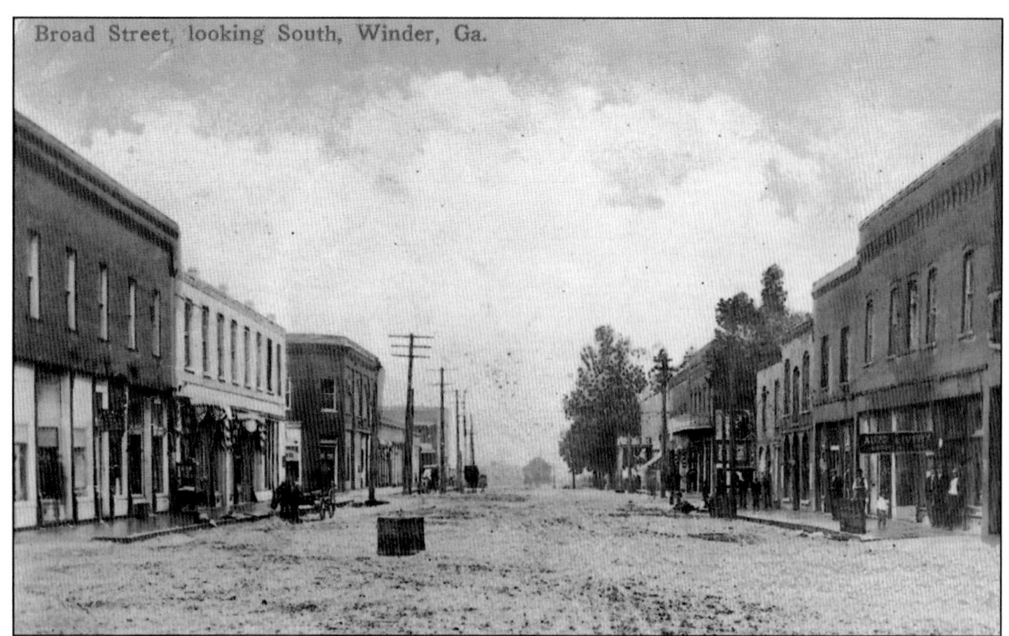

This 1906 postcard shows how Broad Street progressed in about 15 years. Photographed from its intersection with the Gainesville Midland railroad line (present-day Midland Avenue), most of the wooden buildings, leftover from the city's transitional period from Jug Tavern to Winder, are gone. The 1899 Granite Hotel facade and promenade are visible at far right. (Courtesy of Joe Bowen.)

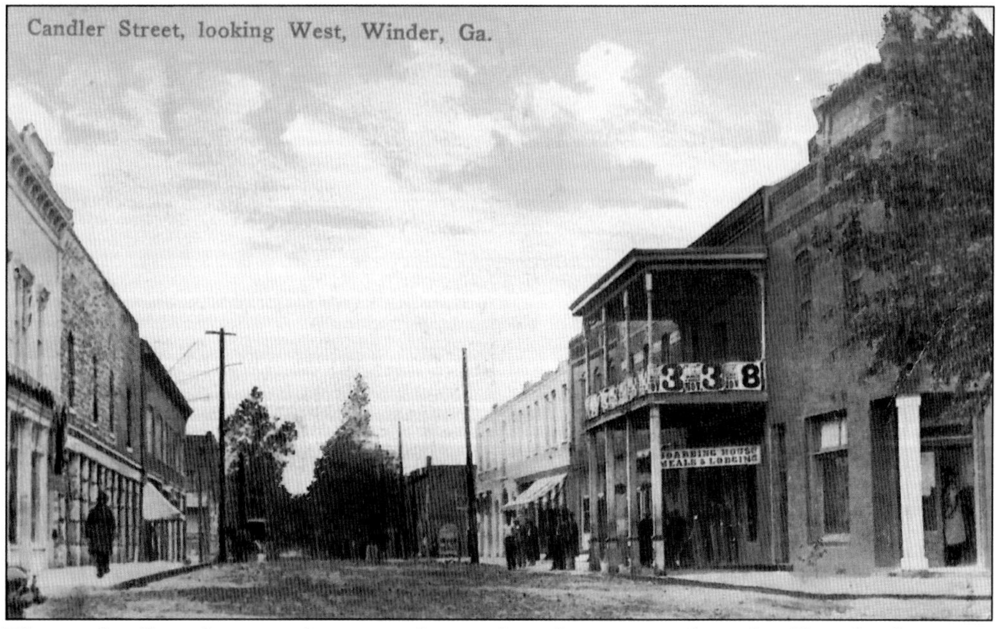

The rapid influx of new residents, travelers, and teachers spawned a rash of boardinghouses in and around downtown Winder. A view of Candler Street looking west toward Broad Street was the subject of this 1906 postcard. Local businessmen like G.W. DeLaPerriere produced postcards of street scenes, the homes of prominent residents, and individual businesses to help promote the growing city to prospective investors. (Courtesy of Joe Bowen.)

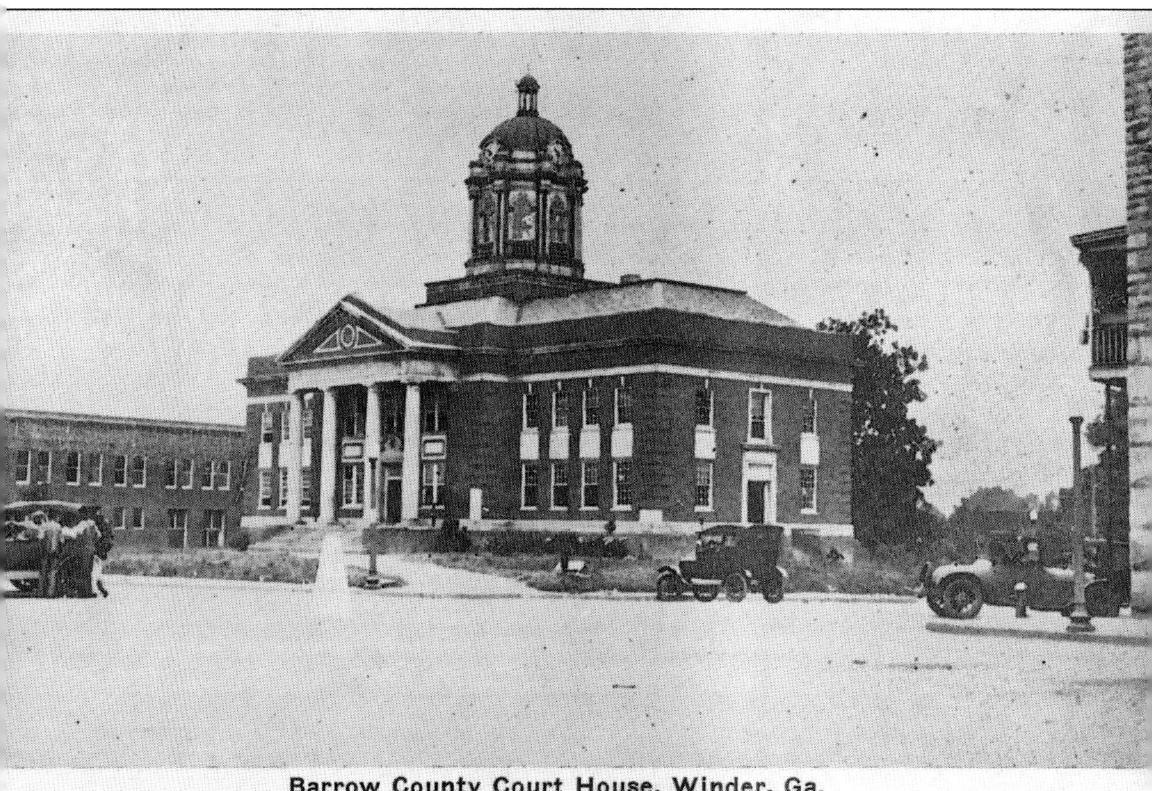

Named for University of Georgia chancellor David Crenshaw Barrow, the county of Barrow was created in 1914 by an act of the Georgia General Assembly. Its largest city—Winder—was chosen as the county seat. This c. 1920 photograph of the newly constructed Barrow County courthouse at the corner of Athens and Broad Streets features a granite obelisk that marked the apex of the three counties. (Courtesy of Joe Bowen.)

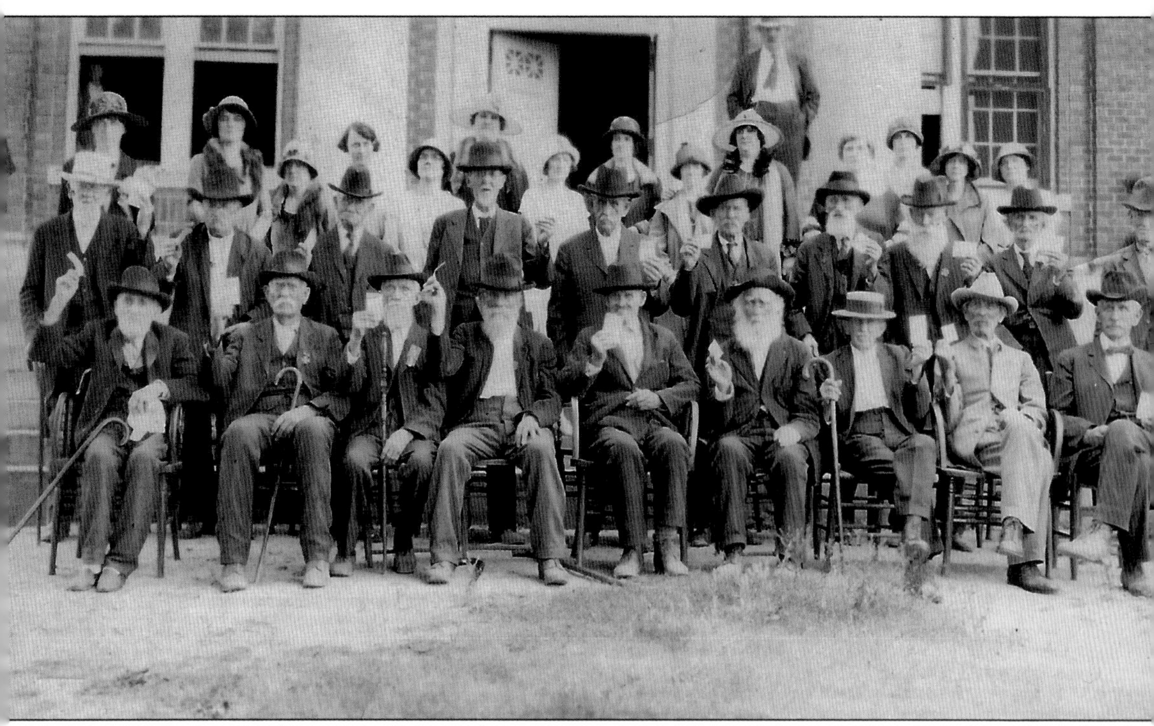

The flurry of building, new faces, and investment in Winder and Barrow County in the early 20th century did not obscure the area's deep connection to the former Confederate States of America. Around 1920, these surviving Confederate veterans were honored in a ceremony on the grounds of the new Barrow County courthouse. Second from left in the second row is James K.P. Arnold of Statham, great-grandfather of one of the authors. (Courtesy of Helen Person.)

Two
WORKING

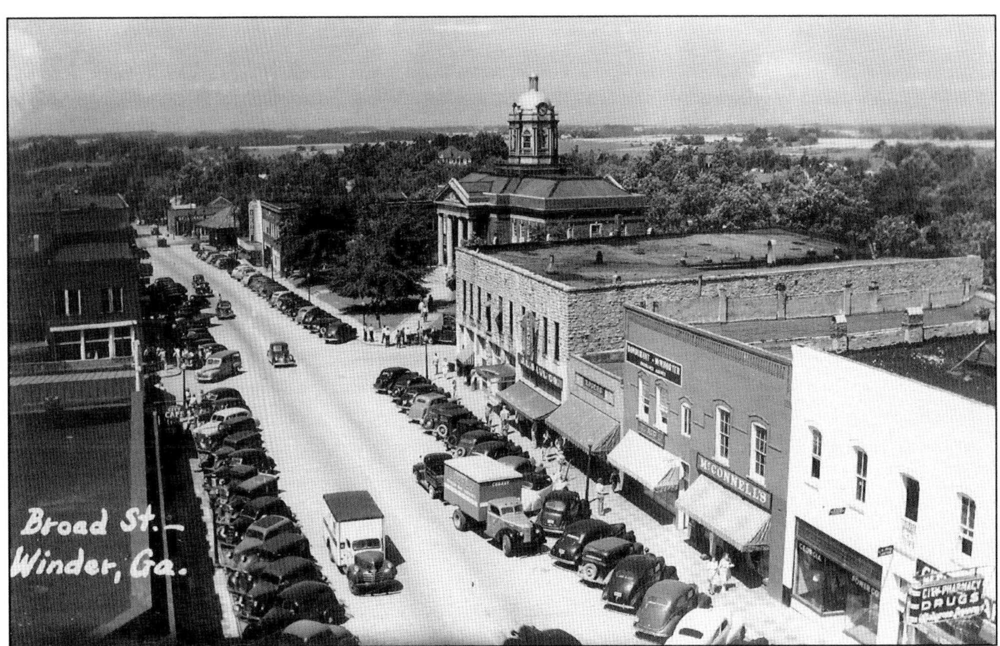

Winder, the "Work Clothes Capital of the World," was a beehive of activity in the epicenter of Barrow County. This c. 1949 image of Broad Street—with not an empty parking space in sight—was taken from the third floor of the Peoples Bank building overlooking the commercial, governmental, and transportation center that employed the workforce of Winder and Barrow County. (Courtesy of Joe Bowen.)

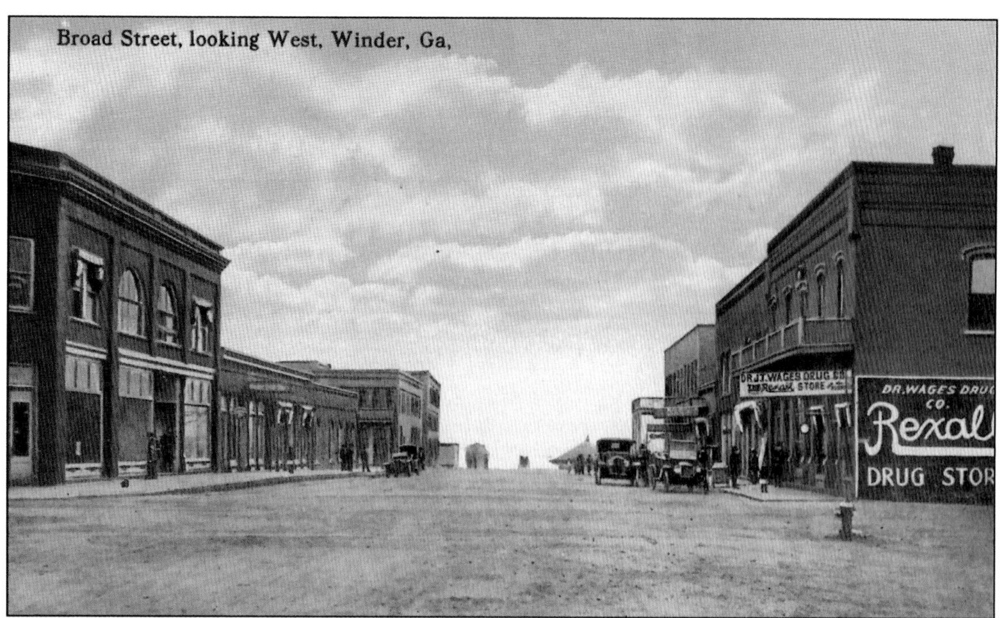

This c. 1915 painted postcard of Broad Street shows dirt-packed streets for the horse-drawn vehicles still prevalent in Winder. The few motorcars in the city were accommodated through unmarked parking suitable for vehicles that were either motorized or powered by one horse. The roof of the Jug Tavern bandstand is visible in the distance. As wood buildings were replaced by brick-and-mortar structures, function trumped form as practicality prevailed. (Courtesy of Joe Bowen.)

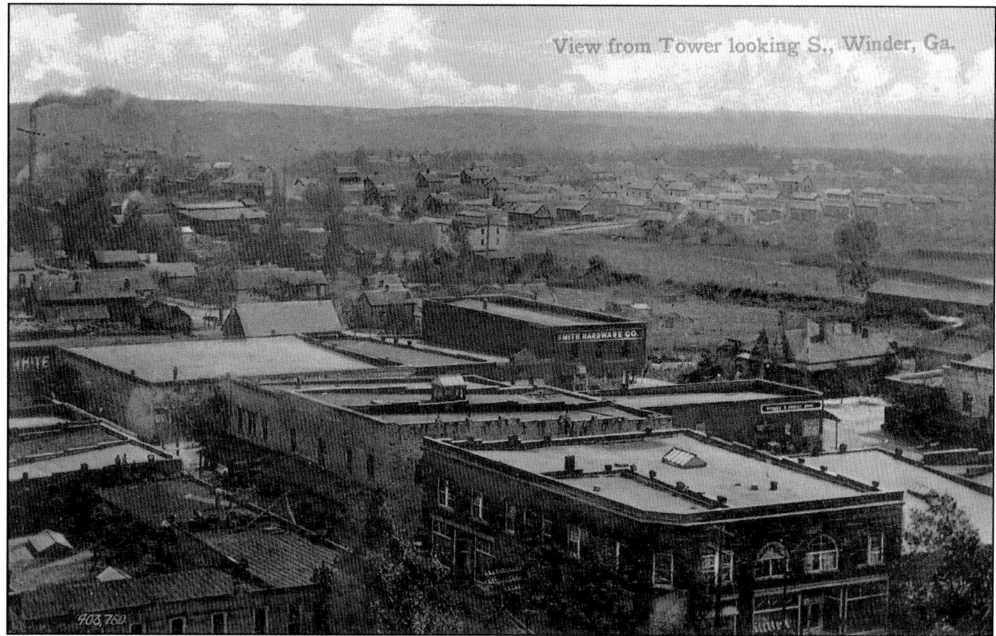

This c. 1912 rooftop image of southeast Winder shows the transition from commercial core to industrial and residential neighborhoods. Winder was not unusual in its development; as new businesses began, their owners lived in boardinghouses, hotels, or on upper floors until the business was established. In Winder, factories encircled the core of downtown while residential areas grew around the places of employment. (Courtesy of Joe Bowen.)

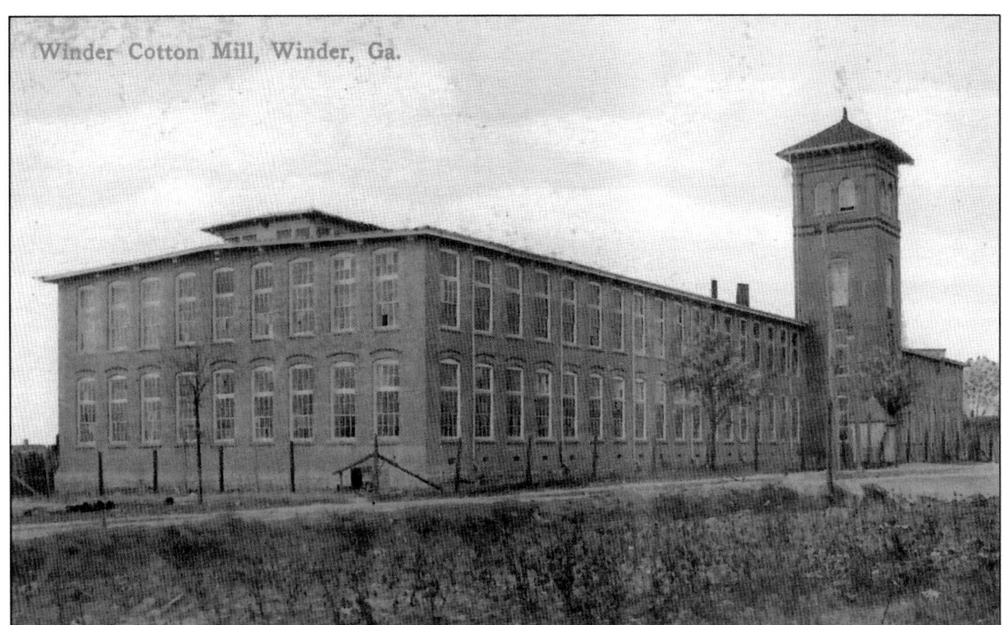

Built in 1898 as the Winder Cotton Mill, this dignified brick manufacturing facility on the eastern outskirts of Winder's commercial core was established by Col. George W. Scott of Decatur, Georgia. Cotton was king among Barrow County's agricultural concerns. The Winder Cotton Mill was one of 10 textile manufacturers operating during Winder's reign as "Work Clothes Capital of the World." (Courtesy of Joe Bowen.)

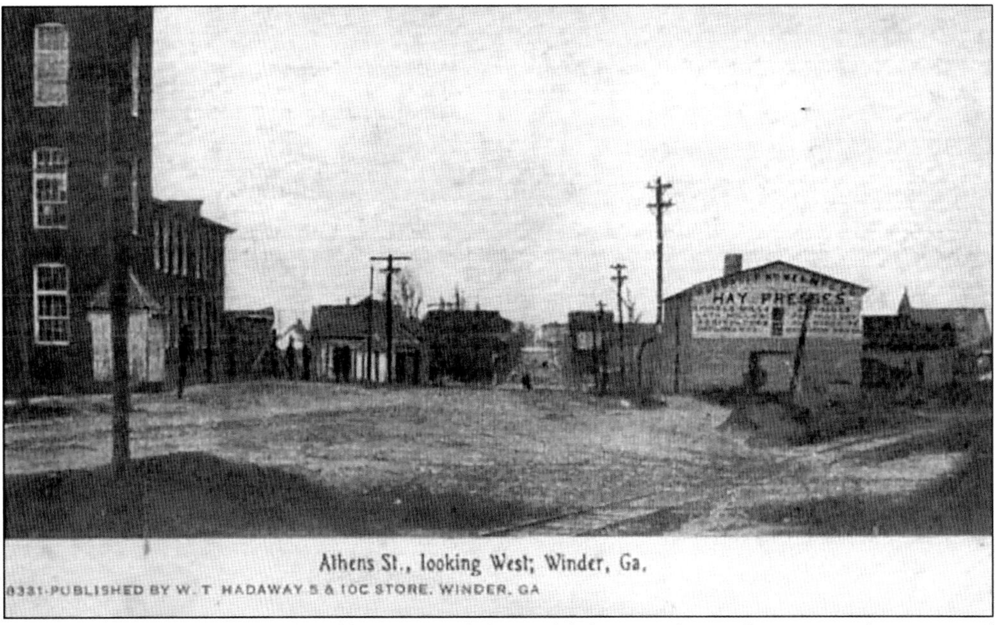

The Gainesville Midland Railroad line inspired the establishment of manufacturing and commercial industries near rail transportation facilities. The Winder Cotton Mill neighborhood included support in the form of the Glenwood neighborhood, developed in the early 1900s, and the Mill Village, where many of the factory workers lived. A nearby cotton gin, feed and hardware store, and other businesses supporting the mill also populated the area. (Courtesy of Joe Bowen.)

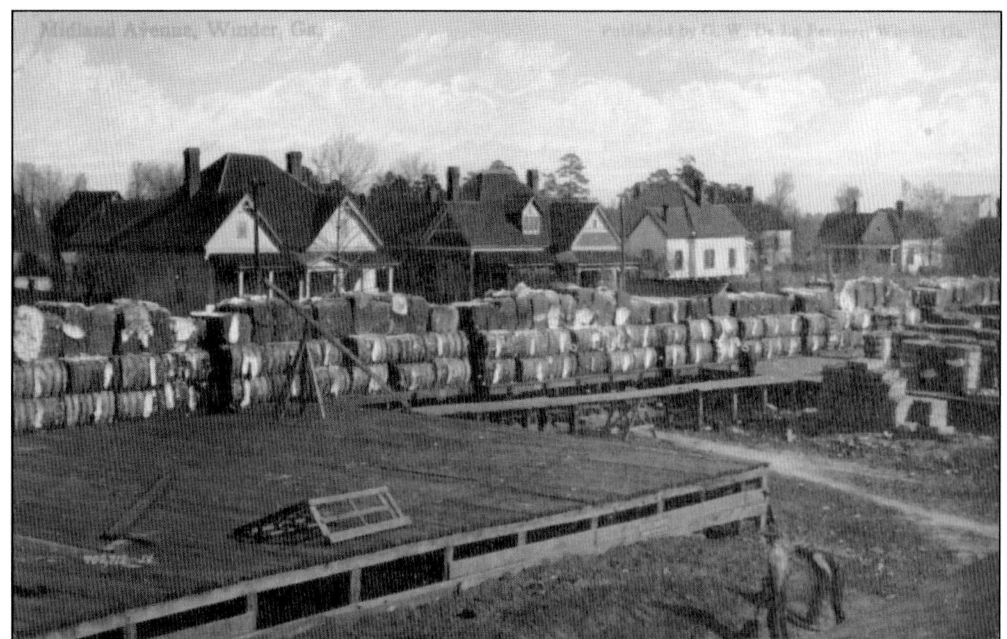

Industrial, commercial, and residential districts shared neighborhoods just one block off Winder's main thoroughfare—Broad Street. This c. 1915 postcard shows bales of picked cotton stacked on the Gainesville Midland freight platform. Growers in communities along the rail line shipped their crops to gins to be made into thread for use by the many textile factories throughout north Georgia in the late 19th and early 20th centuries. (Courtesy of Joe Bowen.)

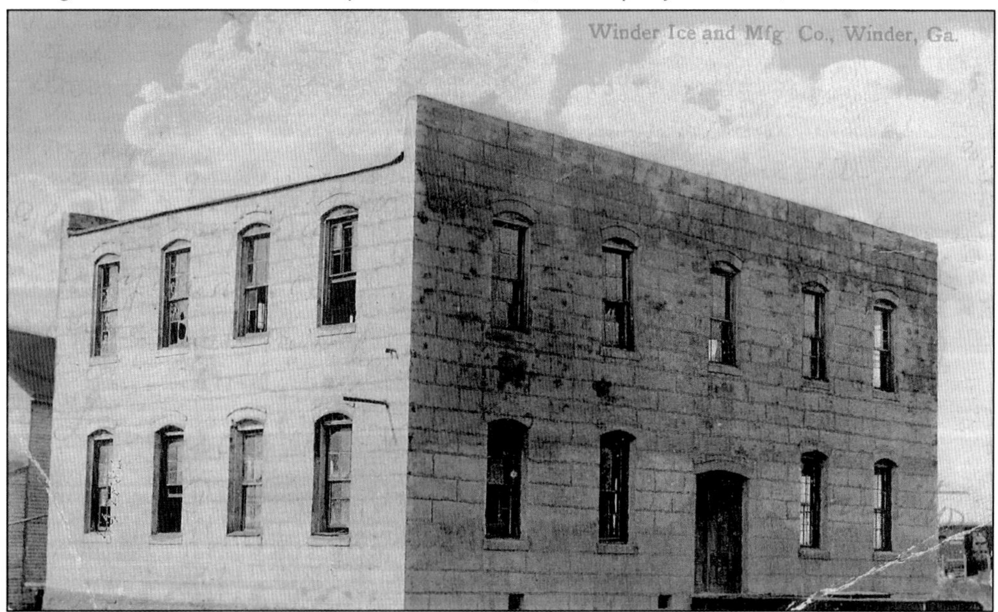

Built in 1908, the Winder Ice Co. contained a 10-ton Columbus ice-making plant. The simple, granite, block building with arched windows reflected the dignity of form with the designer focused on the function of the business contained therein. In intermittent operation until 1922, the icehouse operations stabilized as the Winder Ice and Coal Company. Clay Howard operated the icehouse until 1972. (Courtesy of Joe Bowen.)

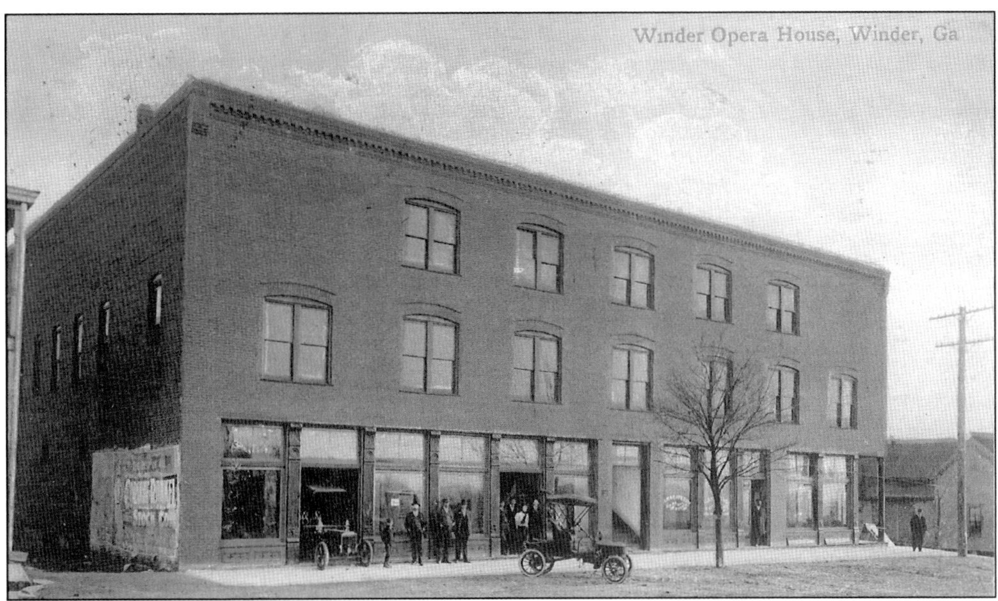

Built in 1906, the Sharpton Opera House was listed in the 1908 *Billboard* index of American theaters and playhouses. Winder's population was shown as 5,000, with the Opera House boasting a 1,000-seat capacity. The street level housed a carriage repository, grocery, and the real estate office of Lamar and Perry. The 1916 construction of the motion-picture house the Strand Theatre relegated the Opera House to alternate uses. (Courtesy of Joe Bowen.)

The Winder Foundry and Machine Works, established in 1900 by R.L. Carithers and J.M. Hood, created ornamental cast-iron storefronts found on many local buildings, as well as commercial storefronts around the southeastern United States. This face, one of the signature pieces from the Winder Foundry and Machine Works, is particular to the Sharpton Opera House. Reminiscent of a Native American princess, the face recalls Winder's earliest days as the Creek community of Snodon. (Courtesy of Helen Person.)

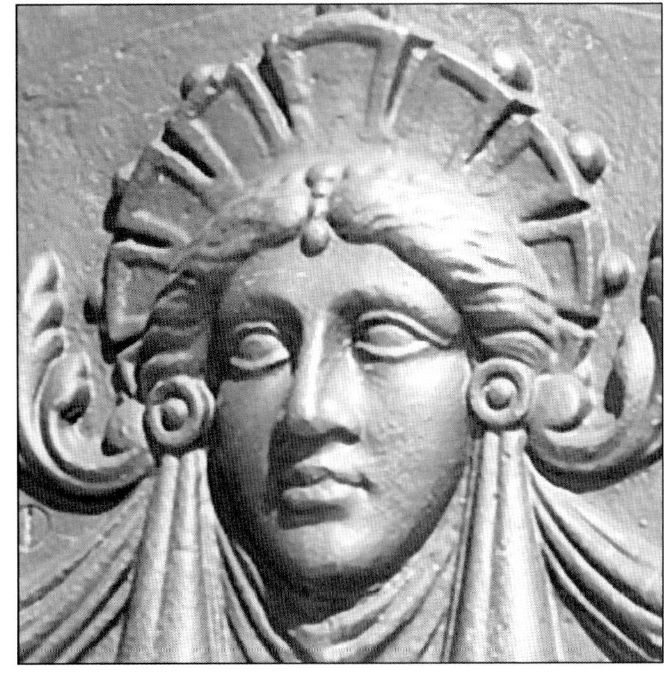

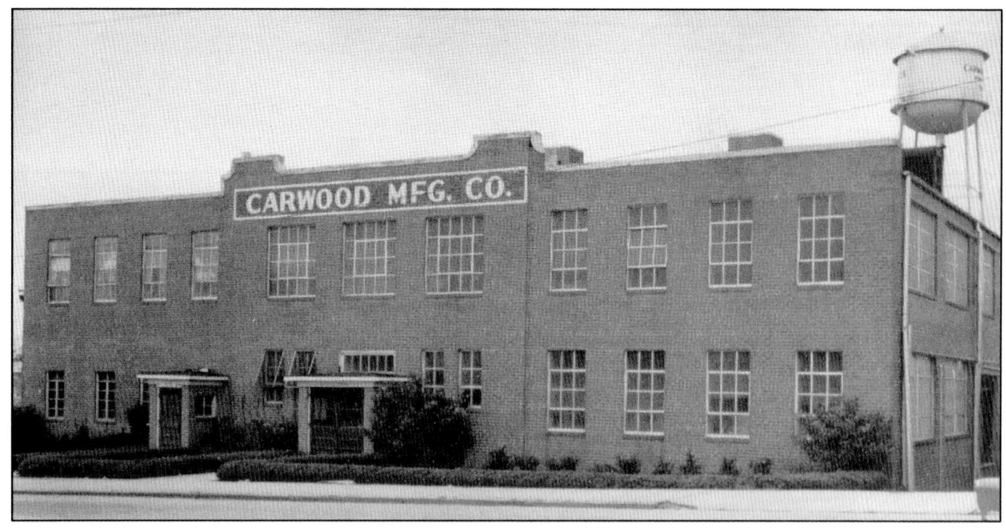

Following the organization of Barrow County in 1914, the Sharpton Opera House served as a temporary courthouse from 1914 to 1920. It also served as the temporary home of Carwood Manufacturing Company, founded in 1927. Carwood was the result of a partnership among Robert L. Carithers, Hugh A. Carithers, George W. Woodruff, and W. Clair Harris. Carwood was later merged with O'Bryan Brothers Co., the founders of the Duck Head clothing company, to create the Duck Head Apparel Co., which established headquarters in Winder in 1989. (Courtesy 1958 Winder-Barrow High School *Panorama*.)

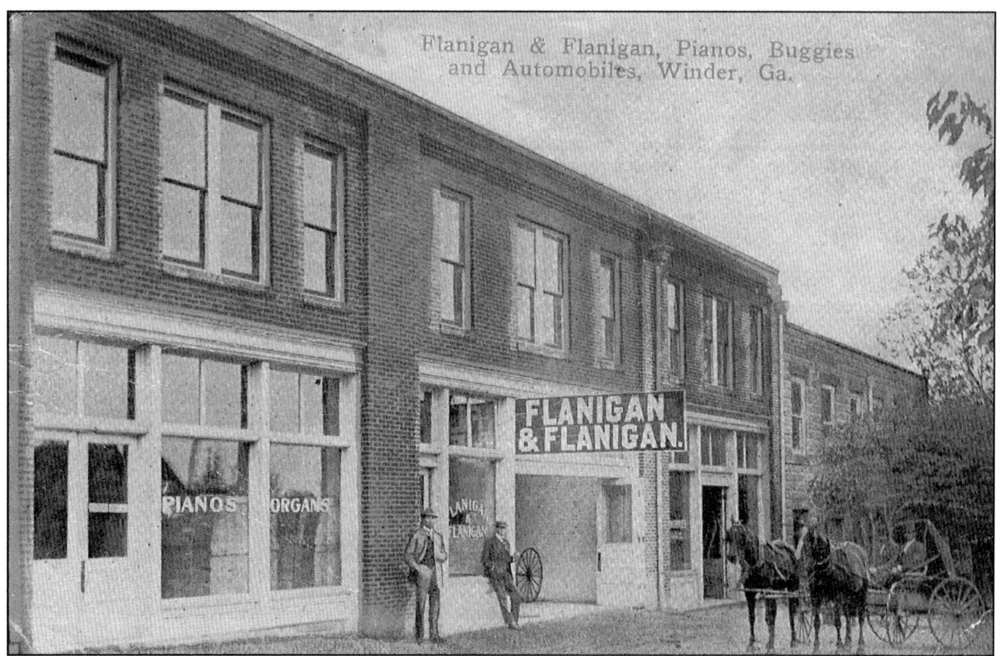

Flanigan and Flanigan Pianos, Buggies, and Automobiles was located on Candler Street, east of Broad Street and near the Winder Ice House. The Flanigan brothers' business was a sign of the times, ushering out horse-drawn buggies as motorized conveyances (available in any color, so long as it was black) began appearing on the streets of cities like Winder. (Courtesy of Joe Bowen.)

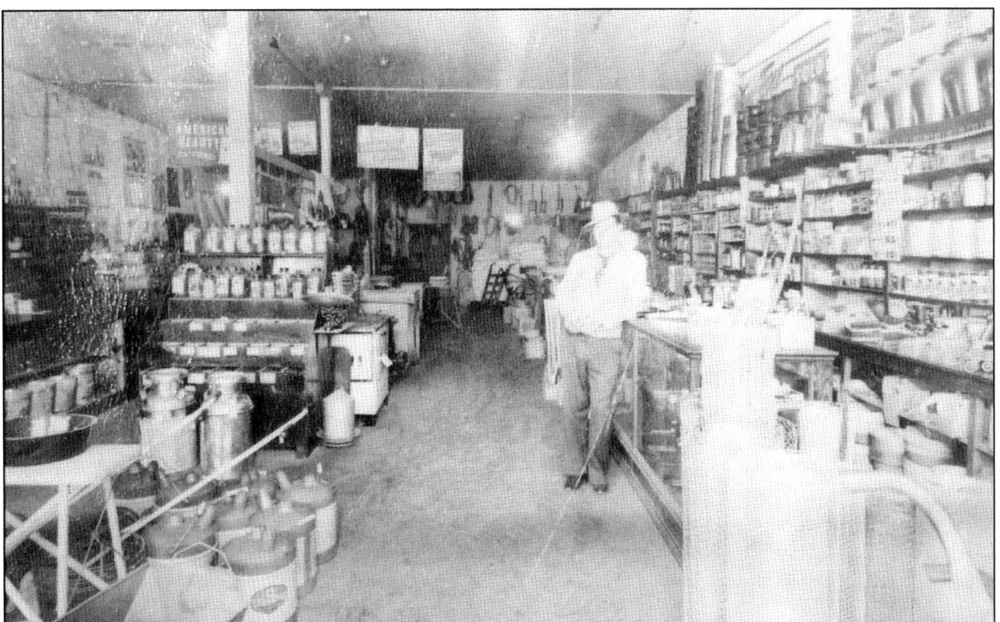

In 1918, George W. Garner organized a general mercantile that came to be known as Cash Supply. Cash Supply specialized in hardware and farm supplies, as well as feed and seed. When Cash Supply moved to the former Flanigan and Flanigan location in 1940, the three storefronts lent themselves well to the major product categories sold by Garner and his son-in-law Robert A. Hill. Like many of Winder's commercial buildings, Cash Supply's street facade consisted of large, plate-glass, showcase windows to utilize natural light. Until joined in the business by Hill, Garner and his wife, Annie, operated their hardware and farm supply business together as they catered to the area's vast agricultural community. Below, Garner (right) is shown with Robert Beckum in this 1933 photograph. (Both images courtesy of Bob Hill.)

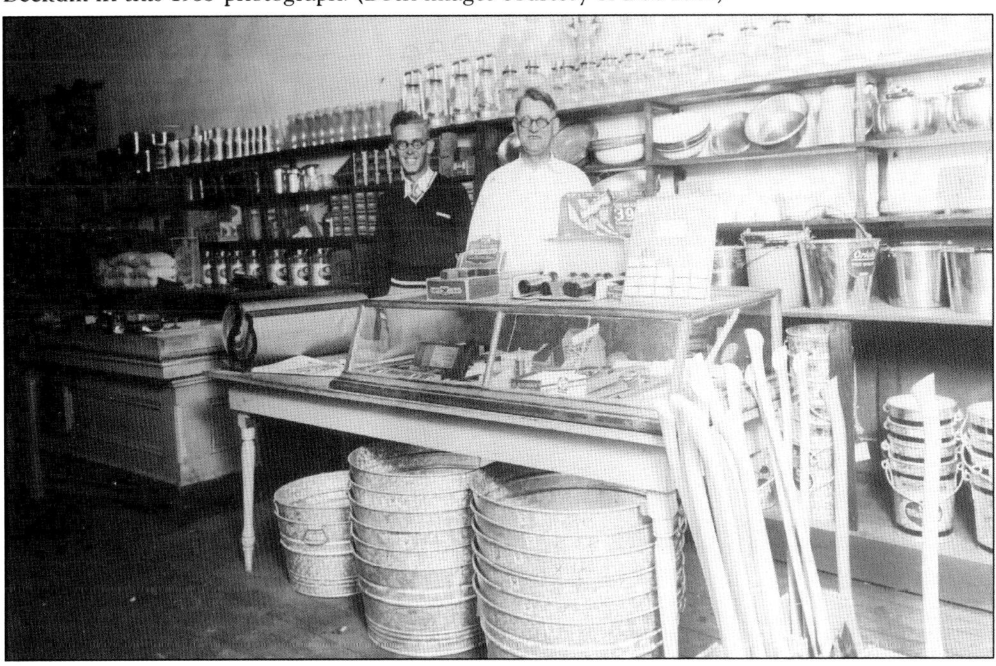

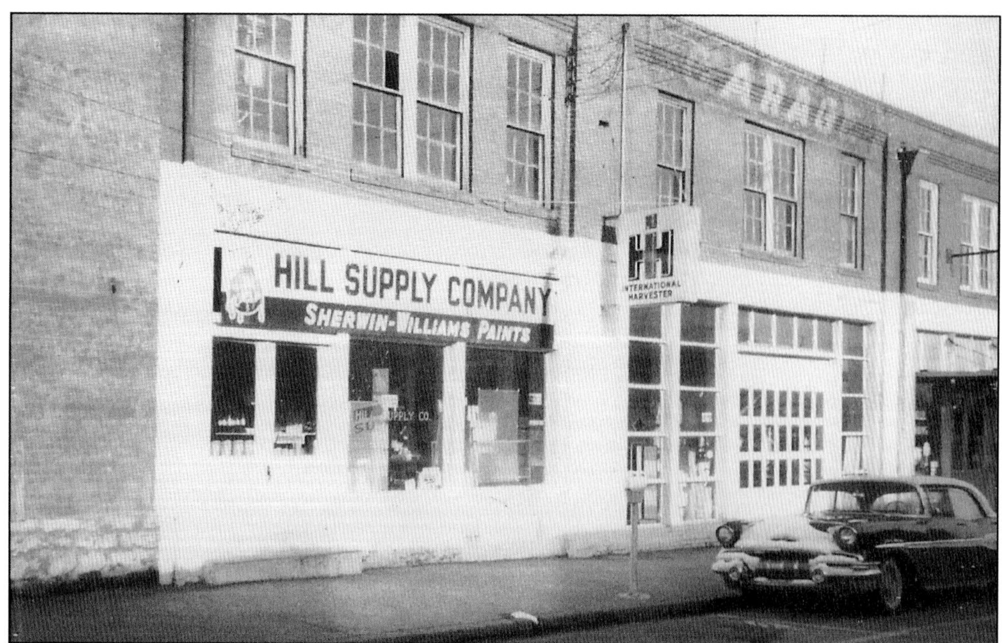

Following Garner's death in 1945, Robert Hill changed the name of Cash Supply to Hill Supply Company. The company's inventories were expanded to include lumber and building supplies following the purchase of R.C. Jones' Building Supply Company. Typical of postwar trends, the brick storefront was painted white for a sleeker look while new, lighted signage completed the transition into contemporary, mid-20th century commerce. (Courtesy of Bob Hill.)

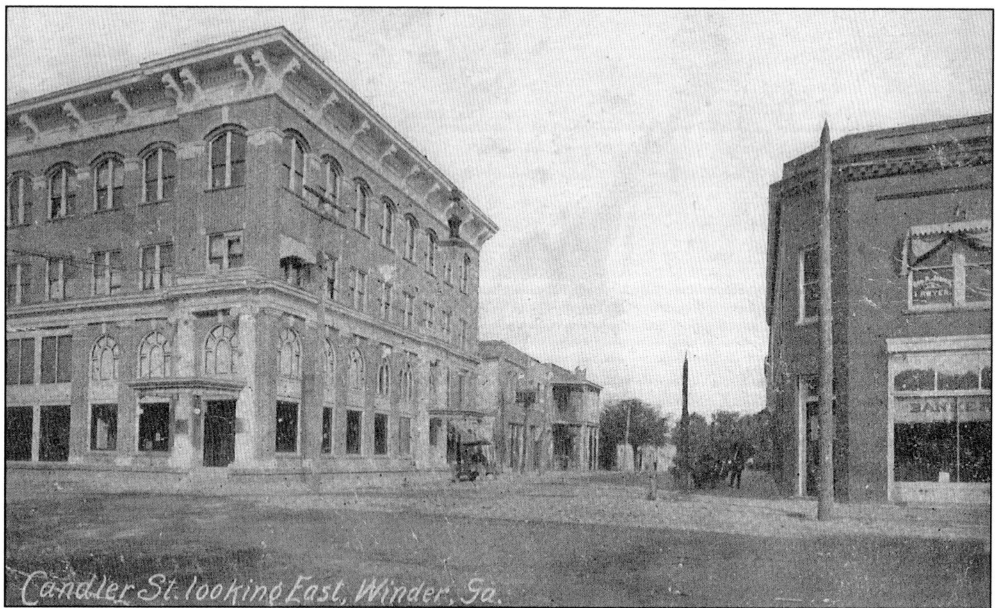

The Winder Banking Company was organized in 1899 on the corner of Broad and Candler Streets. Its first home was a wood frame building. This impressive four-story Italianate building was completed in 1908. The 1909 Sanborn map shows the bank, a grocery store, and a bowling alley occupying the ground floor. Professional offices for doctors, dentists, and attorneys populated the upper floors. (Courtesy of Joe Bowen.)

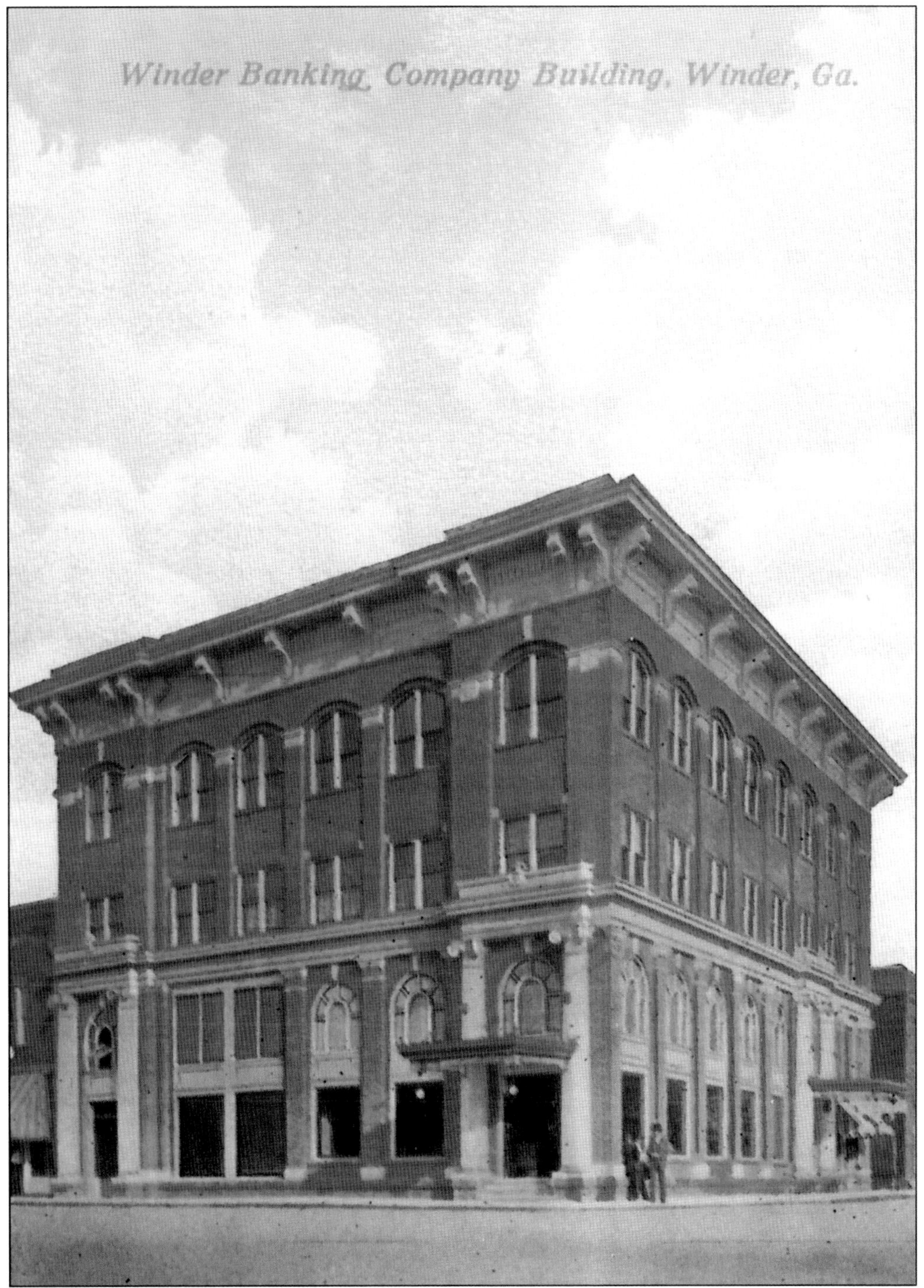

Early 1900s postcards produced by a variety of publishers featured photographs of prominent Winder businesses. The elegant new Winder Banking Company image advertised the prosperity of this young city. Officers at this time were Thomas A. Maynard (president) and Charles O. Maddox (cashier). The bank building was designed to be a presence of dignity and affluence amid a foundation of simplicity and practicality. (Courtesy of Joe Bowen.)

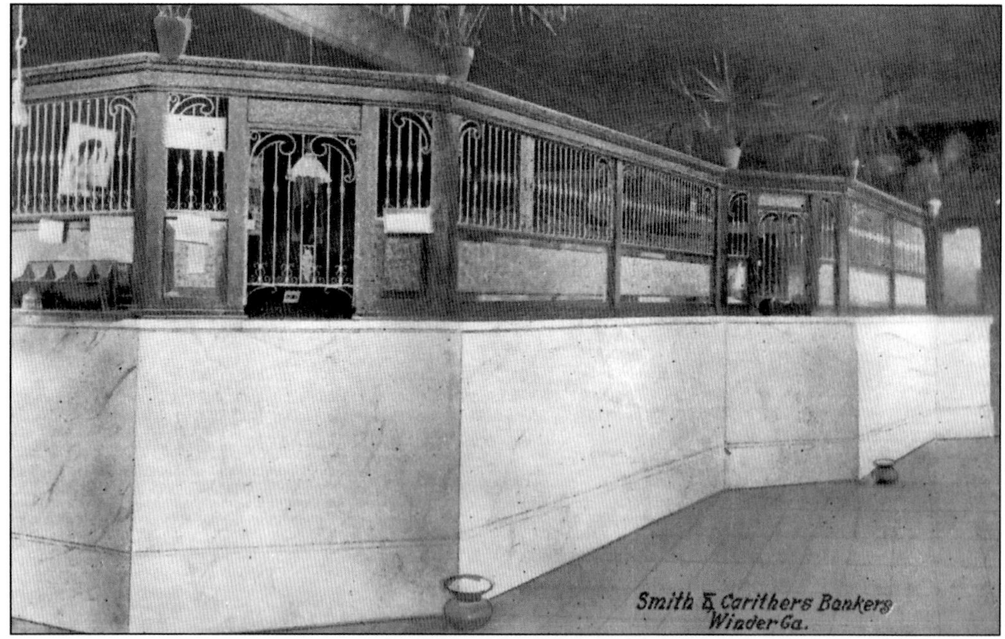

Banking institutions were plentiful in Winder. The Winder Banking Company's neighbor across Candler Street was Smith and Carithers bankers, established c. 1900, on the corner of the J.T. Strange Department Store. The Smith and Carithers teller line was the epitome of taste and elegance, with marble counters, decorative bronze grilles, and unobtrusive brass spittoons. Potted palms softened the institutional atmosphere. The bank was closed by 1921. (Courtesy of Joe Bowen.)

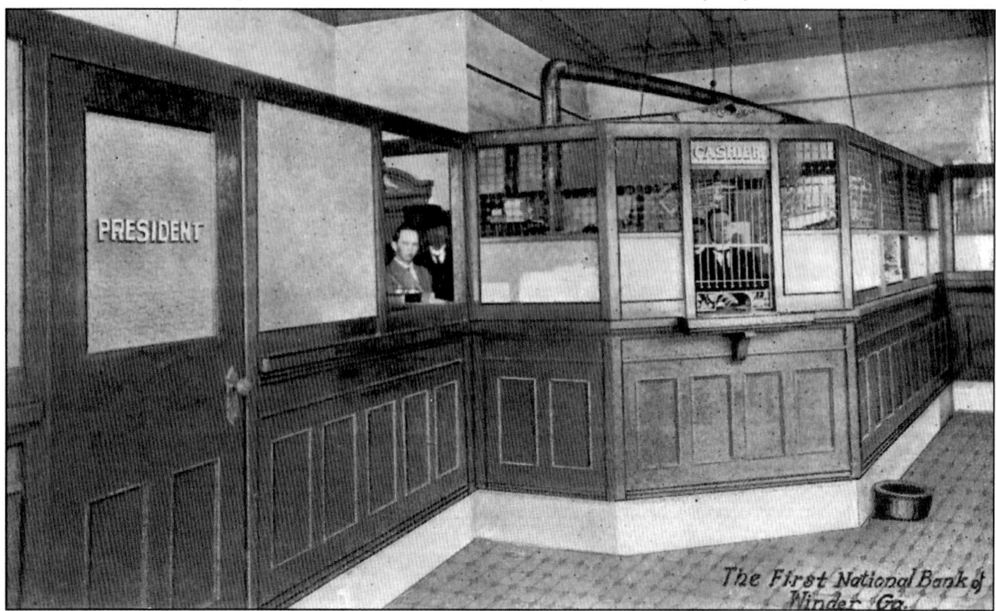

In 1908, the First National Bank of Winder was organized with capital of $50,000, and W.H. Toole was the president. With a picture frame–style wainscoted teller line and in-line president's office door, the First National Bank presented an image of accessibility and practicality aimed toward a no-nonsense approach to attracting the typical Winder resident's business. The appearance contrasted with Smith and Carithers's more elegant aesthetic. (Courtesy of Joe Bowen.)

In 1916, the Winder Banking Company was converted into a national bank, as indicated on this reprint of the bank's postcard with the changed imprint "Winder National Bank." The Winder National Bank became one of many victims of the Great Depression when the institution was dissolved on December 30, 1932. The building then became home to The Peoples Bank, with former cashier C.O. Maddox as president. (Courtesy of Joe Bowen.)

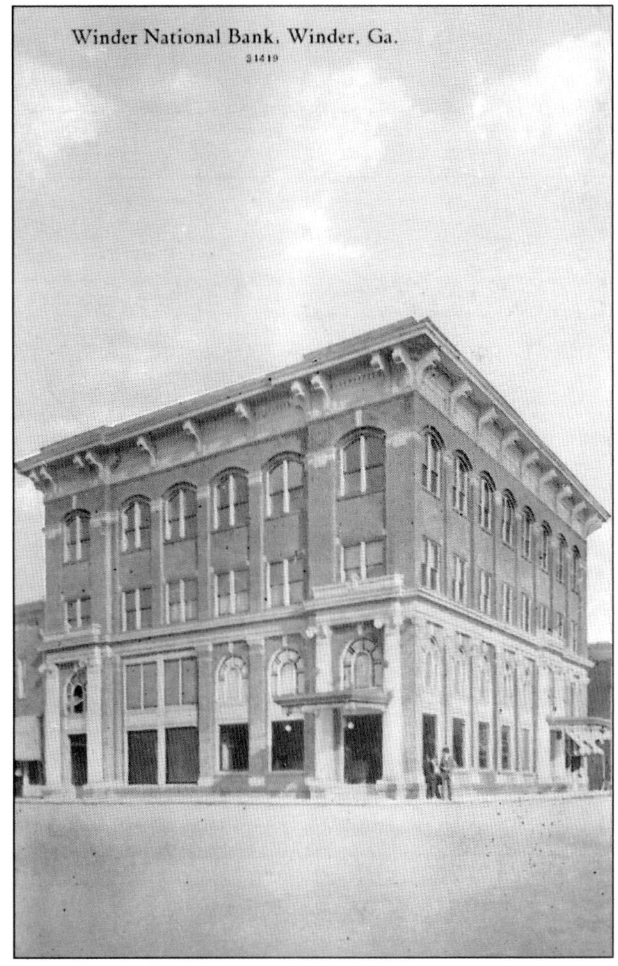

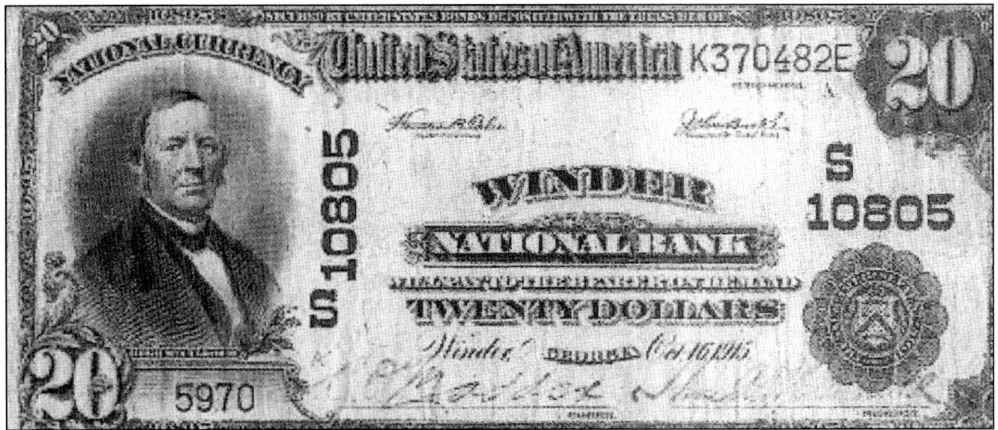

During its 33-year existence, the Winder National Bank was one of the two local institutions that issued currency. This $20 note from 1915 bears the signature of cashier C.O. Maddox and bank president Thomas A. Maynard. The bank's charter number was 10805. Winder National Bank currency, considered rare national bank notes, carries a value upward of $400 in today's market. (Courtesy of Joe Bowen.)

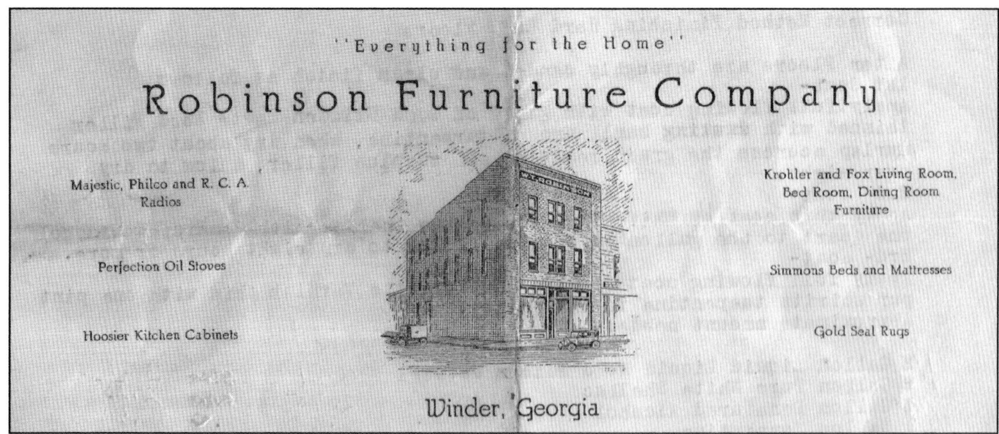

William T. Robinson opened his furniture store on the corner of Candler and Jackson Streets around 1905, according to Sanborn Fire Insurance maps. The two-story granite building featured a cast-iron storefront fabricated by the Winder Foundry and Machine Works. Plate-glass windows and a recessed entry on Candler Street welcomed patrons to the store. The third floor, with its brick facade, was added around 1912. This letterhead provided an imprinted image of the Robinson Furniture building, along with a listing of product lines represented at the leading Winder retail establishment. Below, Oscar E. Summerour (left), Bert Roberts (center), and William Taylor Robinson posed for this c. 1921 photograph taken inside the store. (Both images courtesy of Bill Summerour.)

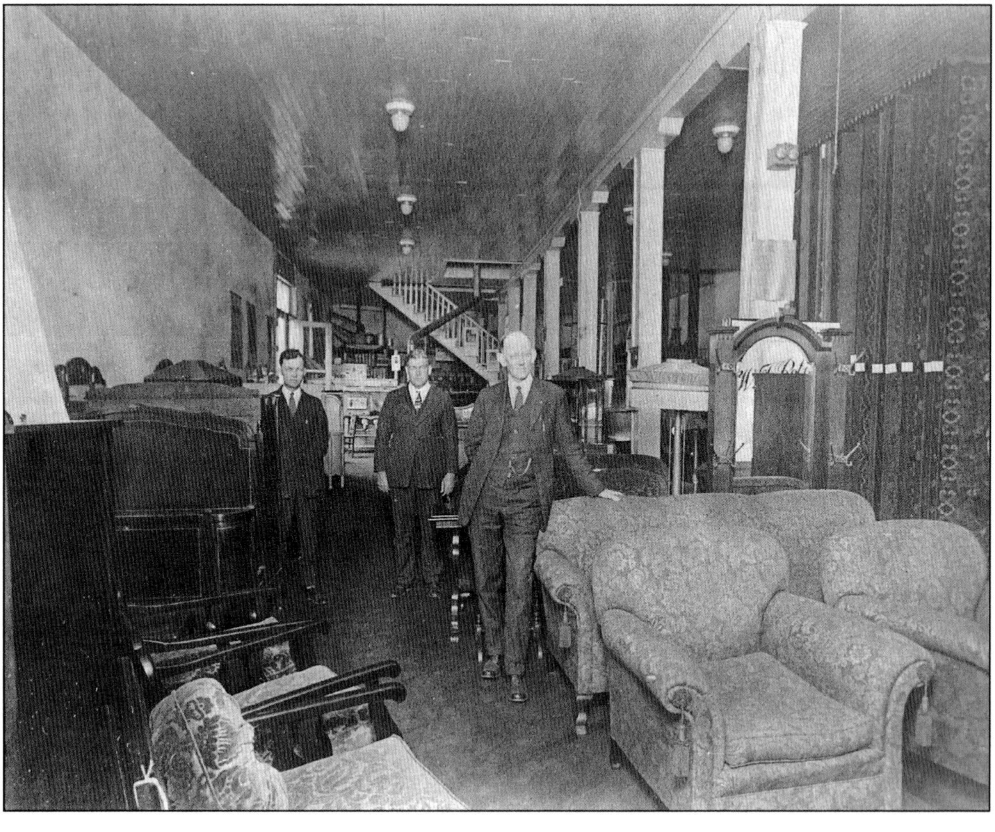

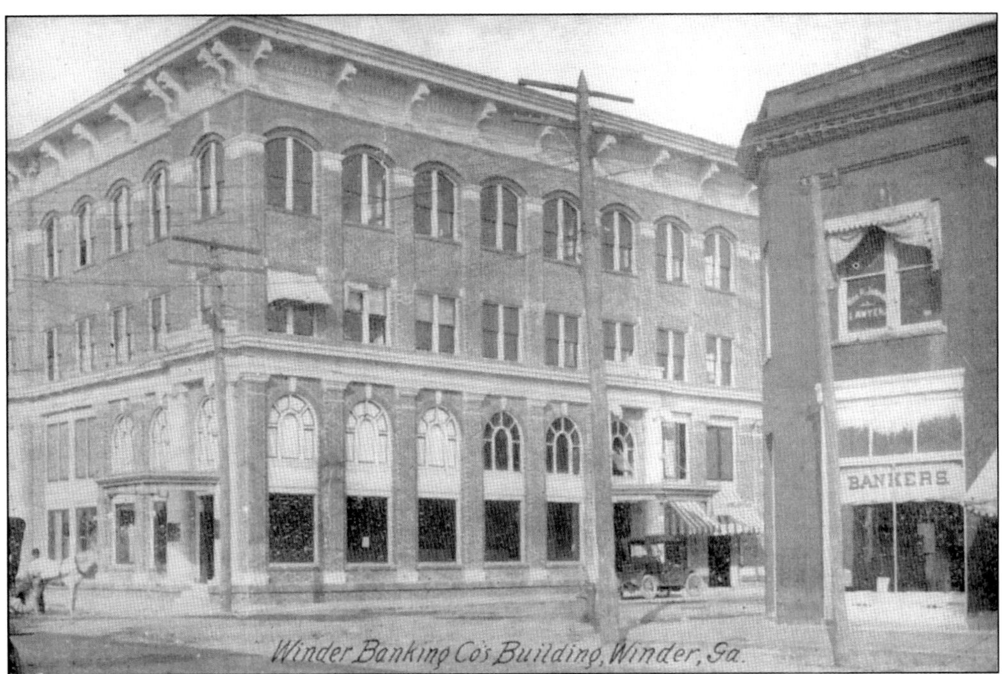

The intersection of Broad and Candler Streets was home to two banks, a department store, and two pharmacies. J.T. Strange and Co. Department Store was established around 1885. The modern two-story brick building with corbelled cornice and glass display windows was built in 1903. It housed the retail operation, a grocery store on Candler Street, and Smith and Carithers bankers. Families from all walks of Winder society shopped at the Strange Co. This 1894 receipt for Mrs. J.R. Coker is dated two years after the reincorporation of the town as Winder. The Cokers were one of Winder's original families. Mrs. Coker was the mother of Charles M. "C.M." Ferguson. (Both images courtesy of Joe Bowen.)

J. T. STRANGE. SMITH CARITHUS & CO.

Bought of J. T. Strange & Co.

—DEALERS IN—

Dry Goods, Notions, Shoes, Clothing and Hats.

Paid J. T. Strange & Co 3.48

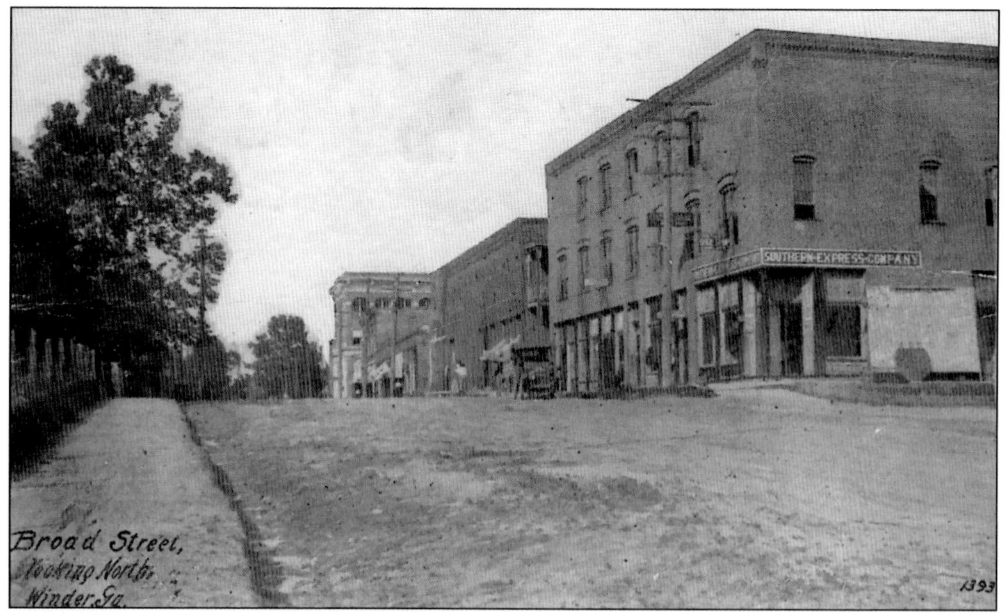

The 20th century dawned in Winder with rapid development, a flood of new residents, and an avalanche of construction. This c. 1910 photograph of Broad Street, taken from the Seaboard Air Line railroad depot on South Broad Street, shows the Sharpton Opera House and the Winder Banking Company in the distance. Streets had not yet been paved because automobiles were scarce in the area. (Courtesy of Joe Bowen.)

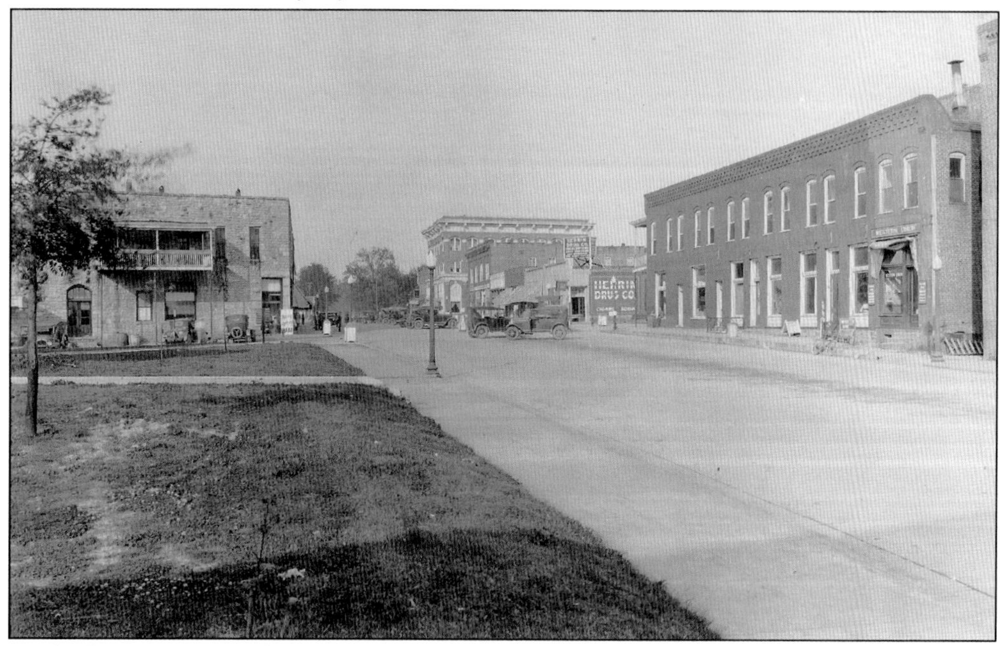

By the late 1910s, Broad Street had been paved to accommodate the automobiles using the city streets. This photograph, taken for a 1920 engineering study, shows vehicles parked in the middle of the street, as well as parallel to the sidewalks. The photograph appears to predate the construction of the 1920 Barrow County Courthouse due to the absence of a shadow from the imposing building. (Courtesy of Joe Bowen.)

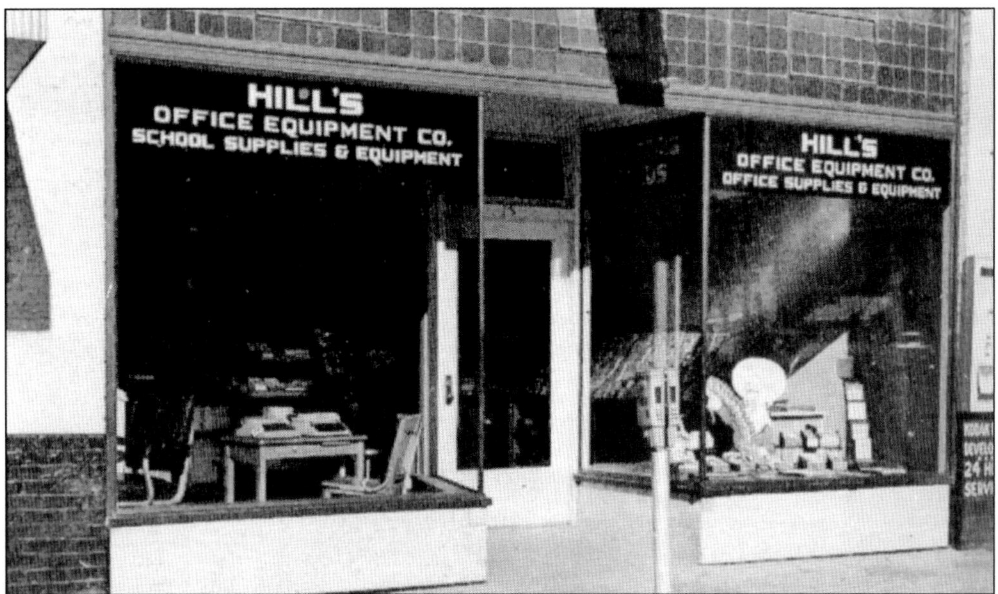

In the mid-19th century, American foundries discovered the art of prefabricating architectural elements out of cast iron. More durable and readily available than the site-fabricated, terra-cotta ornamentation installed on commercial buildings, cast-iron elements could be created in a factory and shipped to the construction site. Cast-iron ornament fell out of vogue in the post-Depression years. Many building owners opted for sleek metal storefronts devoid of the ornamental detail, like that of the Sharpton Opera House and many of the Broad Street storefronts in Winder. As America sought to distance itself from the fussiness of the Victorian period, architects began discarding such details as the multipaned transoms of B.C. Hill's Office Equipment Co. (pictured above) and installing designs containing simple lines of glass and metal. (Both images courtesy of Joe Bowen.)

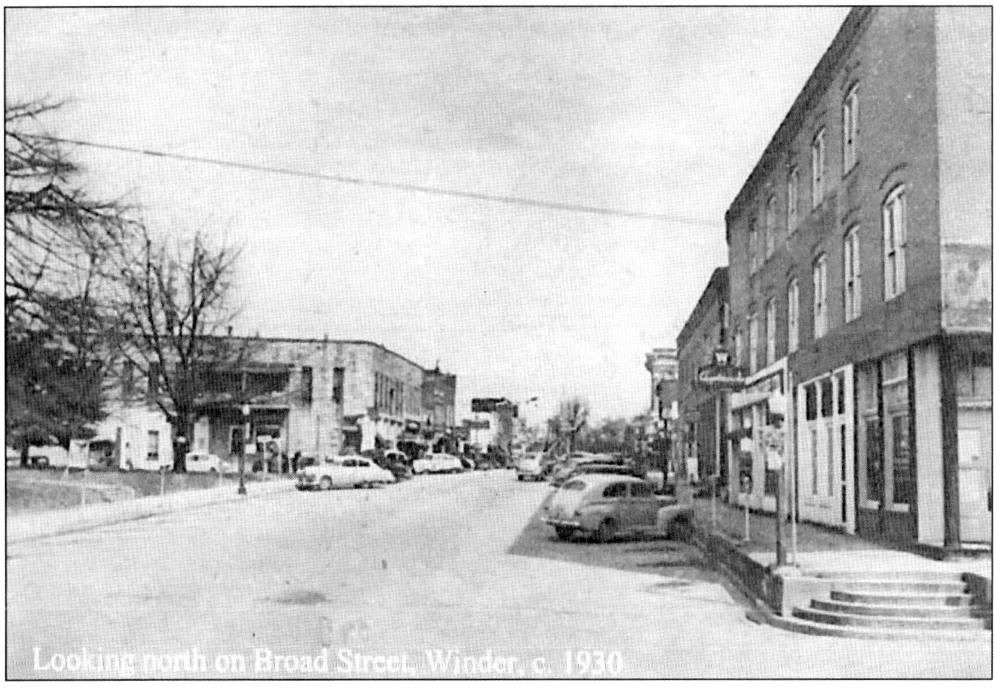

Looking north on Broad Street, Winder, c. 1930

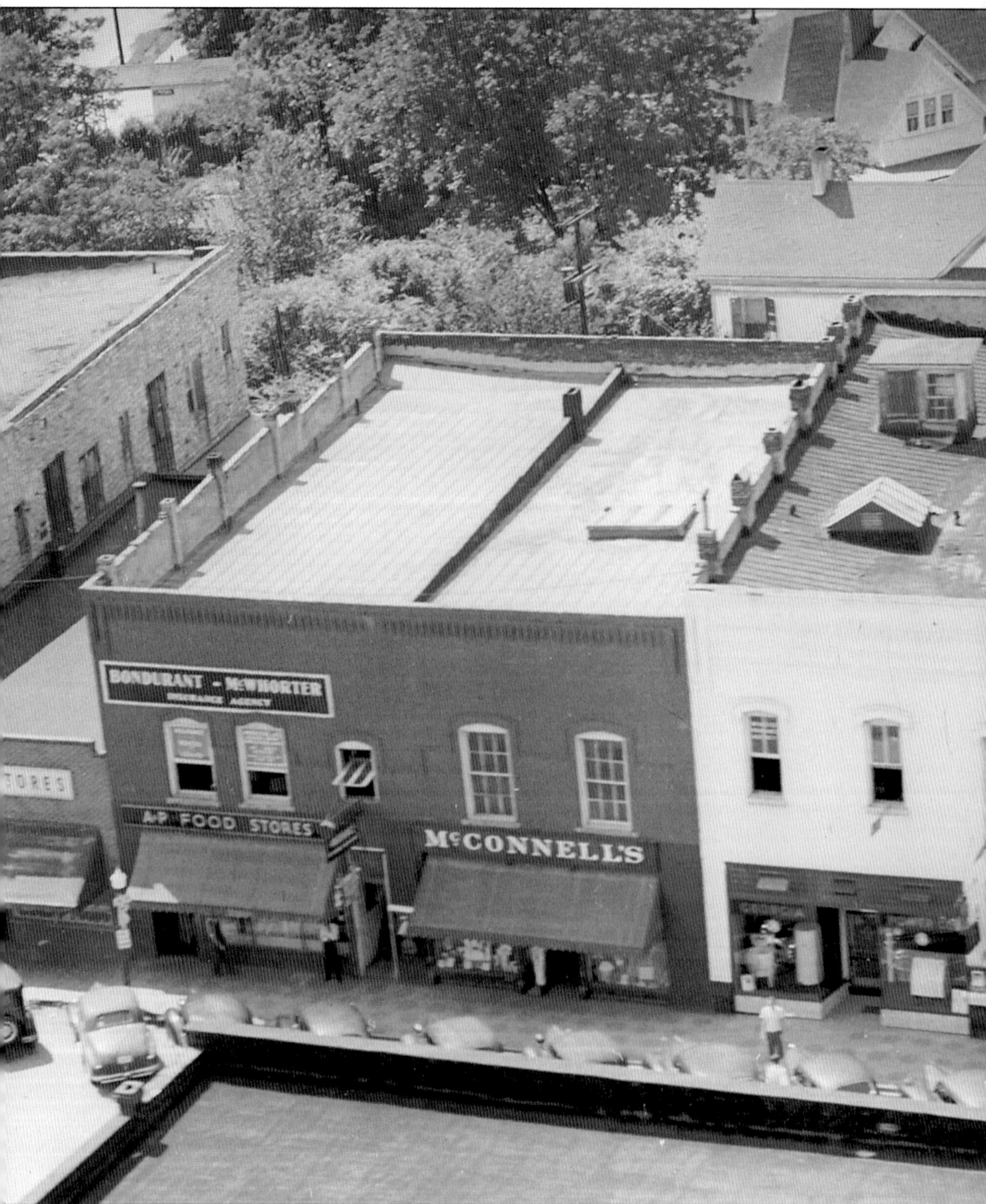

This 1948 aerial photograph of Candler Street west of Broad Street illustrates the proximity of residential areas to downtown Winder. The asymmetrical orientations and varying rooflines of the houses on Candler Street marked the residences of the Albert A. Camp (center) and Robert L. Carithers (far center) families. Both families were prominent early residents before the organization of Jug Tavern as a city. Robert L. Carithers and Hugh A. Carithers built Jug Tavern's first brick

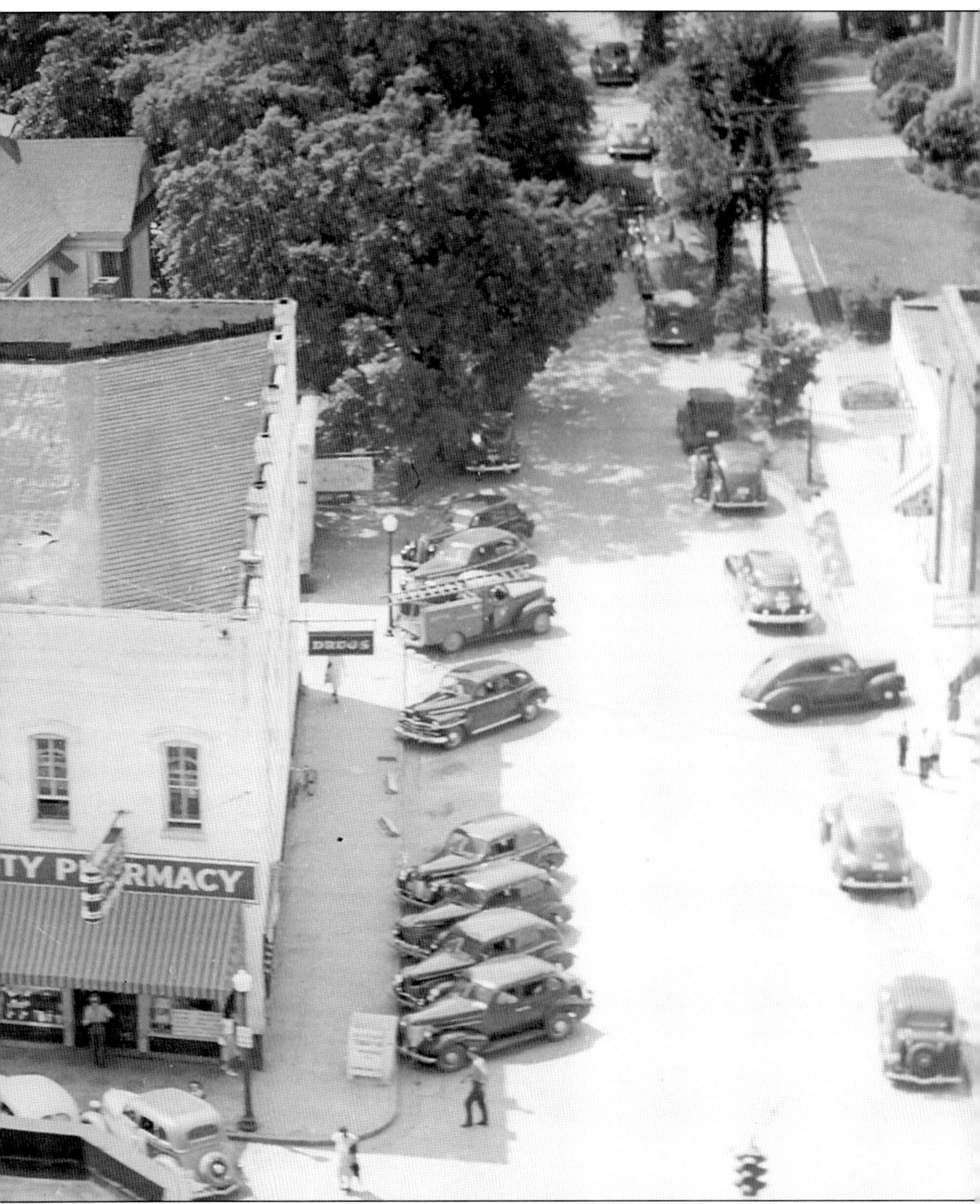

building at the corner of Broad and Athens Streets. R.L. Carithers served as Barrow County's first elected representative and played in the Jug Tavern Brass Band. He was also chairman of the 1911 committee appointed to promote creation of the new county, later known as Barrow. Albert A. Camp was a Jug Tavern merchant and, later, Winder's first postmaster. (Courtesy of Evelyn Arnold.)

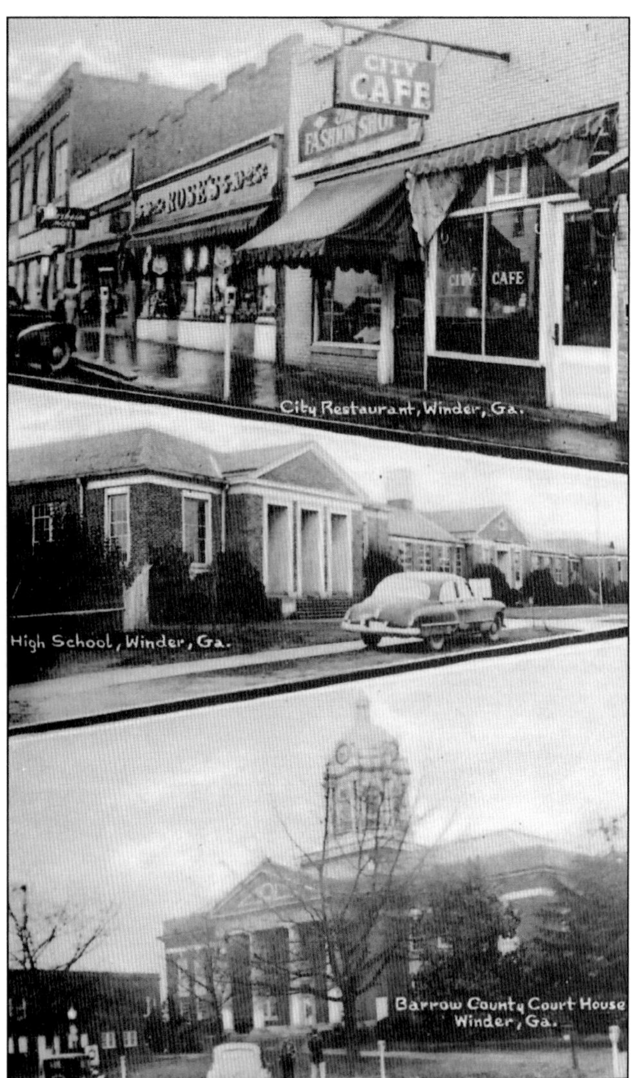

By the early 1940s, Winder's Broad Street contained a new City Café and the debut of a regional five-and-dime store: Rose's. The Barrow County Courthouse continued as the governmental center, and a recently constructed high school offered a new beginning for Winder City School System students. Postcards were still a popular promotional item, with visitors sending greetings featuring images of Winder's progress. (Courtesy of Joe Bowen.)

In the 1940s, Empire 5, 10, and 25 Cent Store (below) on Athens Street installed a stationary marquee-style canopy. Display windows framed in ceramic tile completed a contemporary presentation unlike any ever seen in Winder. As facade wraps made of aluminum or ceramics achieved popularity, many traditional commercial buildings began losing their visible identities as brick was painted or covered completely in favor of a more modern look based on suburban shopping centers. (Courtesy of 1959 Winder-Barrow School *Panorama*.)

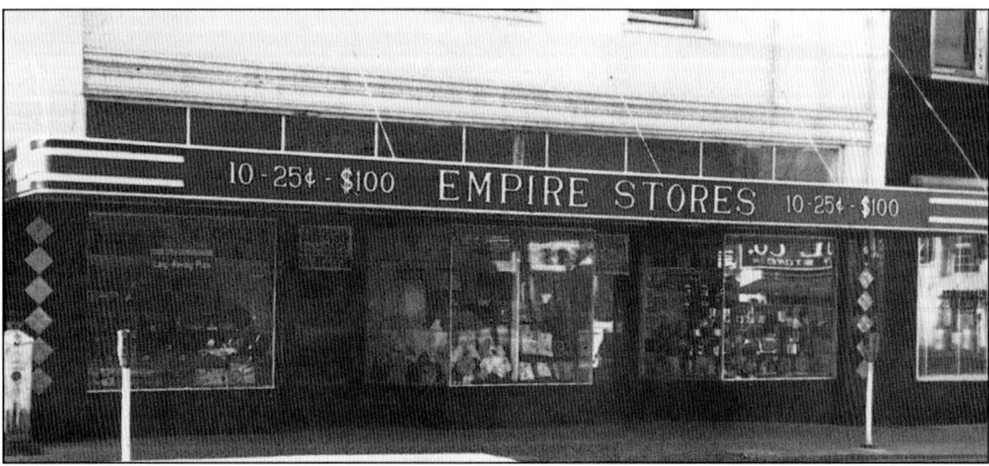

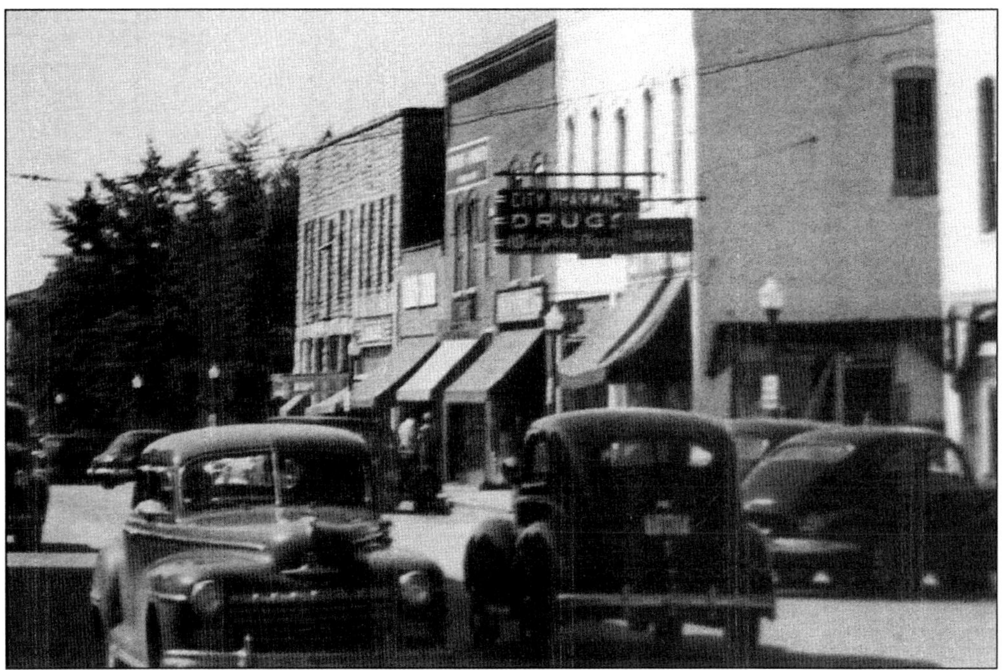

As World War II drew to a close, Winder was experiencing the loss of its first generation of citizens. The second generation returned to resume their adult lives as business owners, professionals, and community leaders in their hometown. The "Town that Bush Built" (*Atlanta Constitution*, 1924) launched a new round of growth as manufacturing orders increased, new residents moved to the area for jobs, and retailers spruced up their storefronts with new awnings, modern appointments, and up-to-date accoutrements. Considered the middle of downtown, the intersection of Broad and Candler Streets continued to be as much a hotbed of activity in 1948 as it was in the mid-1910s in this photograph of the City Pharmacy building. Three decades later, state highways brought in more automobiles, and locals were joined by travelers pausing on their journeys to visit Winder. (Above, courtesy of Evelyn Arnold; below, courtesy of Joe Bowen.)

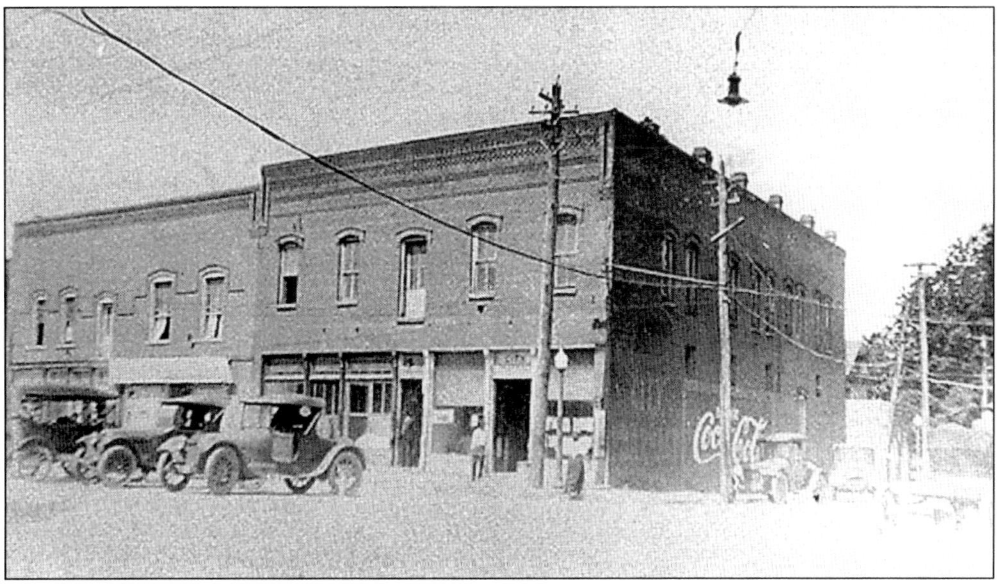

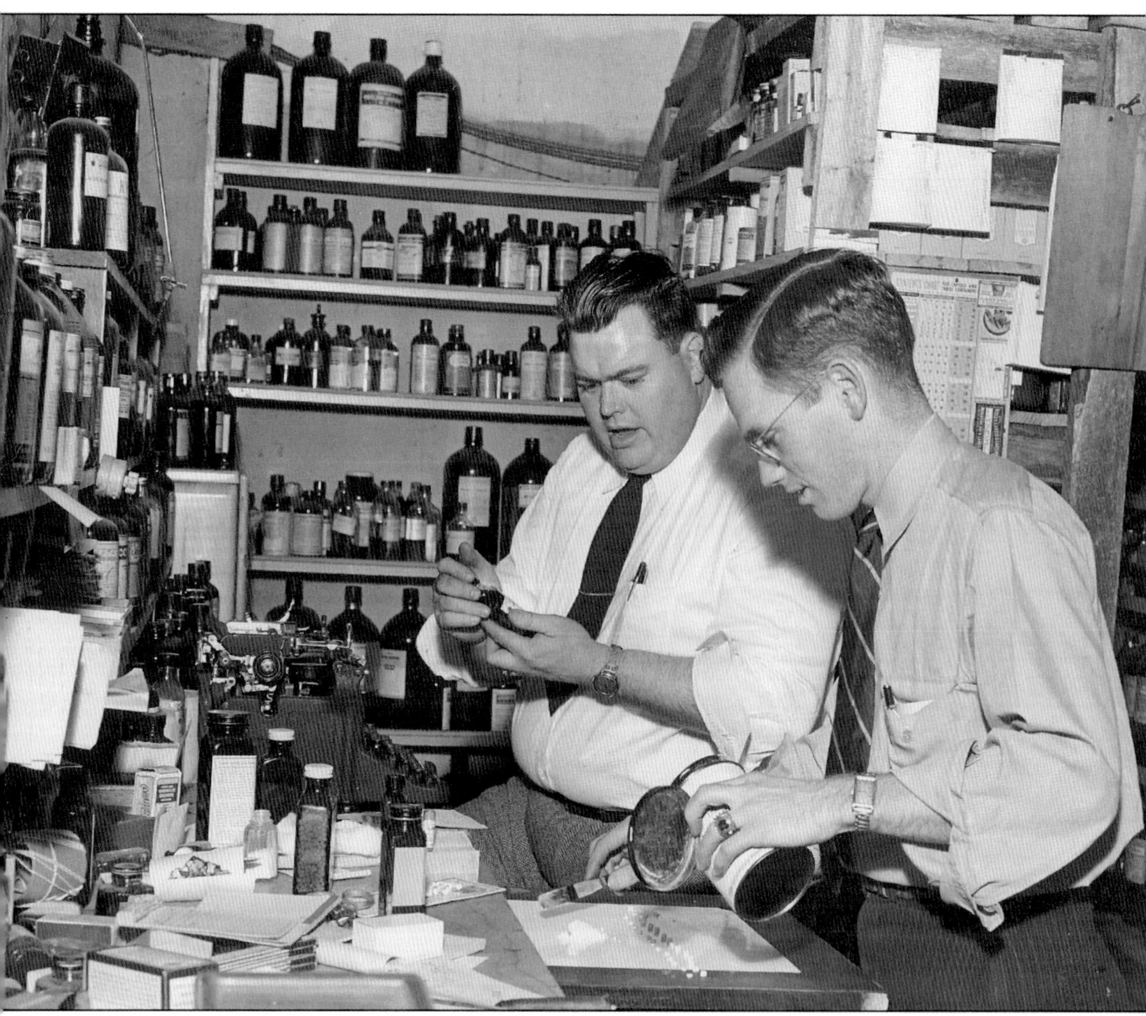

In 1945, Haase Arnold returned from the US Navy to pursue his dream of becoming a community pharmacist. With his brother Sells Arnold, he purchased City Pharmacy in downtown Winder. Pictured with pharmacist Joe Harrell, Haase Arnold (right) drew on his high school and college experiences working with Harold M. Herrin at neighboring Herrin Drugs. The independent pharmacies in Winder were a delightful blend of tradition and innovation. (Courtesy of Evelyn Arnold.)

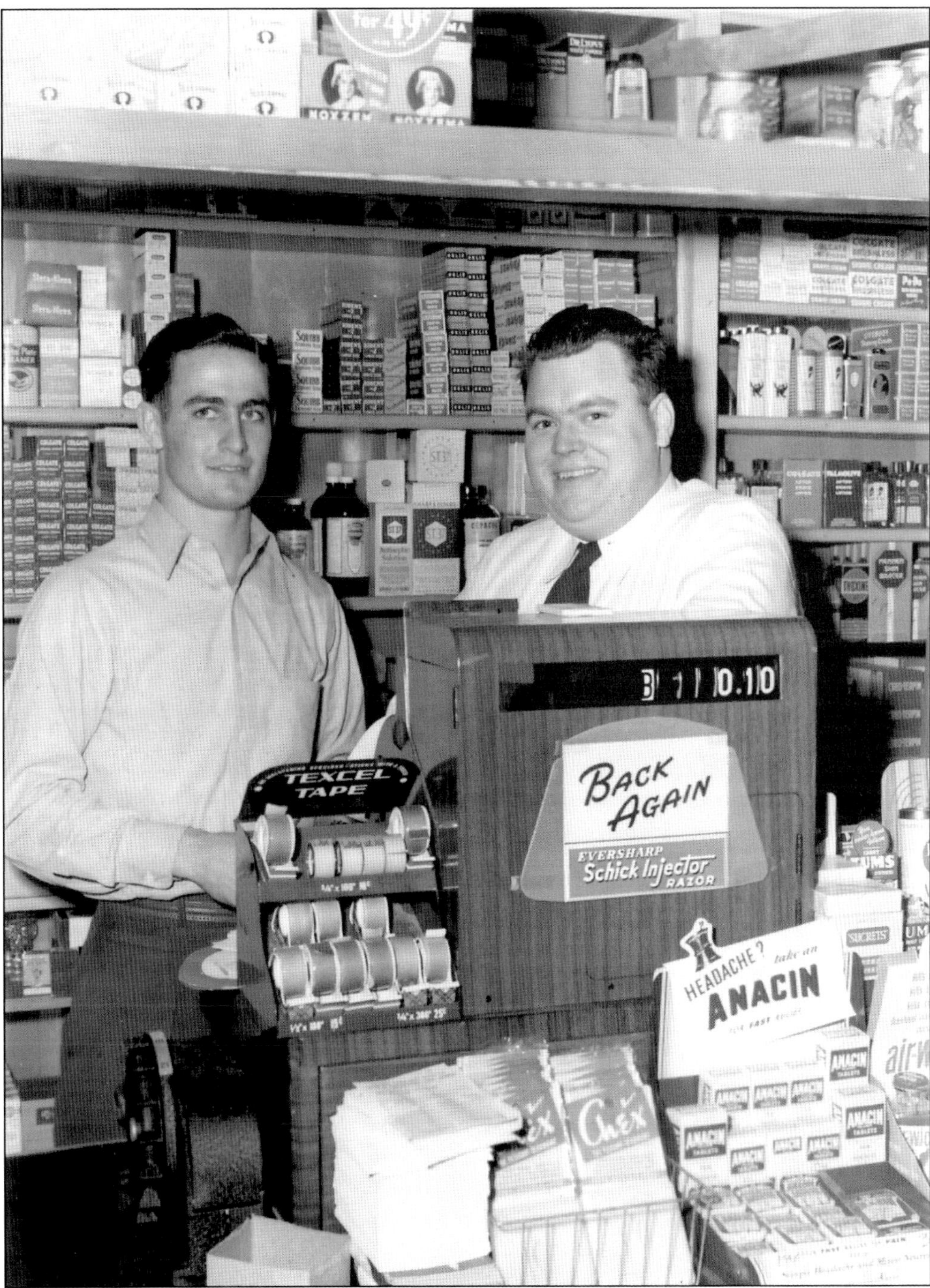

City Pharmacy was representative of the traditional corner drugstore filled with medications, potions, sundry, and novelty items. The shelves and counters were laden with products of all shapes, sizes, and purposes as Ralph Lee (left) and Joe Harrell worked to serve patrons. Practicality reigned in the pharmacy, with friendly, professional service being the highest priority. Following the death of Sells Arnold in 1947, his younger brother became sole proprietor of the store. Arnold's 44 years of ownership was the longest in the pharmacy's 106-year history. (Courtesy of Evelyn Arnold.)

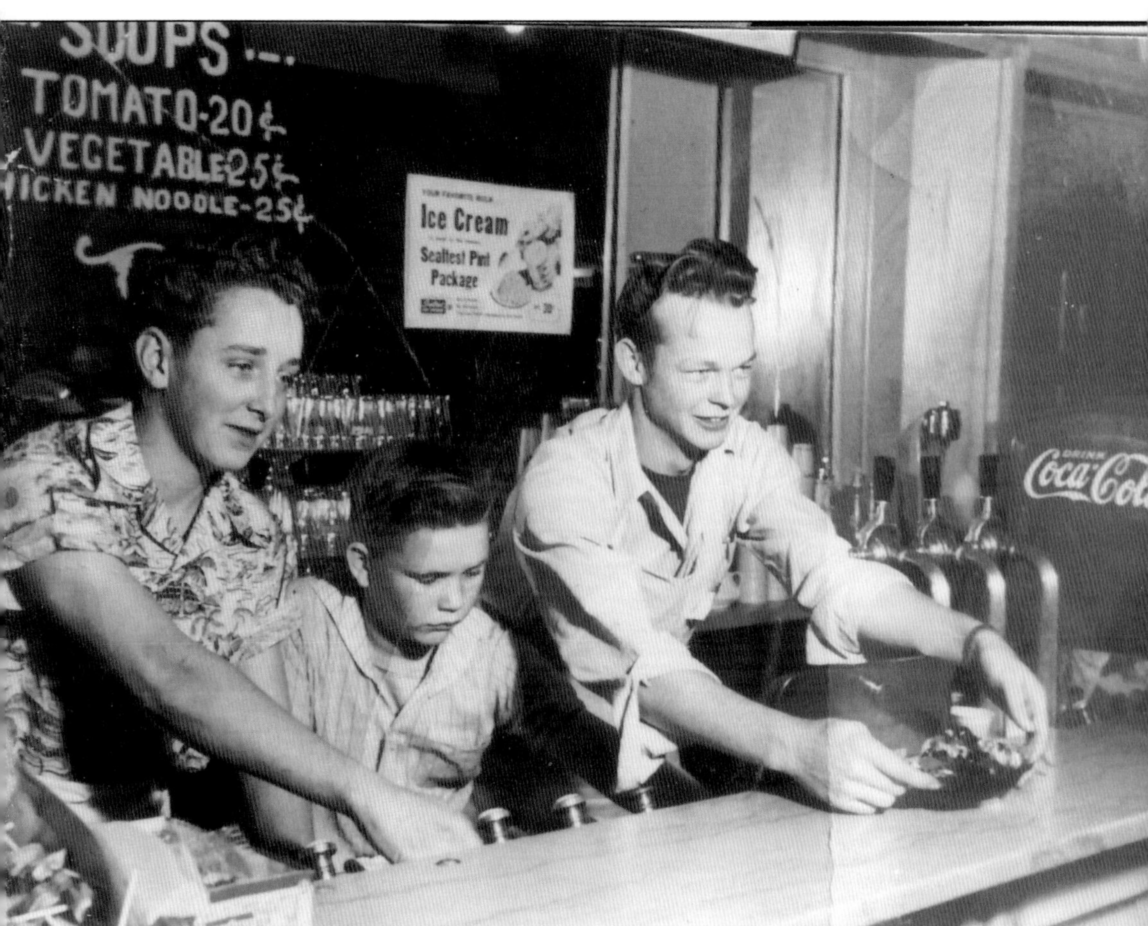

For generations, the soda fountain was synonymous with a trip to the drugstore. After all, who does not feel better after consuming a Coke float? Joe Haynie (left) and Talmadge Phillips (right) were joined by a young Gene Hopkins as they served banana splits, malts, milk shakes, sandwiches, and Coca-Cola confections to customers. Among their patrons were Clyde "Hoot" Gibson and his ice cream–eating Chihuahua. (Courtesy of Evelyn Arnold.)

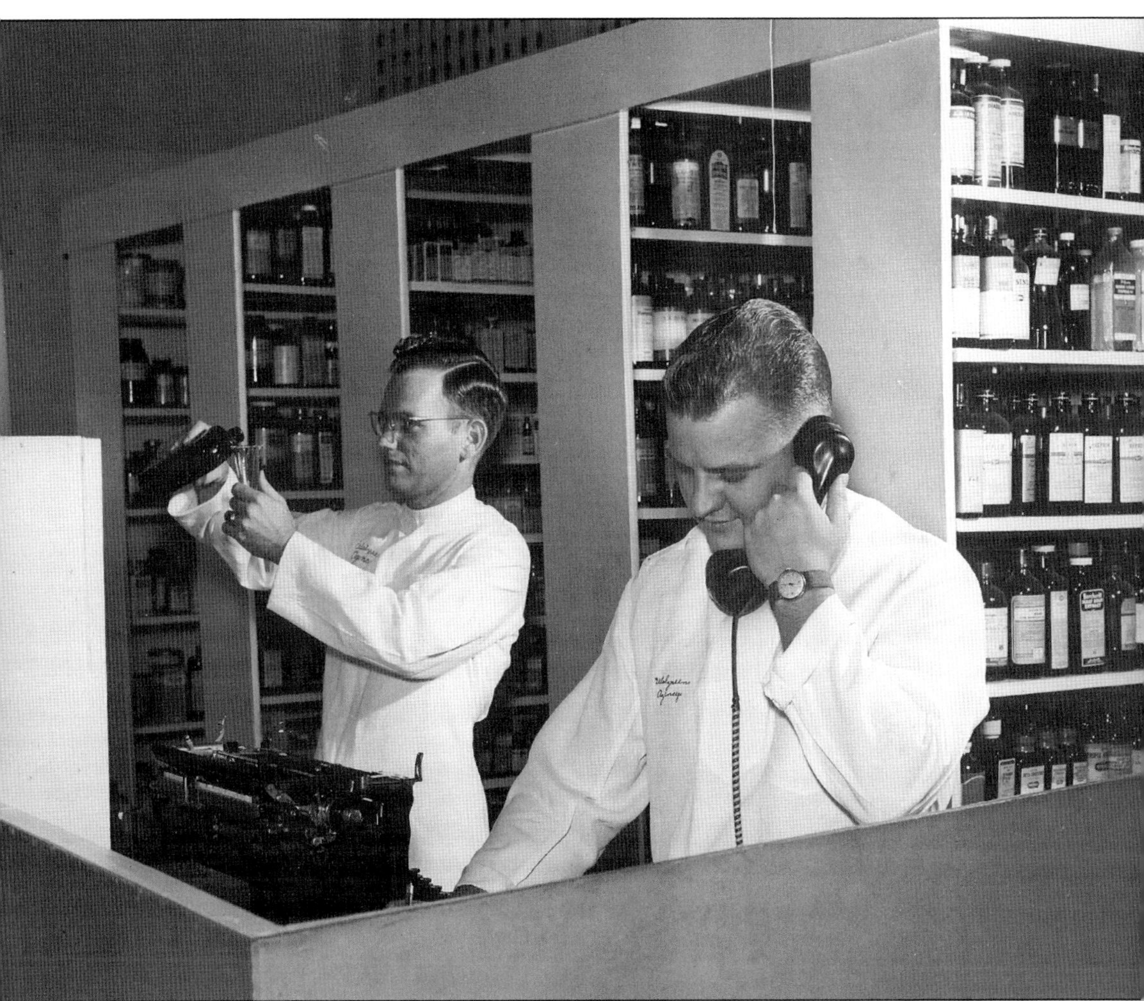

In 1958, City Pharmacy remodeled the display fixtures throughout the store to aid in providing up-to-date professional service for the store's patrons. This image shows owner C. Haase Arnold (left) and James H. "Jim" Farmer at work filling prescriptions for the people of Winder. Just as Harold Herrin assisted Arnold in his 1945 purchase of City Pharmacy, Arnold assisted Farmer with the opening of Farmer's Prescription Shop in 1960. (Courtesy of Evelyn Arnold.)

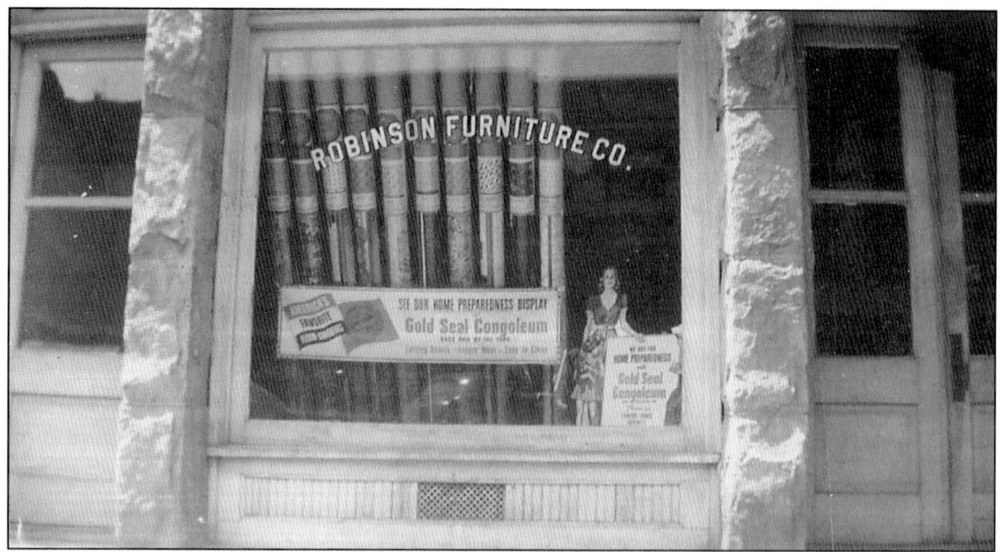

As the second generation of local business families assumed leadership, Robinson Furniture Co. was no exception. Expansion into neighboring buildings gave the Robinson family a stronger hold in the Winder home furnishings market. This photograph of the display window shows the granite block storefront with a recessed double-door entry. Ferguson Funeral Home was a neighboring business. The granite storefronts extended west on Candler Street to the rear of the J.T. Strange Building. By the time of this c. 1950 photograph, Gallant-Belk had purchased the Strange Building and continued the department store tradition at that location. (Courtesy of Caroline Robinson Stallings.)

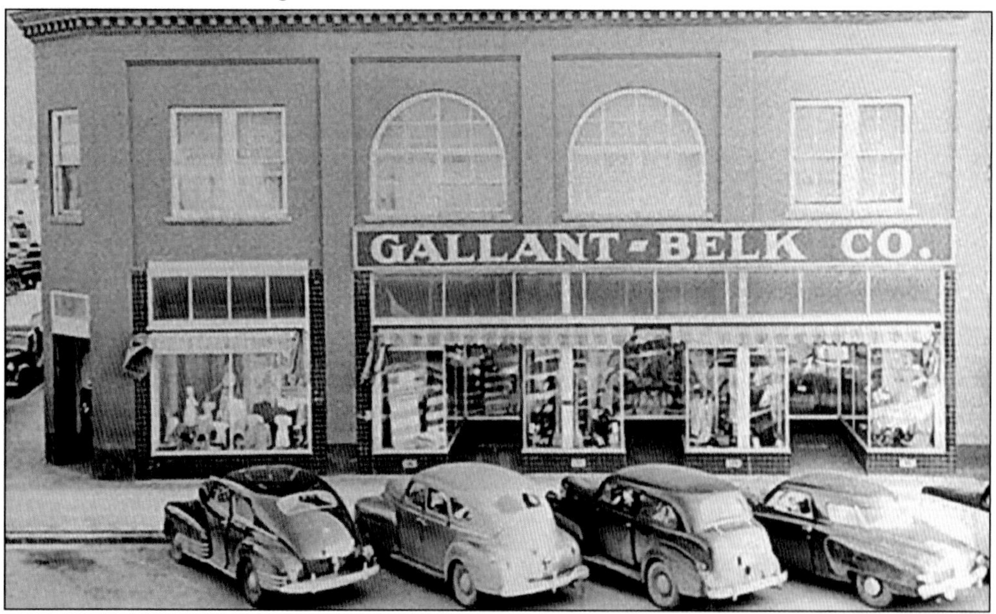

J.T. Strange and Co. ceased operation after the death of its owner and namesake in 1934. The Gallant-Belk Company, a regional department store chain, purchased the building from Strange's widow, Lida. This c. 1940 photograph shows the building's arched second-floor windows and corbelled cornice. The cast-iron storefront had been replaced with modern plate-glass display windows surrounded with Art Deco–style ceramic tile. (Courtesy of Joe Bowen.)

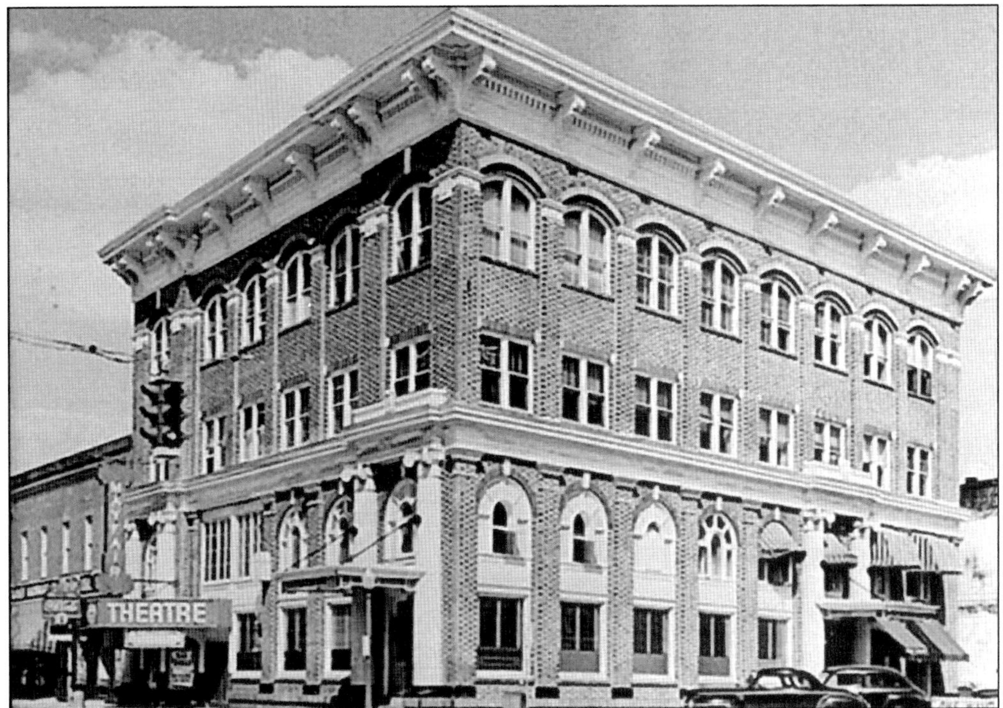

By the mid-1940s, the Mayfair Theatre was located in the north section of the ground floor of the Peoples Bank building. An intimate theater, the long, narrow space ran the length of the structure. Professional tenants like dentist Dr. Carlos A. Shaw opted to add striped awnings to their office windows, adding a touch of personalization to their spaces in the bank building. (Courtesy of Joe Bowen.)

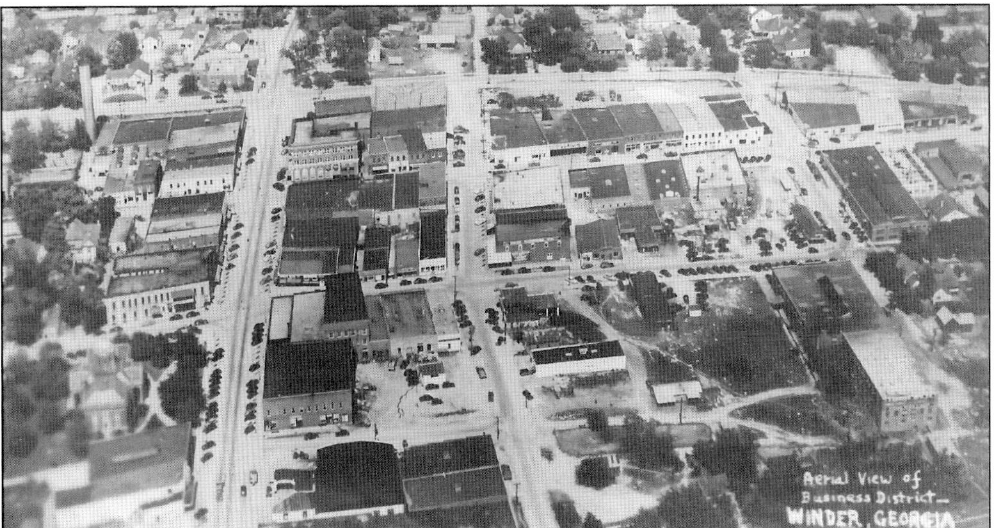

The water tower (upper left) was built for the steam-powered Gainesville Midland Railroad. Having provided an excellent vantage point for monitoring the growth of Winder, the tower was removed after the railroad ceased operation in the 1950s. For this photograph, Winder pilot, merchant, and community leader Robert A. Hill took to the air with photographer Pierson Stell to take a series of aerial images of the Winder of the mid-1950s. (Courtesy of Bob Hill.)

BANK OF BARROW

"YOUR FRIENDLY PROGRESSIVE BANK"

Member of F.D.I.C.

13 Athens Street **Winder, Georgia**

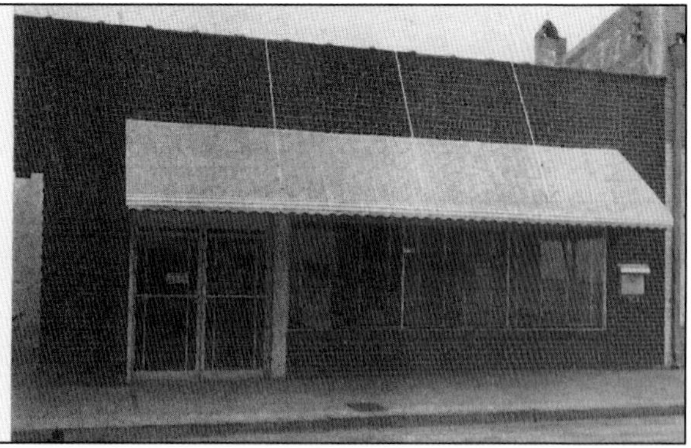

Continuing the Winder tradition of being the home for new financial institutions, the Bank of Barrow opened on East Athens Street in 1951. The simple redbrick storefront was all about function rather than form and fanfare, as with other financial institutions in the city's past. Simple fixtures and furnishings inside the straightforward one-story building indicated to patrons that the institution's priority was service rather than frills. (Courtesy 1958 Winder-Barrow High School *Panorama*.)

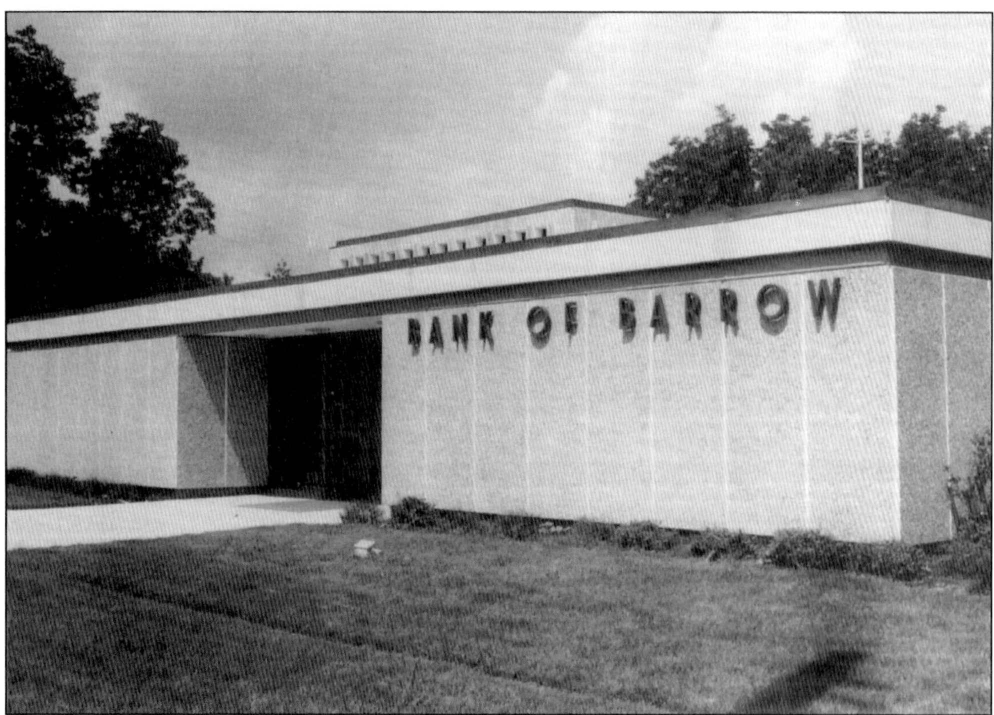

Maintaining its lean, sleek image, the Bank of Barrow moved to its new Moderne-style facility on North Broad Street in 1964. Increasingly, new buildings of the 1950s and 1960s embraced the long and low Moderne style, with its emphasis on interior appointments as opposed to exterior ornament. The Moderne architectural style gained popularity for commercial use because of its no-nonsense appearance, which was popular with financial institutions. (Courtesy 1972 Winder-Barrow High School *Panorama*.)

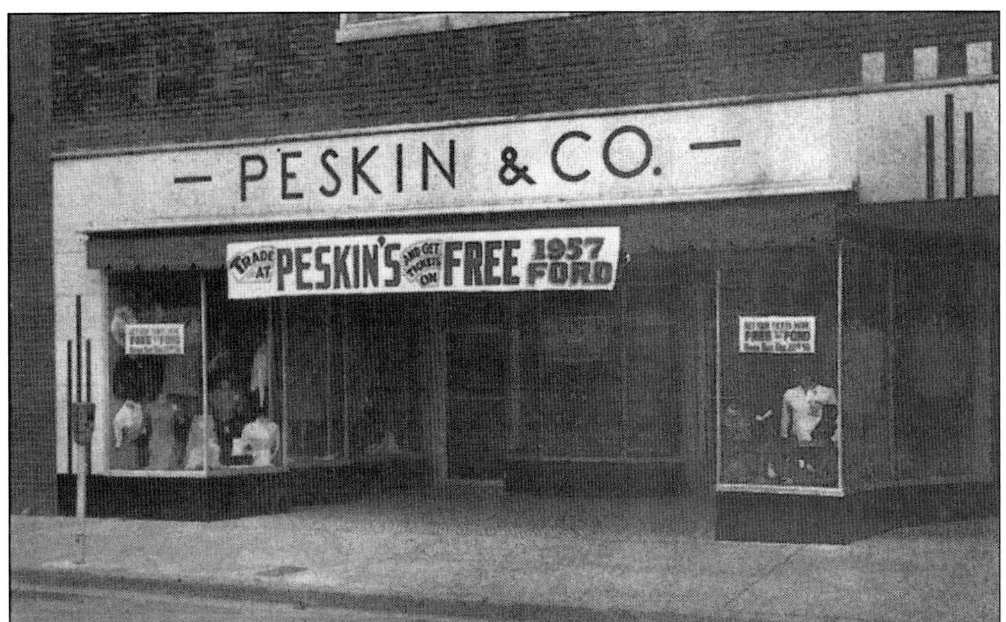

Completed in 1924 as the home for Winder FAM Masonic Lodge No. 333, the three-story brick building on East Athens Street is best known as Peskin's Department Store. Henry Peskin moved to Winder from his native New York, bringing with him an undying community spirit and inspiring retail acumen. Peskin was one of the first merchants to modify his storefront with glass display peninsulas and an aluminum-wrapped facade. (Courtesy of 1957 Winder-Barrow High School *Panorama*.)

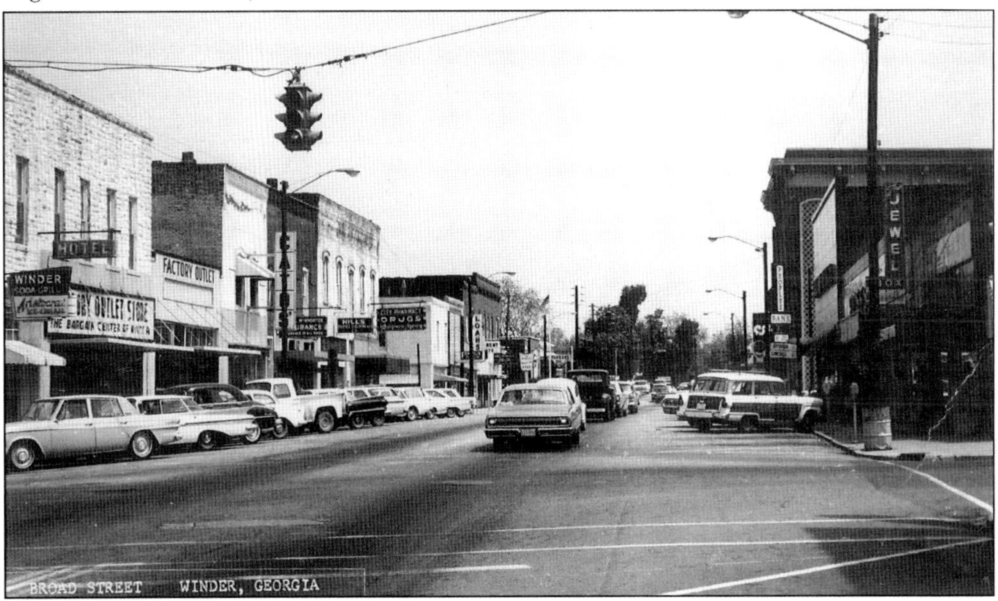

The 1960s in downtown Winder brought increased traffic as more American households became owners of more automobiles. The popularity of Winder's downtown was due to the sales of everything from sewing thread to lawn mowers. Broad Street became a retrospective of 20th-century American architecture with its mix of modest corbelled low-rise brick buildings and the modernized storefronts wrapped in aluminum, ceramic tiles, and heavy plastics. (Courtesy of Joe Bowen.)

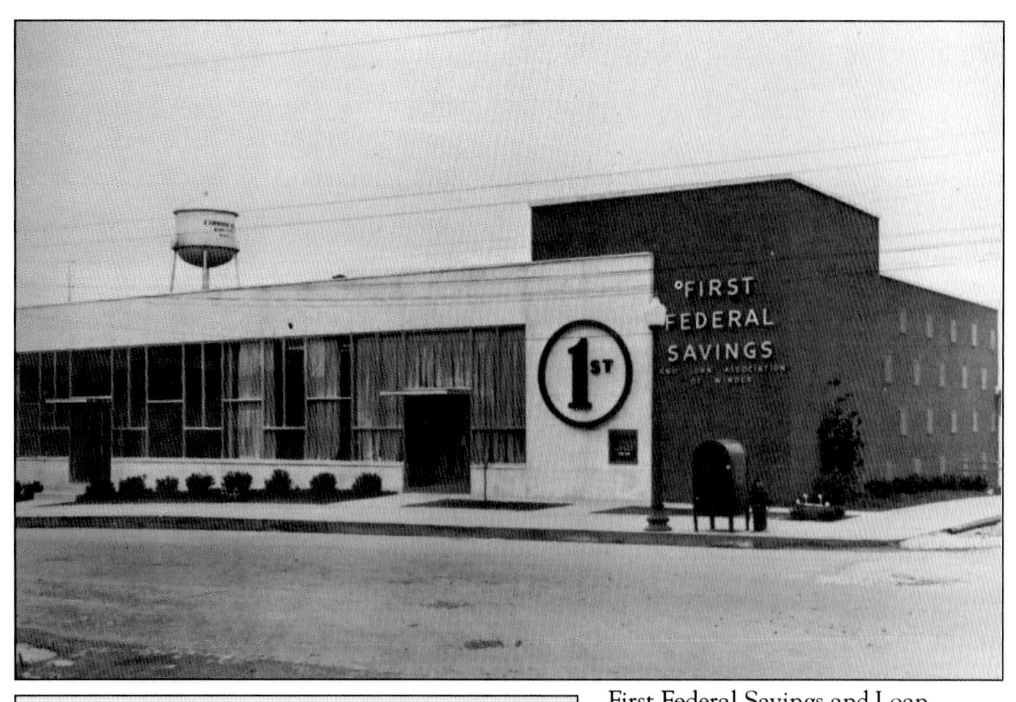

First Federal Savings and Loan Association opened for business in 1941 with modest capital of $25,000. With assets totaling $115,000 by the end of 1942, however, the locally owned mutual thrift and home-financing institution was on its way to a bright future. First Federal constructed this Moderne-style office on the corner of East Athens and Jackson Streets around 1955, signaling its solid place in Winder's financial community. (Courtesy 1959 Winder-Barrow High School *Panorama*.)

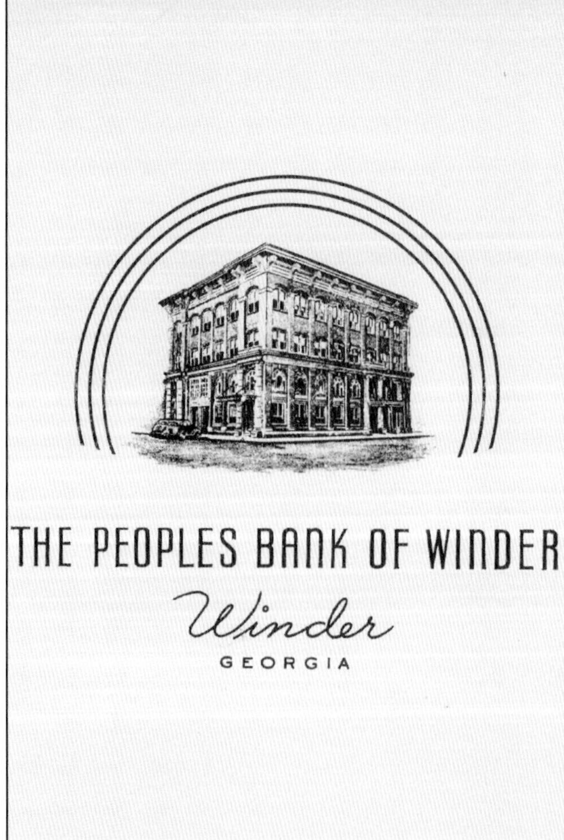

In the late 1950s, tradition prevailed in industries such as banking. With new institutions on the horizon and society's interest in associating with modern businesses, the Peoples Bank was on the cusp of change. This 1959 advertisement in the Winder-Barrow High School yearbook spotlighted the traditional appearance of the bank that would inspire comfort and security in the familiar as graduates began managing their own financial affairs. (Courtesy 1959 Winder-Barrow High School *Panorama*.)

The former Winder National Bank building became the headquarters for the Peoples Bank in 1933. Major events like the Great Depression and World War II triggered waves of modernization as America attempted to distance itself from anything "old-fashioned." In the early 1960s, the Peoples Bank remodeled its Italianate facade to present a more contemporary, Moderne-inspired image. (Courtesy of Joe Bowen.)

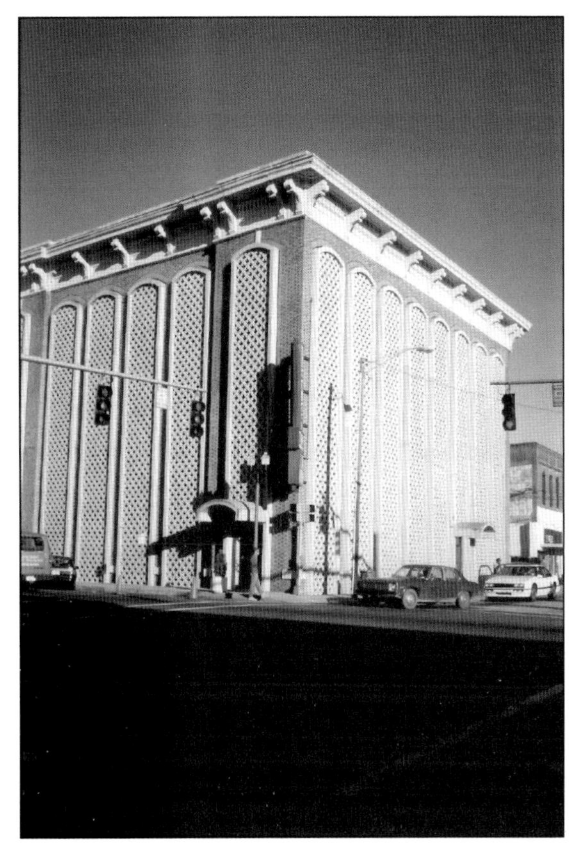

With automobile ownership on the rise and more households becoming dependent upon two incomes, Winder families turned to local restaurants—first, for a dining treat and, later, as a substitute for cooking on week nights. Capitalizing on the popularity of regional drive-in restaurants like the Varsity in Atlanta, Howard Langford took a triangular-shaped piece of property, a fabulous pizza recipe, and opened the wildly popular Triangle Drive-In on May Street. (Courtesy 1959 Winder-Barrow High School *Panorama*.)

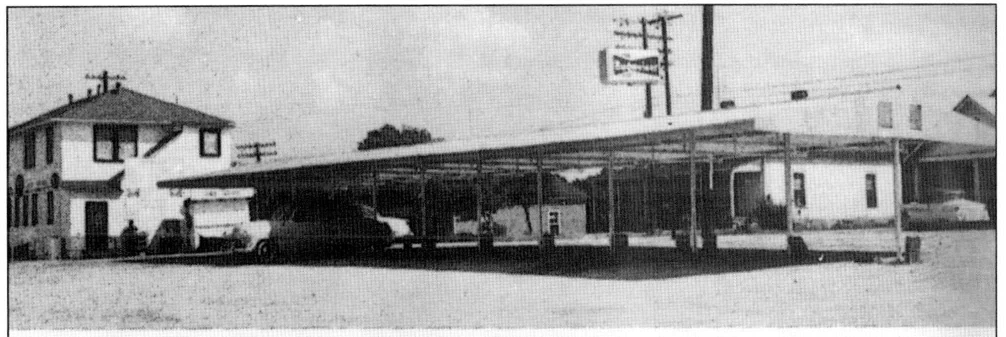

Triangle Drive-Inn Restaurant

DELICIOUS SANDWICHES - SHORT ORDERS

Private Dining Room by Appointment

Prompt Curb Service — Phone from Your Car System

Winder's Leading Drive-Inn Restaurant

Athens Highway Winder, Georgia

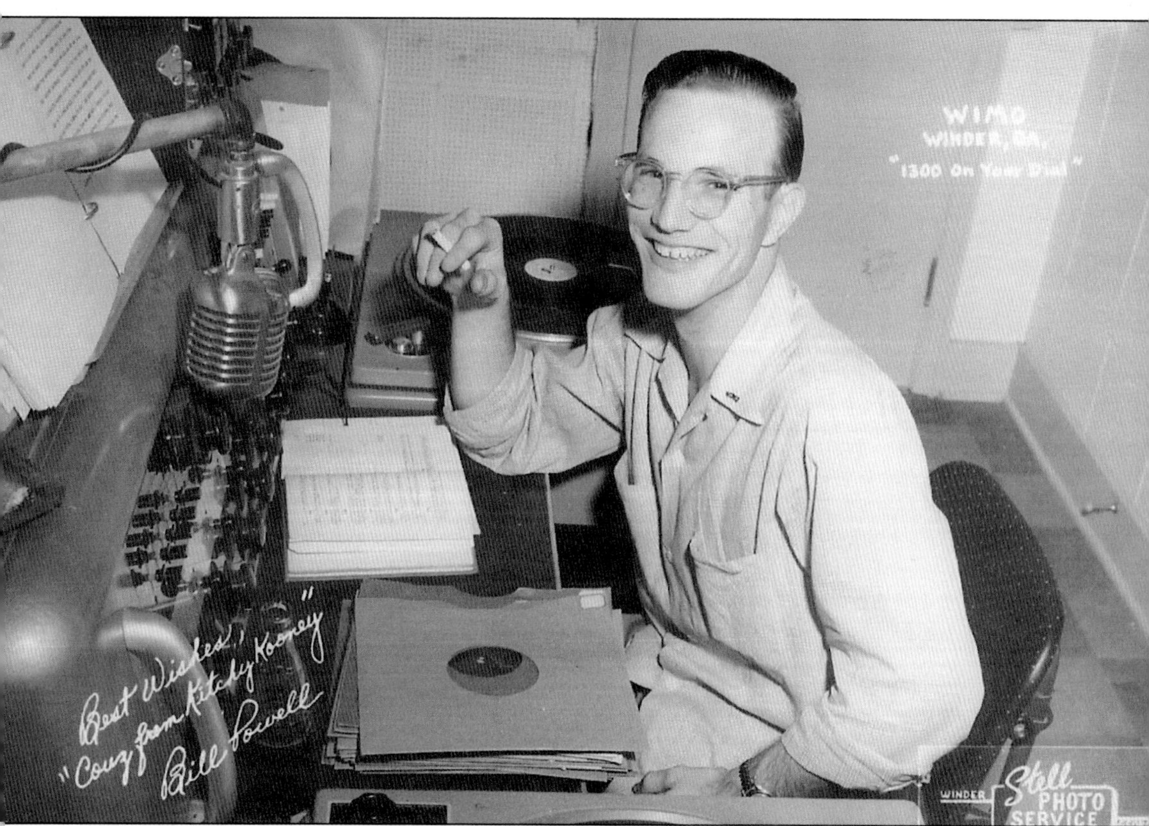

The Winder-Monroe Broadcasting Company began broadcasting at 1300 AM on the radio dial in November 1952 with the call letters "WIMO." Owned by Cecil H. Grider and W.C. Woodall, the station broadcast a mix of locally produced and syndicated music, news, and informational programs. Bill Powell "spun platters" for WIMO in the station's early days; its daylight-only hours are still in effect six decades later. (Courtesy of Caroline Robinson Stallings.)

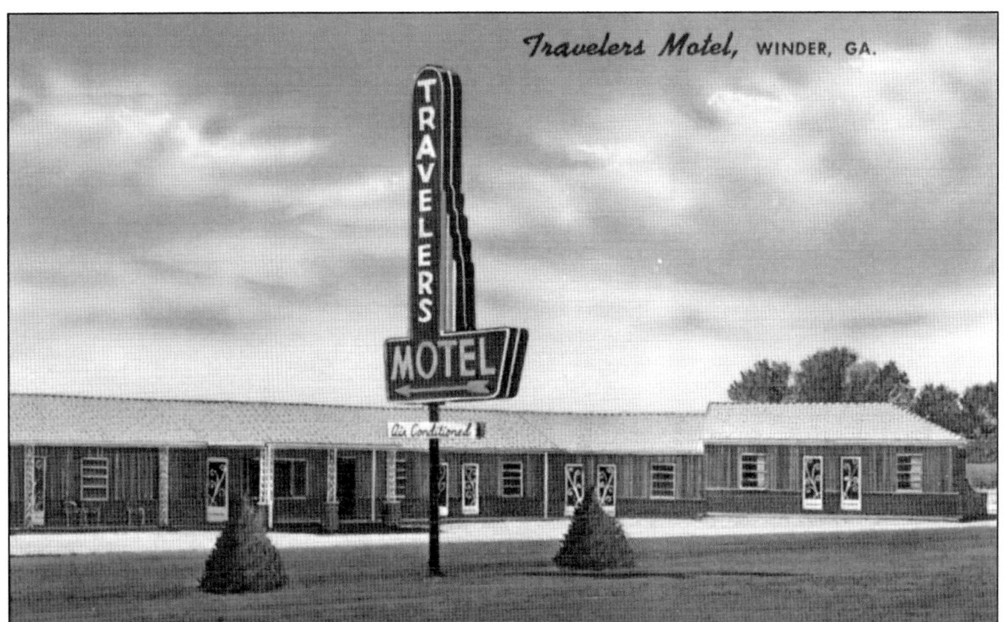

The Travelers Motel opened for business on May Street, also known as US Highway 29, in 1954. The Travelers was recommended by gourmet food and travel expert Duncan Hines in his *Lodging for a Night* directory. The modern, air-conditioned motel, with dedicated parking spaces for each room, was particularly popular with business travelers in town to work with local manufacturers, corporations, and retail establishments. (Courtesy of Joe Bowen.)

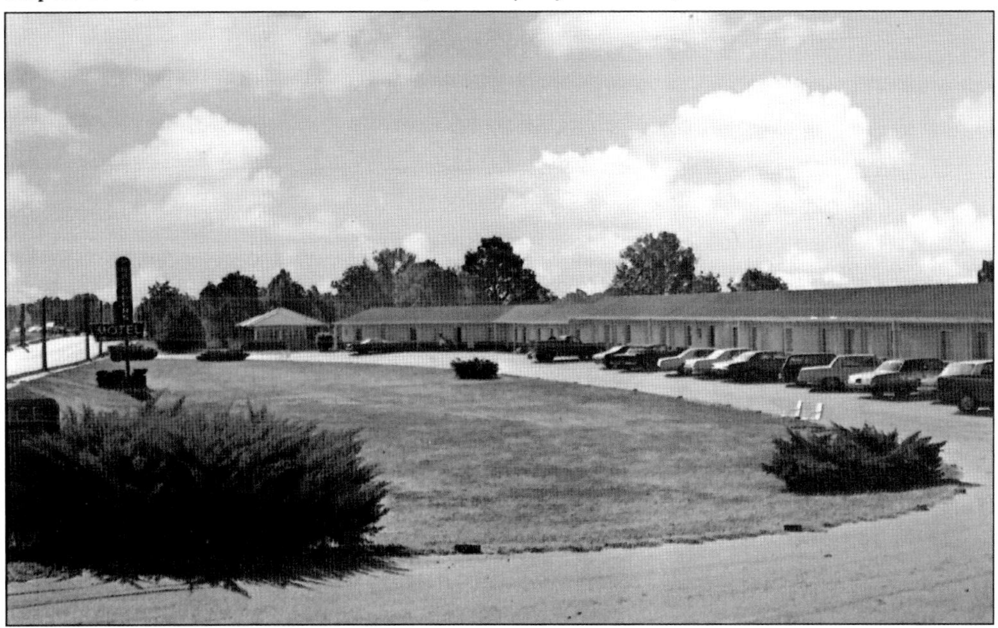

Long, one-story motels had become the style for overnight lodging facilities after World War II. Evolving from the auto camps of the 1920s and 1930s, the motor inn was popular with business and leisure travelers using automobiles to travel from place to place. The Travelers' strategic location on a major highway secured its success as its neon sign beckoned weary drivers needing lodgings. (Courtesy of Joe Bowen.)

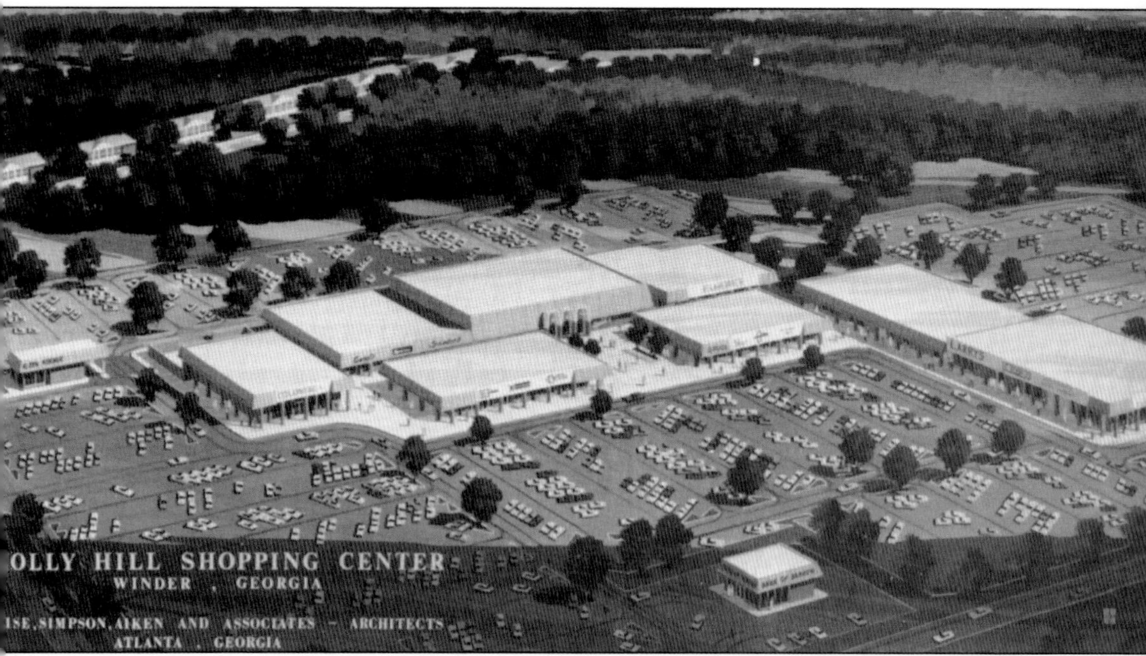

The introduction of several small strip shopping centers in and around Winder proved popular as automobile travel increased through the 1960s. In 1971, local real estate developer J.W. Maynard opened Winder's first venture into the suburban shopping center. Holly Hill Mall opened with Belk Department Store and Big Star Supermarket, a movie theater, a Hallmark card shop, the Boutique, and other retail establishments. (Courtesy of 1972 Winder-Barrow High School *Panorama*.)

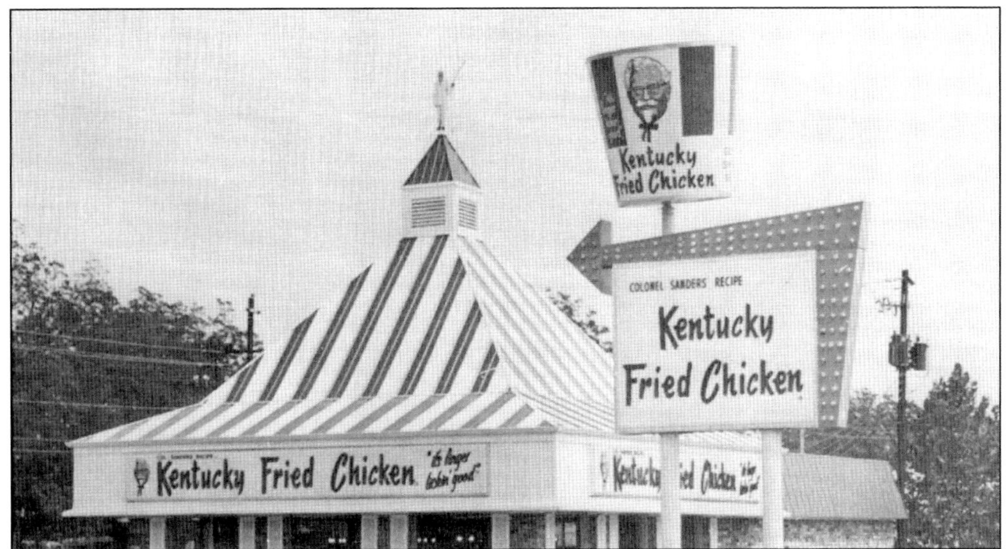

By the late 1960s, quick-service restaurants were making impressions across America. Unique architectural features, paint schemes, signage, and uniform store templates served as marketing tools for national restaurant chains like Kentucky Fried Chicken. The red-and-white pyramid-shaped roof with miniature cupola, reminiscent of the Queen Anne and Neoclassical houses prevalent in the 19th- and early 20th–century South, helped cement the look of the KFC franchise in the American psyche. (Courtesy of 1972 Winder-Barrow High School *Panorama*.)

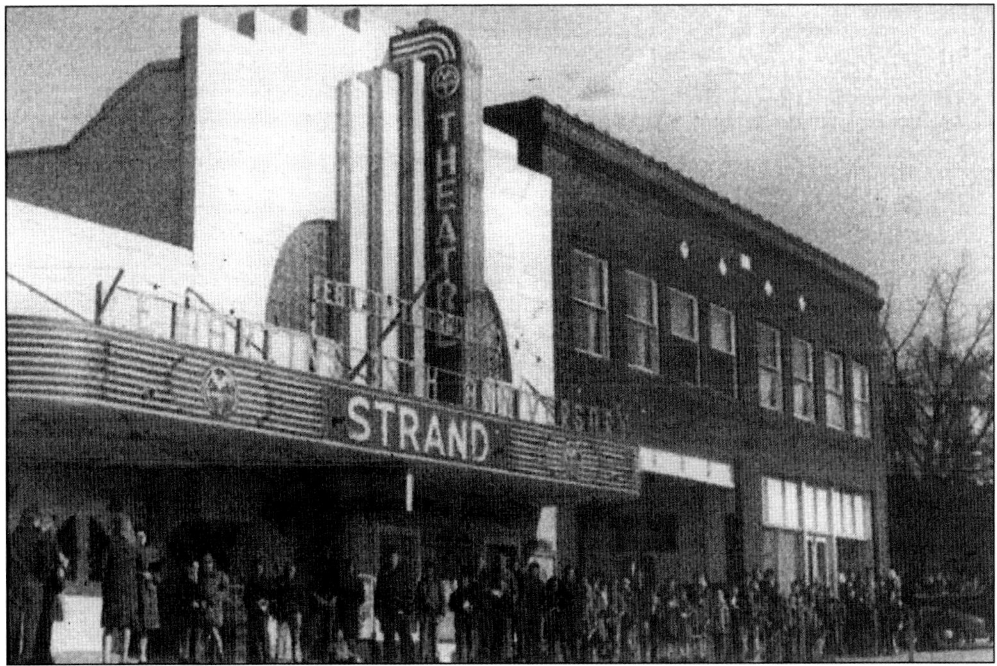

Built in 1916, the Art Deco Strand Theatre hosted motion pictures as well as live stage shows until it was demolished in the 1970s. Its neon marquee announced shows to generations of Winder residents who, for 25¢ or 50¢, spent Saturday afternoon at "the picture show." The Strand was adjacent to the c. 1905 Bush Building, home of the city police and fire departments, which was demolished in 1990. (Courtesy of Joe Bowen.)

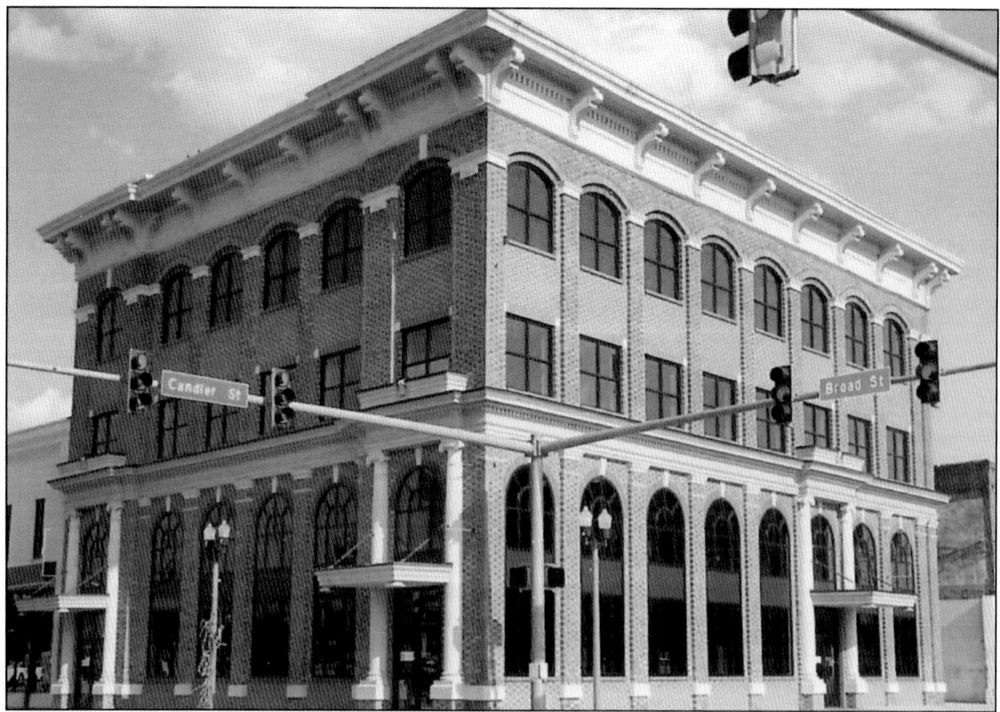

The elegant detailing of the Peoples Bank building spent almost 50 years in hiding after its remodeling in the early 1960s. Fifty years later, the Charles O. Maddox family, owners of the bank, restored the building's exterior to its original grandeur. The Maddoxes restored or rehabilitated two other major buildings as well, setting a heritage preservation standard for Winder. After 84 years of community service, the bank closed in 2010. (Courtesy of Helen Person.)

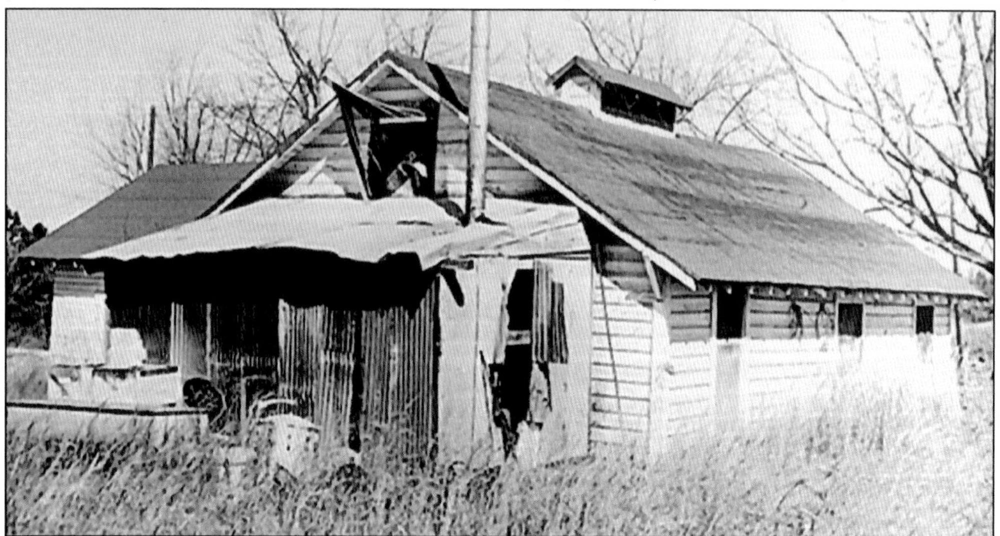

Many old buildings were centers of activity but are not worth the effort and expense of preservation. Take the Cannery, for example. Built around 1930, the Cannery served for 25 years as a processing facility for gardeners who canned and preserved fresh vegetables and fruits. Increasingly available "convenience foods" and better preservation techniques led to the Cannery being demolished in the late 1950s. (Courtesy of Barrow County Historical Society.)

Three
LIVING

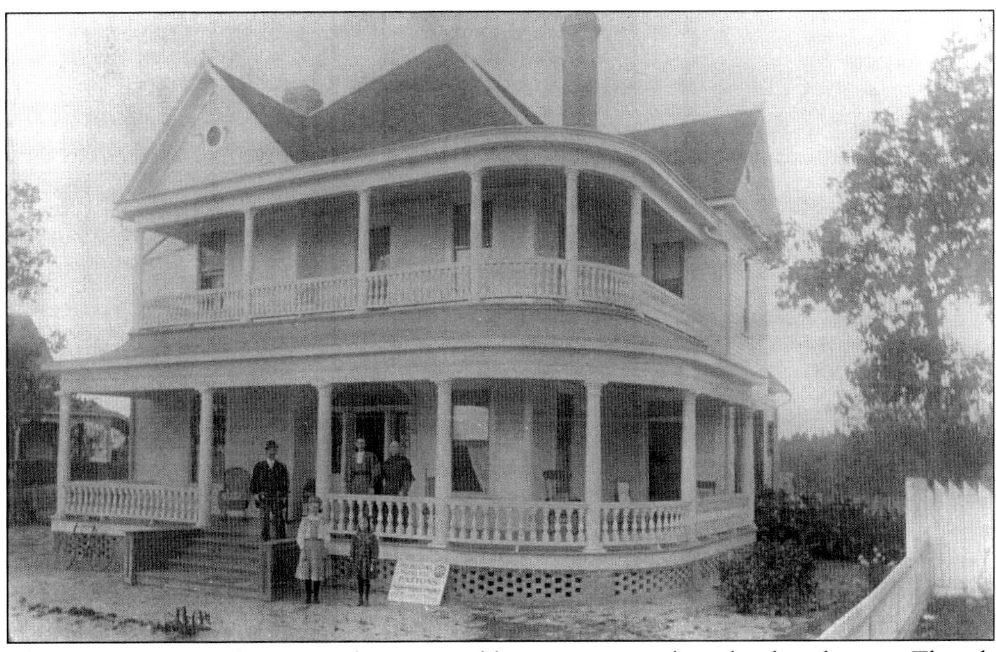

The year 1900 saw a drive toward prosperity like none previously realized in the area. Though Winder was still divided by three counties, the community pulled together as one. William T. Robinson had this magnificent Queen Anne house built for his family on Athens Street in eastern Gwinnett County. Its sweeping wraparound porches and Doric columns make the house a textbook example of the Free Classic Queen Anne. Pictured here are, from left to right, (first row) Lillie Bell Robinson (Summerour) and Montine Robinson (Patton); (second row) C.C. Parr, Mattie Mae House Robinson, and Mary Ann Robinson House. (Courtesy of Bill Summerour.)

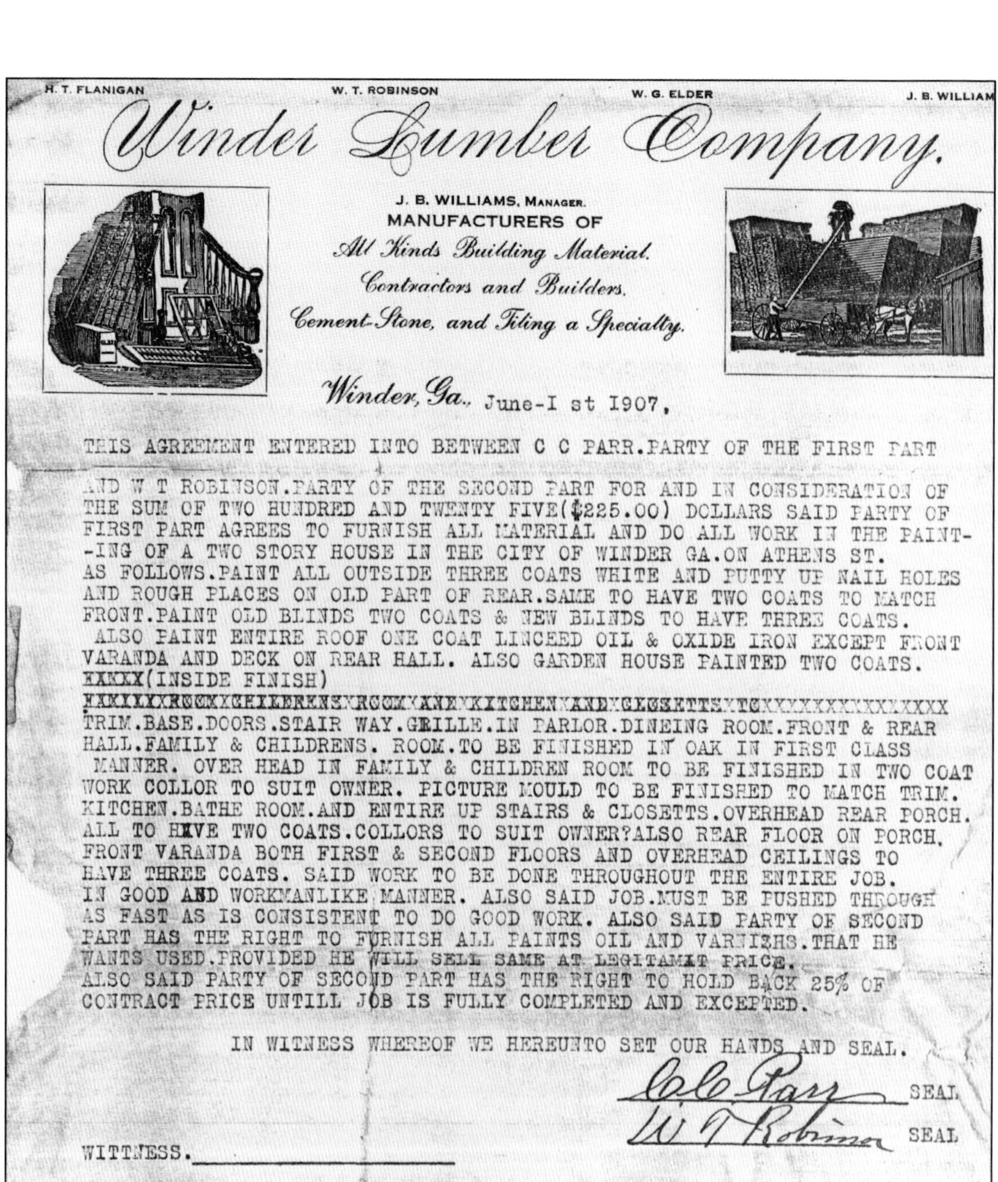

H. T. FLANIGAN W. T. ROBINSON W. G. ELDER J. B. WILLIAMS

Winder Lumber Company.

J. B. WILLIAMS, MANAGER.
MANUFACTURERS OF
All Kinds Building Material.
Contractors and Builders.
Cement-Stone, and Tiling a Specialty.

Winder, Ga., June-I st 1907,

THIS AGREEMENT ENTERED INTO BETWEEN C C PARR.PARTY OF THE FIRST PART

AND W T ROBINSON.PARTY OF THE SECOND PART FOR AND IN CONSIDERATION OF THE SUM OF TWO HUNDRED AND TWENTY FIVE($225.00) DOLLARS SAID PARTY OF FIRST PART AGREES TO FURNISH ALL MATERIAL AND DO ALL WORK IN THE PAINT--ING OF A TWO STORY HOUSE IN THE CITY OF WINDER GA.ON ATHENS ST. AS FOLLOWS.PAINT ALL OUTSIDE THREE COATS WHITE AND PUTTY UP NAIL HOLES AND ROUGH PLACES ON OLD PART OF REAR.SAME TO HAVE TWO COATS TO MATCH FRONT.PAINT OLD BLINDS TWO COATS & NEW BLINDS TO HAVE THREE COATS. ALSO PAINT ENTIRE ROOF ONE COAT LINCEED OIL & OXIDE IRON EXCEPT FRONT VARANDA AND DECK ON REAR HALL. ALSO GARDEN HOUSE PAINTED TWO COATS.
XXXXX(INSIDE FINISH)
XXXXXXROOMXCHILDRENSXROOMXANDXKITCHENXANDXCLOSETTSXTOXXXXXXXXXXXXXX
TRIM.BASE.DOORS.STAIR WAY.GRILLE.IN PARLOR.DINEING ROOM.FRONT & REAR HALL.FAMILY & CHILDRENS. ROOM.TO BE FINISHED IN OAK IN FIRST CLASS MANNER. OVER HEAD IN FAMILY & CHILDREN ROOM TO BE FINISHED IN TWO COAT WORK COLLOR TO SUIT OWNER. PICTURE MOULD TO BE FINISHED TO MATCH TRIM. KITCHEN.BATHE ROOM.AND ENTIRE UP STAIRS & CLOSETTS.OVERHEAD REAR PORCH. ALL TO HAVE TWO COATS.COLLORS TO SUIT OWNER?ALSO REAR FLOOR ON PORCH. FRONT VARANDA BOTH FIRST & SECOND FLOORS AND OVERHEAD CEILINGS TO HAVE THREE COATS. SAID WORK TO BE DONE THROUGHOUT THE ENTIRE JOB. IN GOOD AND WORKMANLIKE MANNER. ALSO SAID JOB.MUST BE PUSHED THROUGH AS FAST AS IS CONSISTENT TO DO GOOD WORK. ALSO SAID PARTY OF SECOND PART HAS THE RIGHT TO FURNISH ALL PAINTS OIL AND VARNISHS.THAT HE WANTS USED.PROVIDED HE WILL SELL SAME AT LEGITAMIT PRICE. ALSO SAID PARTY OF SECOND PART HAS THE RIGHT TO HOLD BACK 25% OF CONTRACT PRICE UNTILL JOB IS FULLY COMPLETED AND EXCEPTED.

IN WITNESS WHEREOF WE HEREUNTO SET OUR HANDS AND SEAL.

C C Parr SEAL
W T Robinson SEAL

WITTNESS.________________

On June 1, 1907, W.T. Robinson contracted through Winder Lumber Company for C.C. Parr to provide extensive painting and remodeling inside and out on his Athens Street house. "First class" oak woodwork, multiple paint coats, "linceed oil and iron oxide" for the red tin roof, and faux graining throughout were to be performed "as fast as is consistent to do good work," according to the specifications of the detailed contract. The contract stated Parr would supply materials, with Robinson providing any specific paints desired, and that Parr would be paid $225 for the job. A prominent furniture merchant, Robinson was careful that his own house and place of business were not only well maintained but stylish. Faux graining was a process employed in locales where specific types of wood or stone were not readily available. The photograph on the previous page shows Parr at the job's completion. (Courtesy of Bill Summerour.)

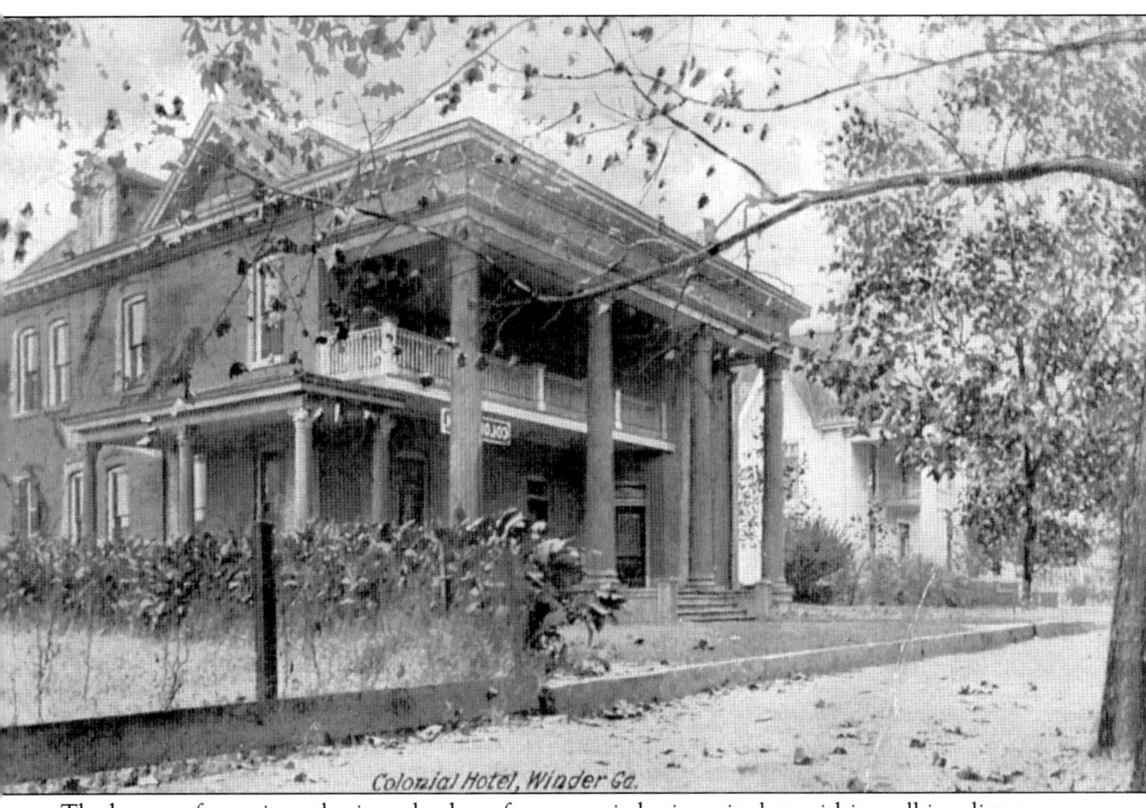

The homes of prominent business leaders often occupied prime city lots within walking distance of their places of business. In a city growing as fast as Winder, businessmen often established their companies before their residences were completed. The Colonial Hotel on West Candler Street was built around 1895 to serve that purpose. The negative for this photograph was reversed during production; note that the hotel sign is backward. G.W. DeLaPerriere and Company in Winder produced several series of images featuring houses and commercial buildings around the city. This c. 1905 postcard shows the hotel that later became the home of Judge and Mrs. G.A. Johns. By the 1890s, the Neoclassical architectural style had grown in popularity for residential, as well as commercial, buildings. The Ionic-columned, full-height entry porch, with second-floor balcony, and porte cochère were prominent features for the Neoclassical style. One parlor window was inserted slightly askew, giving the house additional personality. The house is now home to a professional real estate office. (Courtesy of Joe Bowen.)

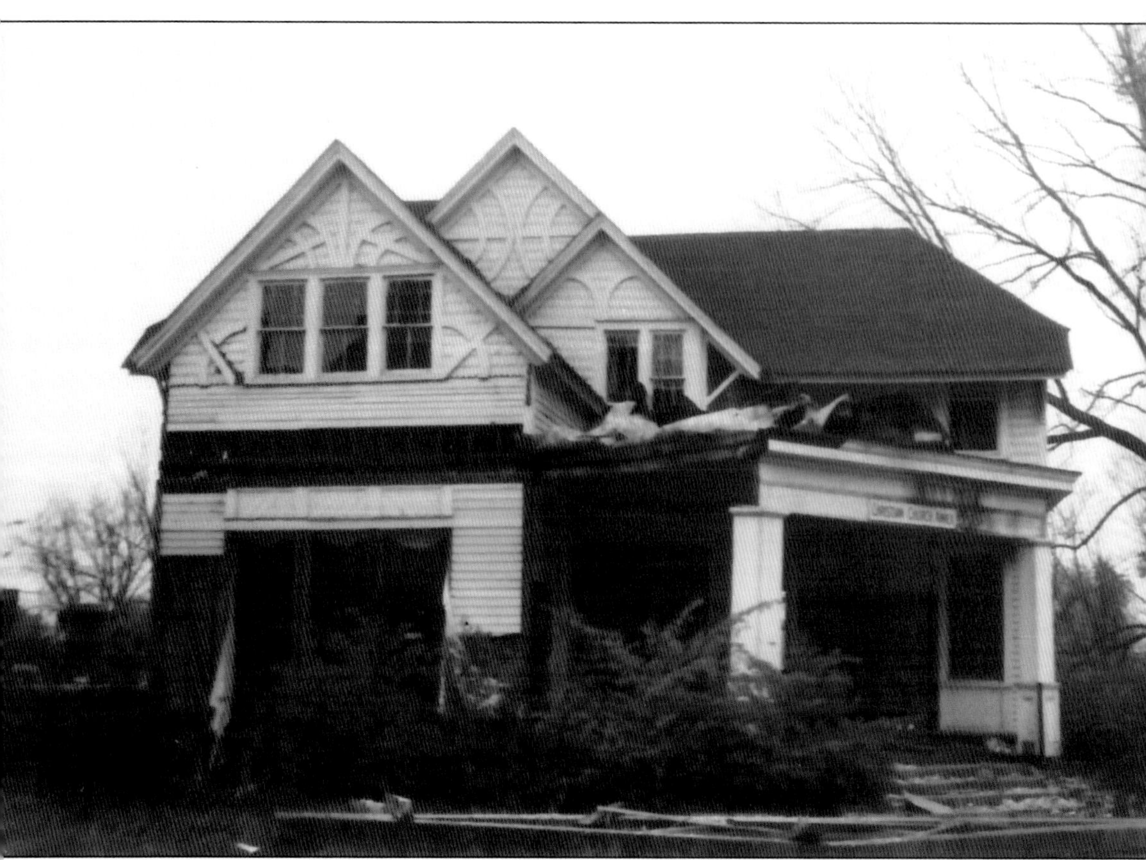

Robert L. Carithers had a Free Classic Queen Anne house built on East Candler Street across from the Colonial Hotel. One of the area's foremost leaders, Carithers's house portrayed its owner's solid foundation and sturdy value system tempered with the forward-thinking philosophy that served him well as an individual and public figure. This photograph belies the c. 1900 house's proud past, with Carithers's family and friends scattered along the full-length wraparound porch. In its later days, the house served as the annex for the neighboring First Christian Church. Both were demolished in 1973, and the site is now a parking lot. (Courtesy of Joe Bowen.)

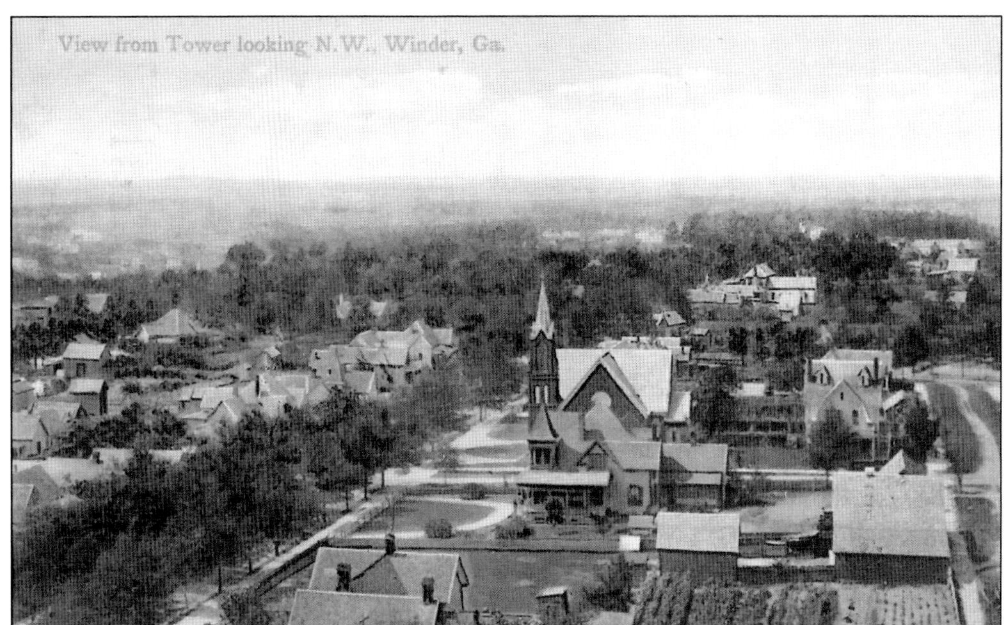

From the Gainesville Midland Railroad tower, this 1909 G.W. DeLaPerriere and Company postcard offers one of several bird's-eye views of Winder during that era. The steeple of the First Methodist Episcopal Church South on West Candler Street towers over the nearby residential neighborhood. Steep pitched roofs of varying heights hint that the Queen Anne style was the dominant choice for Winder residents. (Courtesy of Joe Bowen.)

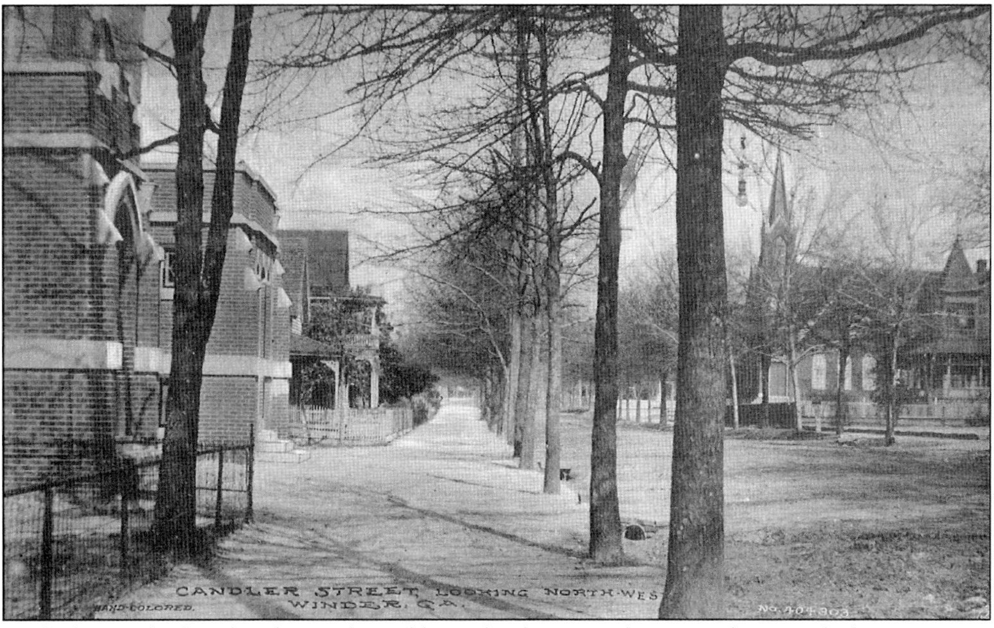

With the Methodist church steeple visible in the distance, this 1908 photograph shows a street-level view of West Candler Street from the First Christian Church on the left. Tree-lined streets were desirable during the early formative years of most towns and cities. With many citizens living within walking distance of the downtown business district, the shade offered by sidewalk trees during hot summer months made the stroll to town pleasurable. (Courtesy of Joe Bowen.)

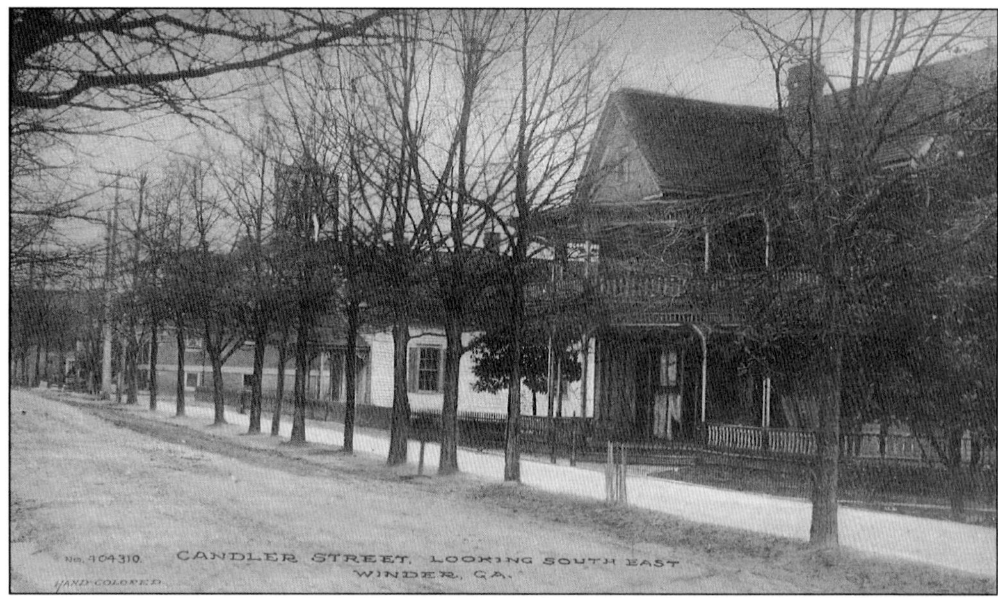

Taken around 1908, this photograph of West Candler Street shows the George W. DeLaPerriere house near the intersection with Sage Street, as well as the tower of the First Christian Church through the trees. Dr. DeLaPerriere's house was built in 1890. The full-height porches swept around the house, typical of the Queen Anne style. With the popularity of the Arts and Crafts movement between 1905 and 1930, the two-story wraparound porch was replaced with a one-story porch with heavy, Craftsman, patterned, concrete piers and square, coupled columns. The house had fallen into a state of disrepair until Buford accountant Tim Grizzle purchased and restored it in 2007. Now owned by Christopher B. "Chris" Maddox, the house was featured on the Barrow Preservation Society's Spring 2011 Tour of Homes. (Above, courtesy of Joe Bowen; below, courtesy of Barrow Preservation Society, Inc.)

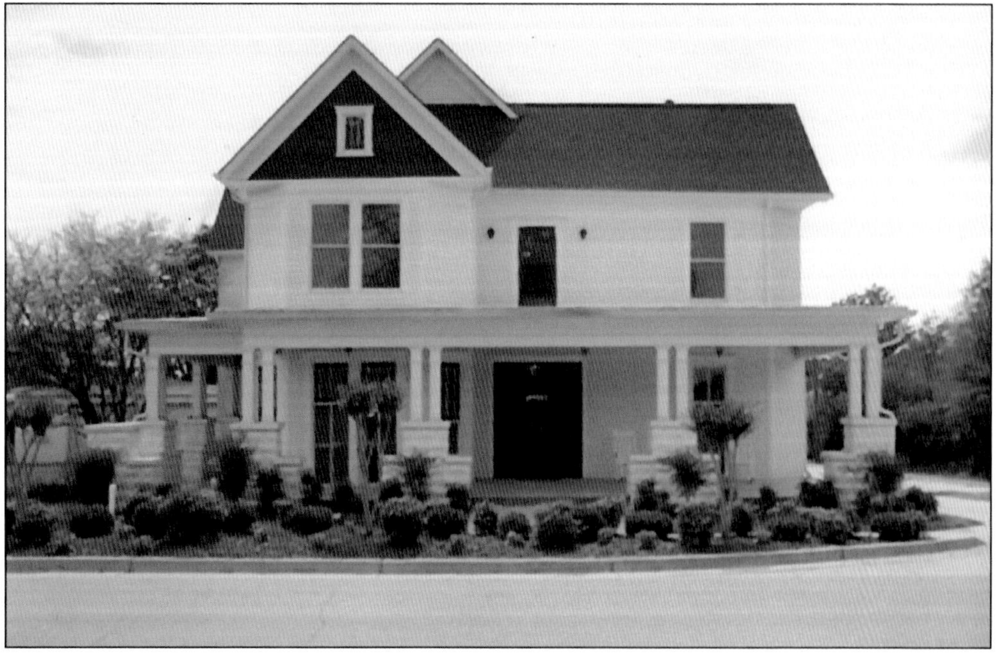

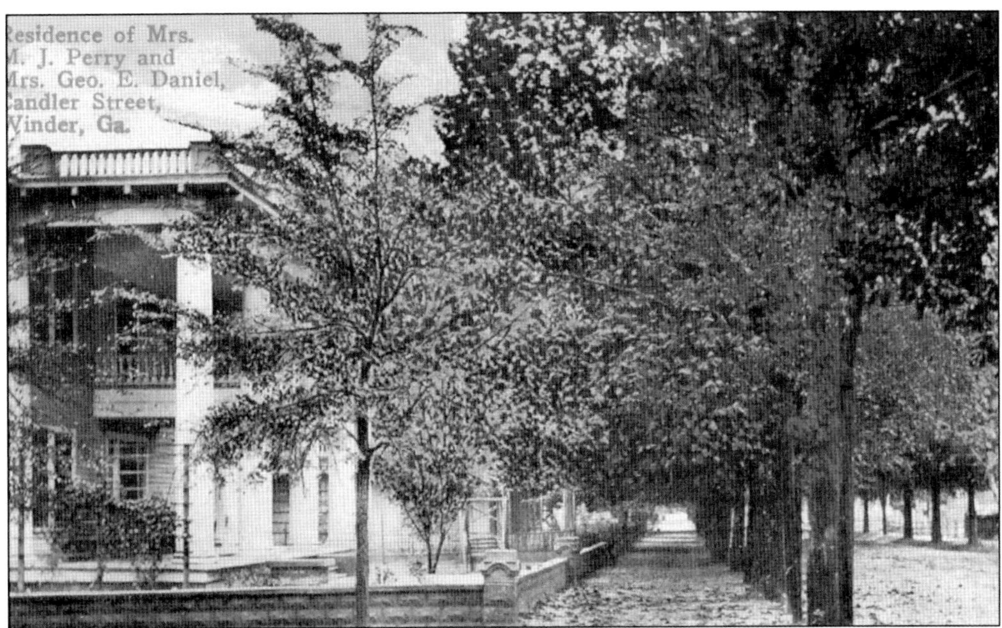

In these 1912 images of West Candler Street, taken from its intersection with Sage Street, the cottage at the corner had been replaced by the stately white Neoclassical house owned by sisters Mrs. M.J. Perry and Mrs. George E. Daniel. The columned, full-height portico with balustrade presented a classic image at a previously modest residential corner. The below photograph, taken in winter, allows the stunning features of the house to be viewed in their entirety. The Perry-Daniel house later became a funeral home before reverting to a single-family dwelling in the 1980s. The DeLaPerriere house, with its spindled Queen Anne porches, is visible beyond the Perry-Daniel house. This block of West Candler demonstrates the evolution from classical, Gothic Revival, and Victorian architectural styles to the sturdy, more relaxed Craftsman style. (Both images courtesy of Joe Bowen.)

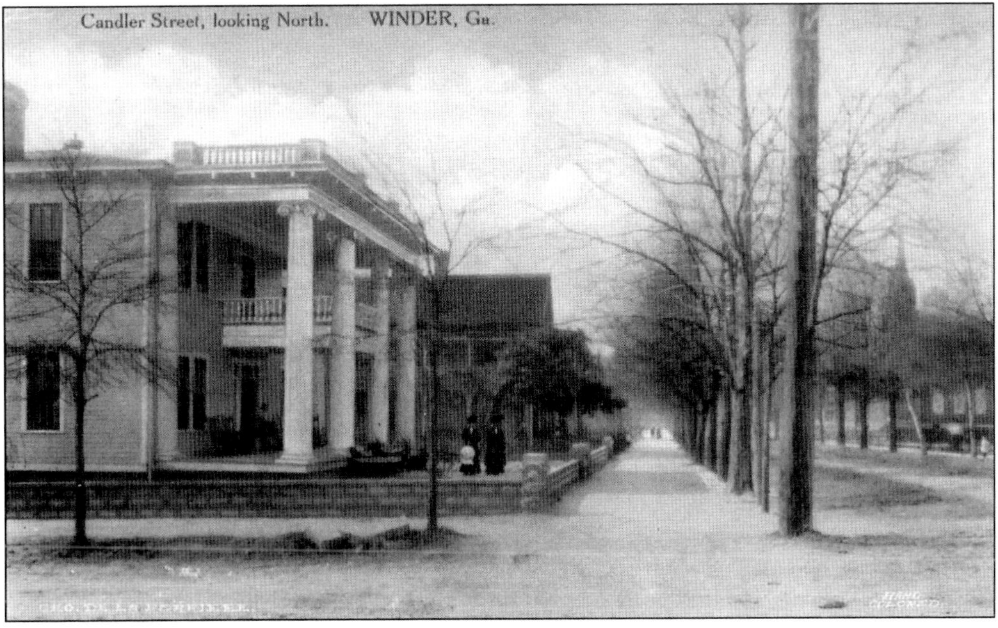

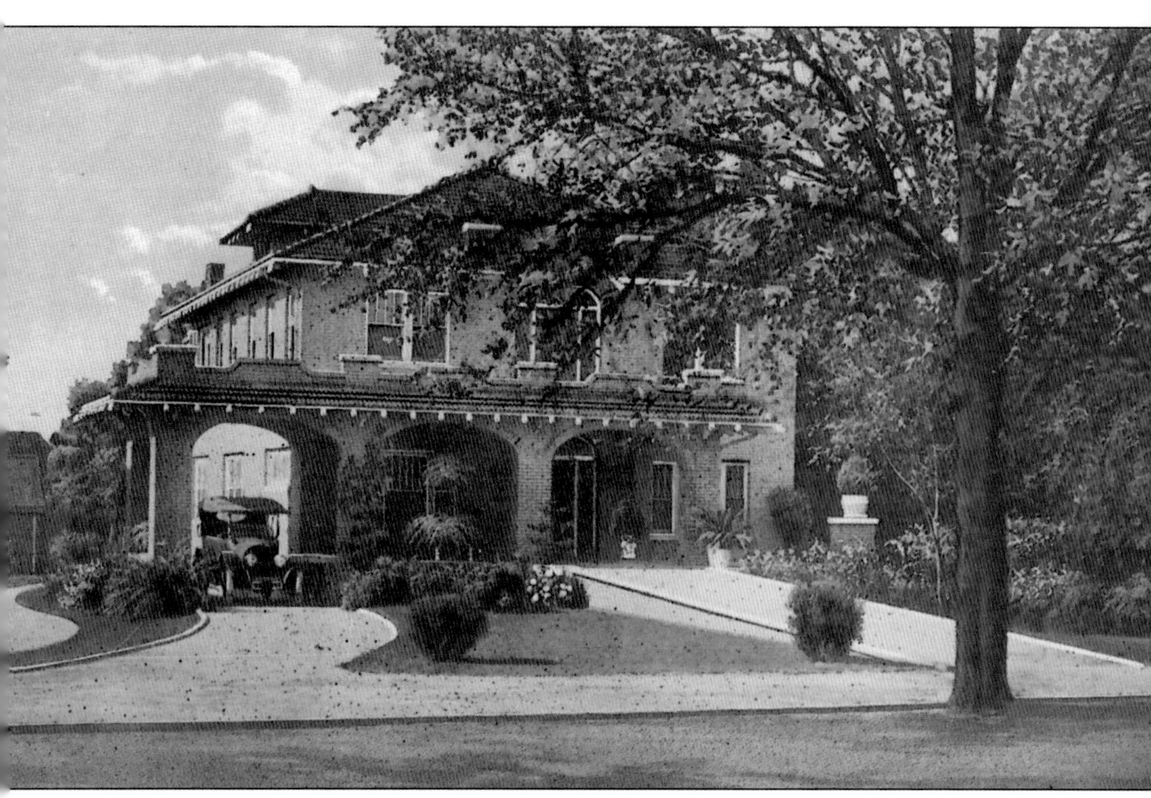

The houses on Candler, Athens, Church, and Melrose Streets are part of the Athens-Candler-Church Street National Register of Historic Places District designated in 1986, as well as the Georgia Register of Historic Places and the City of Winder Historic District. The neighborhood is recognized as an outstanding representation of the establishment of residential districts from the turn of the 20th century through World War II. The variation in architectural styles is a retrospective of trends in house design during that period. The house built in 1918 for W.B. Mathews brought the Prairie to Winder. One of America's only indigenous architectural styles, Prairie is most easily identified by its massive square porch columns, multi-over-single-pane windows, and pyramid-hipped roofs of modern Spanish tile. The home of the law firm of Strickland, Chesnutt, and Lindsay, LLC, the house is a high-style example of the Prairie style. Attorney Michael W. Strickland and his wife, Mace L. Strickland, have been instrumental in the rehabilitation of over 25 historic buildings in the Winder Historic District. (Courtesy of Joe Bowen.)

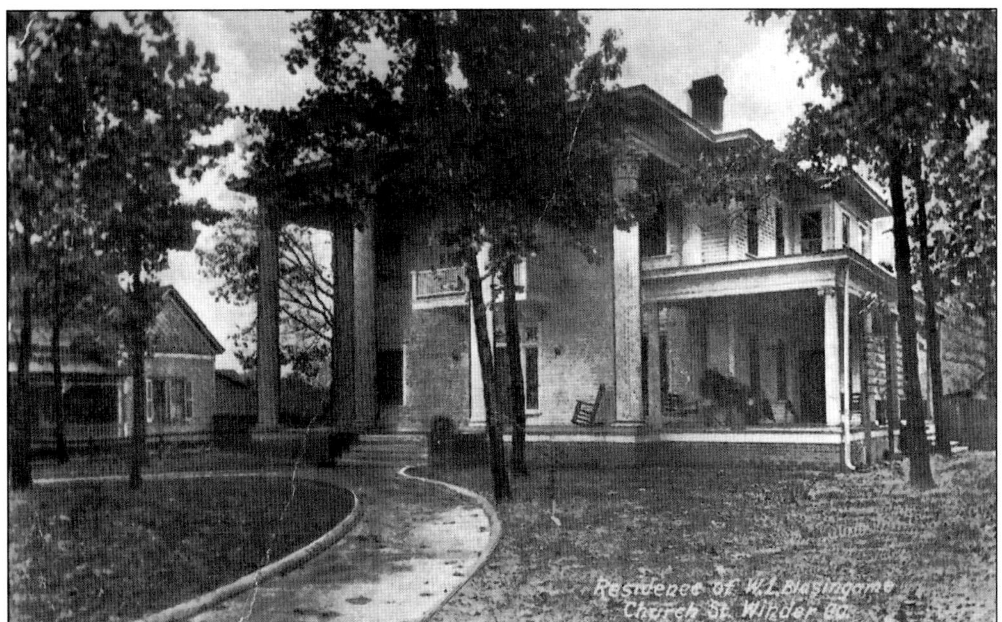

The Neoclassical Luther W. Blasingame house was built in 1910, while its 1912 Craftsman neighbor (below) was constructed by Charles Madison (C.M.) Ferguson. Owner of the Winder Ice and Manufacturing Company and a banker, Blasingame had his house built when he, his wife, Lily Starr Blasingame, and their daughters, Starr and Robbie, moved from neighboring Walton County to the town that was turning heads all over Georgia. Current owner Lee Perkins and her husband, John, restored the house in 2010 when it became Constance Manor Event Center. Already a fixture in Winder, Ferguson was an undertaker, as well as a stonemason and community volunteer. The Ferguson-Robinson House was restored by local preservationists Michael and Mace Strickland and is a single-family dwelling. (Above, courtesy of Joe Bowen; below, Barrow Preservation Society, Inc)

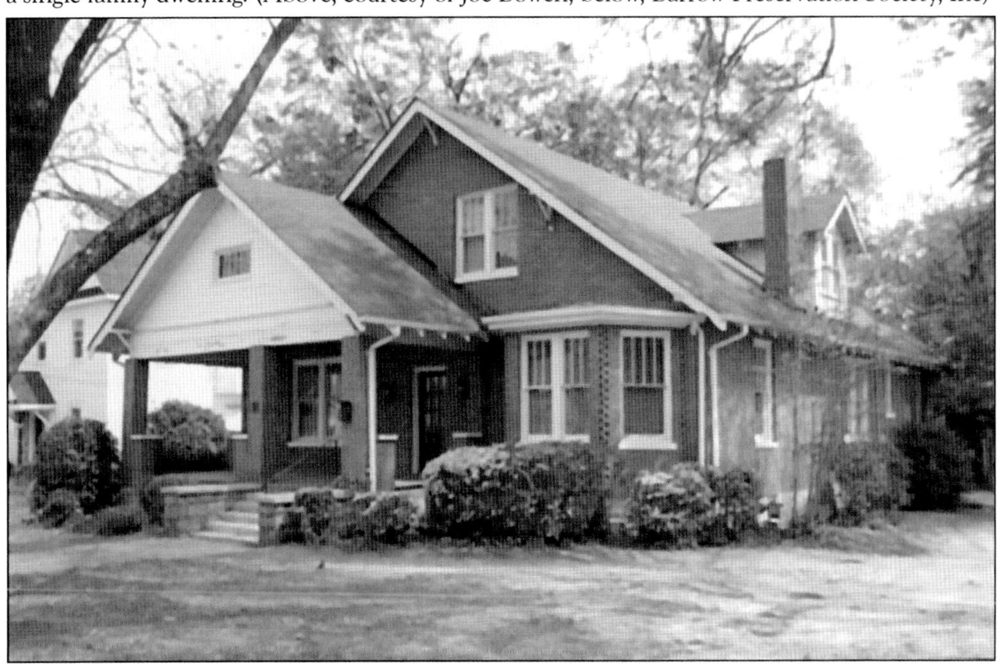

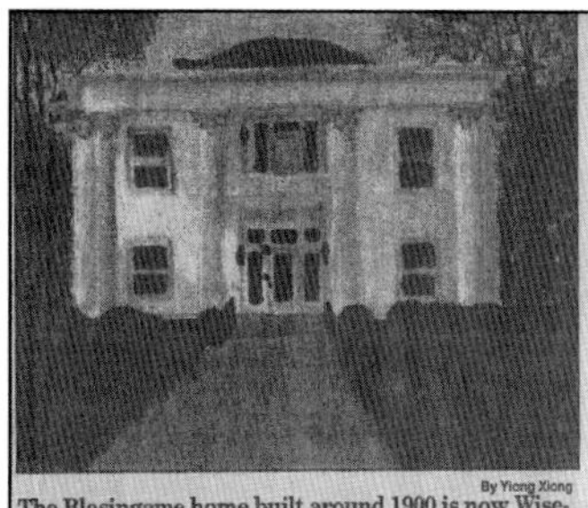

By Yiong Xiong

The Blasingame home built around 1900 is now Wise-Connolly Funeral Home on Church Street

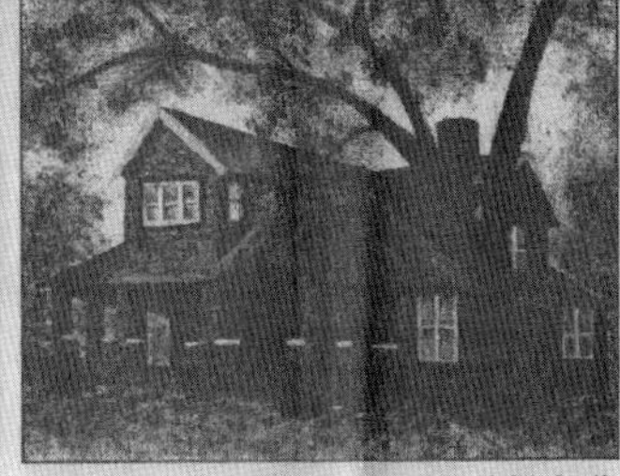

By Amber Reynolds

Brick structure on South Broad between H&S Rental and the office complex of St. Ives Development

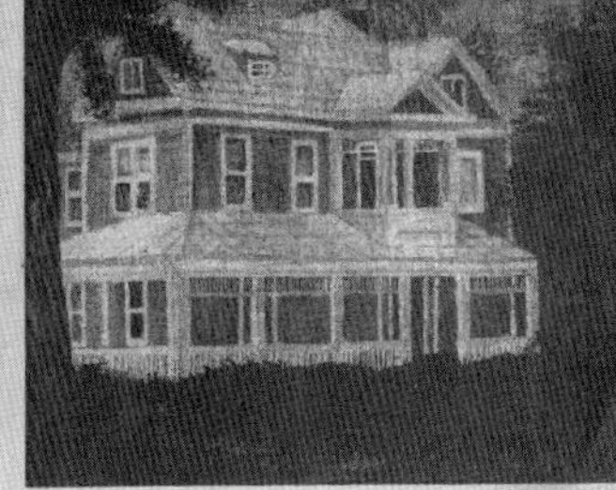

By Maggie Borders

The Millers keep this Candler Street beauty a sight to behold with its beige with blue and reddish accents

By Emily Dorris

Build by Ike Jackson in early 1900s corner of Candler Street and Woodlawn Avenue. From the upper level windows, a glimpse of Stone Mountain is possible on a clear day. Next door to it is the Jackson-Johns House

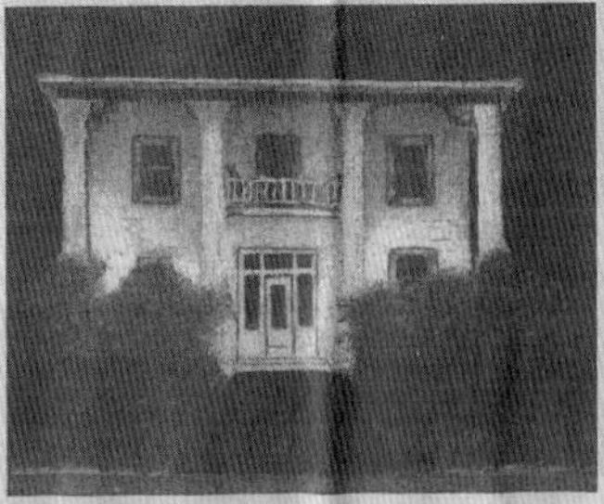

By Jason Pina

This plantation style home on North Center Street was built by Ambrose Jackson and has always been rumored to have a ghost

Barrow County Museum offers a historic look back into community

When you enter the Barrow County Museum in downtown Winder, you immediately capture the sense of history contained within its walls.

C. Fred Ingram is the museum's curator.

And you can take some reminders of history with you with some of the items which are available for sale in the Museum Gift Shop, including: Beadland to Barrow, A History of Barrow County Edited by C. Fred Ingram; Historic Note Cards; Winder Centennial Jugs 1893-1993 (special sale price); Bush Medicine Bottles (with original boxes); Ballad of Barrow by Jeanne Stansell; Mama I Want to Marinate (recollections by Wink Harris); Replica of Train - Gainesville Midland edition); Replica of Museum - Former Barrow County Jail 1916 (limited edition); Fort Yargo Epic by Rev. L.G. Marlin (reprinted by Historical Society); Russell Paper (information about Sen. Russell) printed by The Barrow Eagle; The Barrow County Georgia Cemetery Book compiled by the East Georgia Genealogy Society ; and Images of America, Barrow County, Photographs from the Stell-Kilgore Collection edited by Myles Godfrey.

Additional copies of the brochure "The History of Nodoroc and Tales of the Wog" are now available.

Visit the museum between the hours of 1-4 p.m. to purchase any of these items or call for an appointment.

For more information, call the

Winder's two residential areas that have been listed in the National Register of Historic Districts are replete with exquisite houses of all architectural styles, house types, and sizes. Winder-Barrow High School art students painted some of the contributing houses for a special 1995 exhibition at the Barrow County Historical Society Museum. Three decades after the earliest efforts to raise awareness of the value of historic buildings, a greater emphasis is being placed on preserving the area's heritage. (Courtesy of Joe Bowen.)

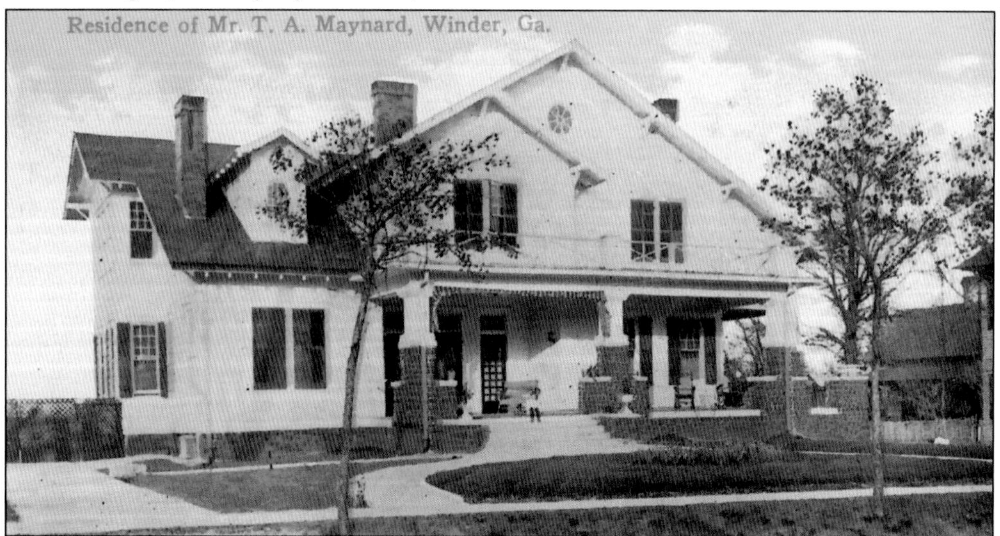

The c. 1905 Thomas A. Maynard house on West Candler Street is a textbook example of the Craftsman style that was so popular in the early 20th century. Befitting an executive, the house was built for the president of the Winder Banking Company. The cross-gabled roof with exposed rafters, square columns anchored by sturdy square brick piers, and nine-over-one windows are distinctive Craftsman architectural features. (Courtesy of Joe Bowen.)

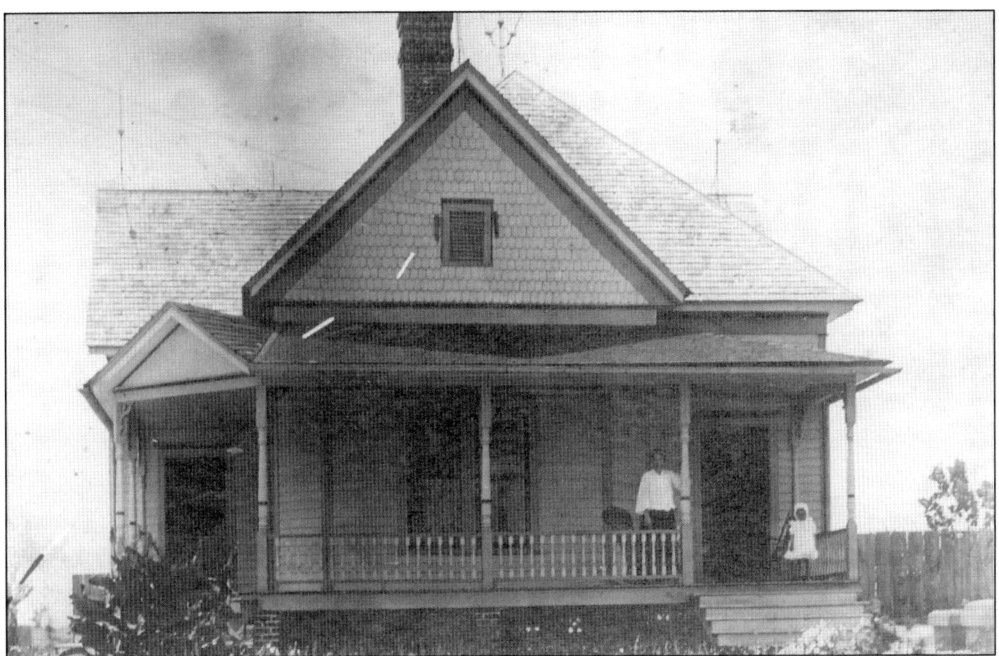

Beulah Maddox lived in this vernacular Queen Anne cottage on North Broad Street. The house, which is no longer standing, exemplified a less ornate take on the style but included the signature asymmetrical personality of the roof lines and porch entrance. Maddox's house was typical of many of the houses constructed in Winder's north and east neighborhoods: neat, modest, and no-nonsense despite the Queen Anne influence. (Courtesy of Bob Hill.)

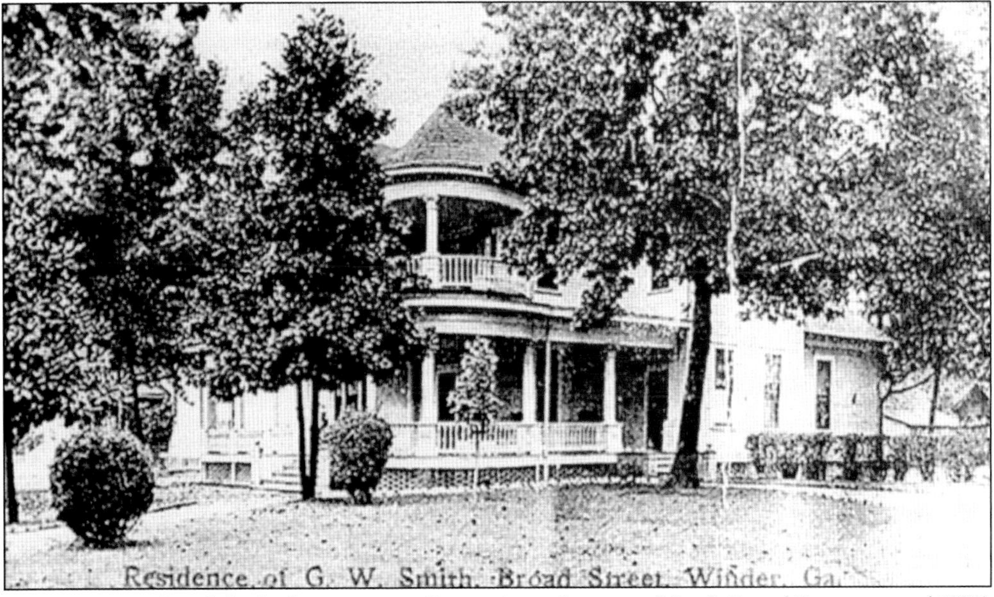

Green Wagner Smith built this exquisite Queen Anne house on North Broad Street around 1885. The turrets and sweeping wraparound porches are distinctively Queen Anne. Befitting Smith's station as a community leader and merchant, the house is sited on a lush city lot with mature Southern magnolia trees bordered by a granite and wrought-iron fence constructed when the streets were widened. (Courtesy of Joe Bowen.)

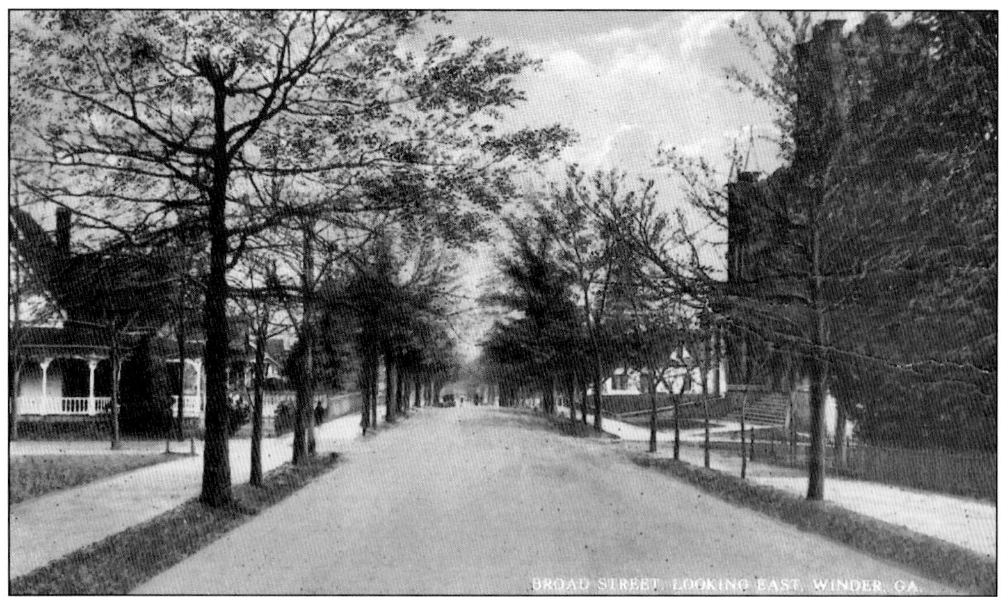

In this c. 1915 postcard, the roofline of the Gothic Revival First Baptist Church is visible at right. Tree-lined thoroughfares were commonplace and highly desirable before the need for wider roadways to accommodate larger vehicles and increased motor traffic. Prominent citizens often built houses on primary streets that were better maintained, facilitating better access between home, downtown, and their neighbors. Pictured below is the 1916 Neoclassical house of the W. M. Holsenbeck family. Holsenbeck served as the first Winder City School superintendent from 1915 to 1921. The Ionic columns, dentil molding, and second-floor partial balcony were archetypical of the Neoclassical style. After being purchased by the First Baptist Church in 1967, the house was demolished shortly thereafter; the site is now vacant. (Both, courtesy of Joe Bowen.)

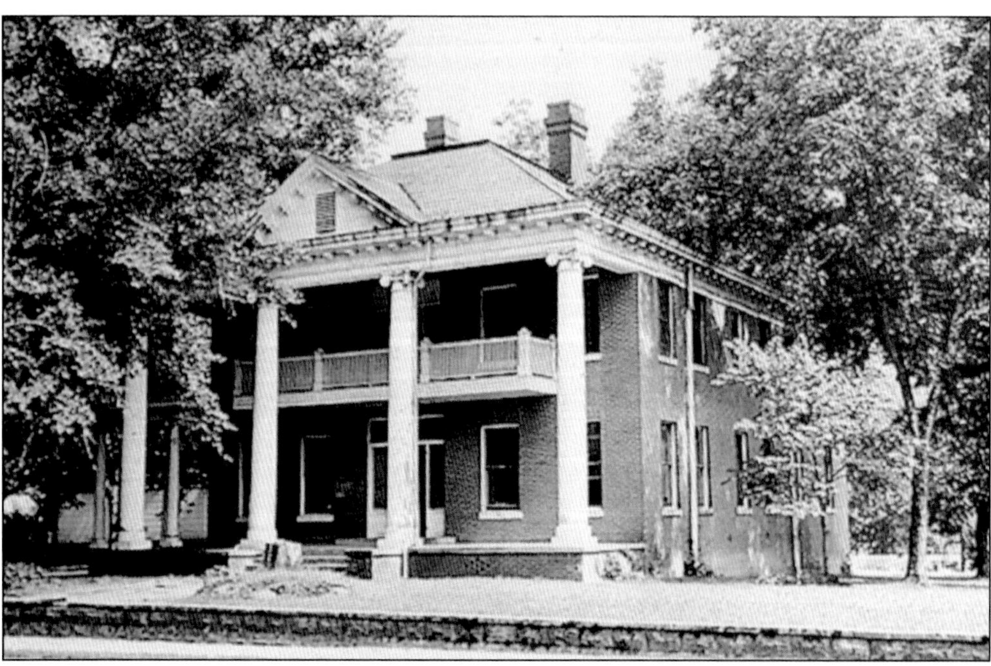

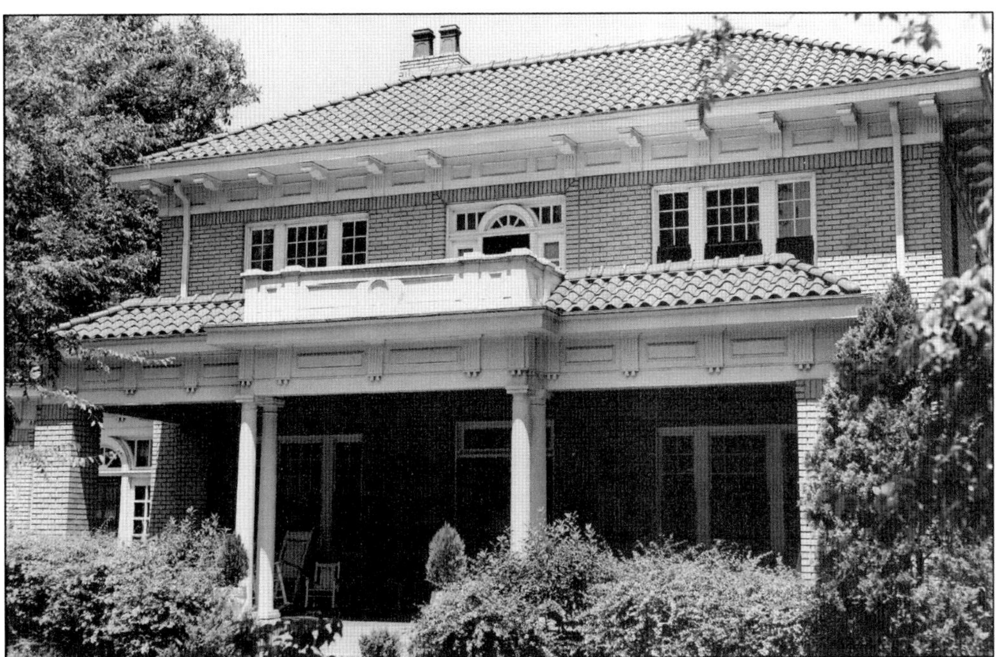

This 1918 Colonial Revival house with heavy Italian Renaissance influence was built for the Camp family before being sold to Russell W. Jones and, finally, to Claude Tuck Jr. The house reflects the early 20th-century celebration of the Adam and Federal styles prevalent on the Atlantic Seaboard. The house is an anchor of the North Broad Street District, which is listed in the National Register of Historic Places. (Courtesy of Elaine Smith Dickens.)

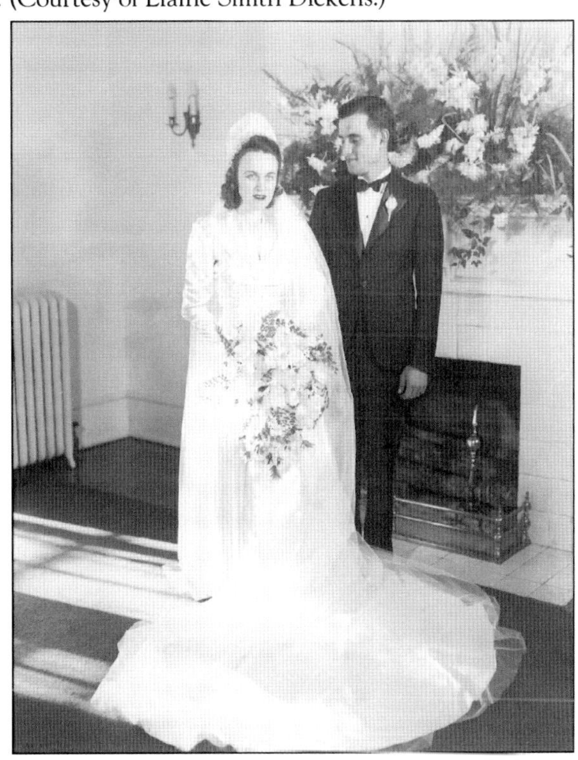

Kathryn Jones and George W. Smith were married in the First Baptist Church on December 6, 1941. They and their guests walked across North Broad Street to the wedding reception at the Jones house. This photograph of the newlyweds in front of the living room fireplace offers a glimpse of the interior details of a typical Colonial Revival house. The ceramic tile hearth and fireplace is topped by a heavy wood mantel with picture frame decorative molding. Freestanding steam heaters like the one to the left of the couple provided heat for the house. (Courtesy of Elaine Smith Dickens.)

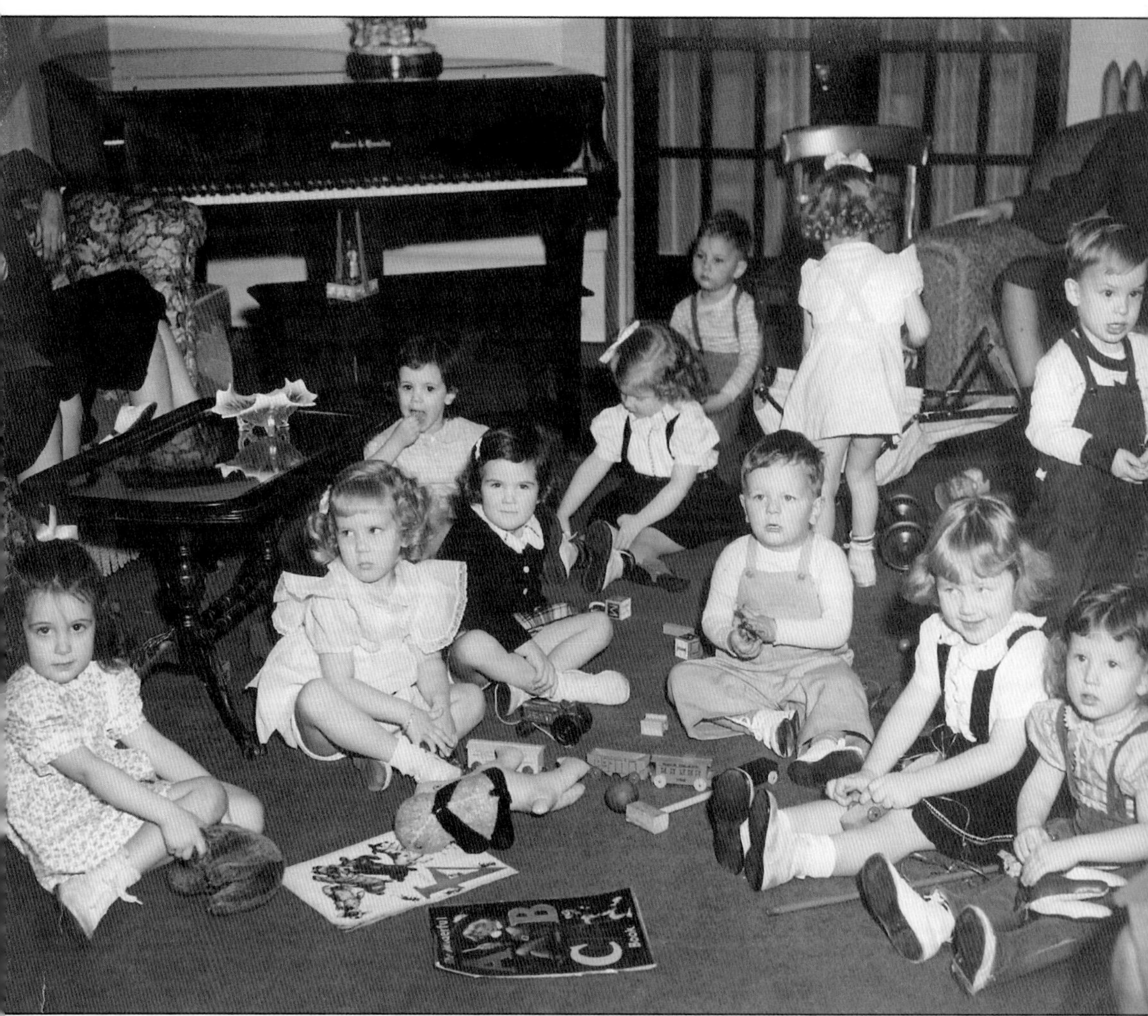

The Russell W. Jones house not only served as the family residence and site of the Jones daughters' wedding receptions but as host to important family events. Held in the living room of her Grandmother Jones's house, Elaine Smith's third birthday party in 1948 was well-attended by children whose parents were contemporaries of her parents. These children became lifelong friends, attending school together through their graduations from Winder-Barrow High School in the early 1960s. (Courtesy of Elaine Smith Dickens.)

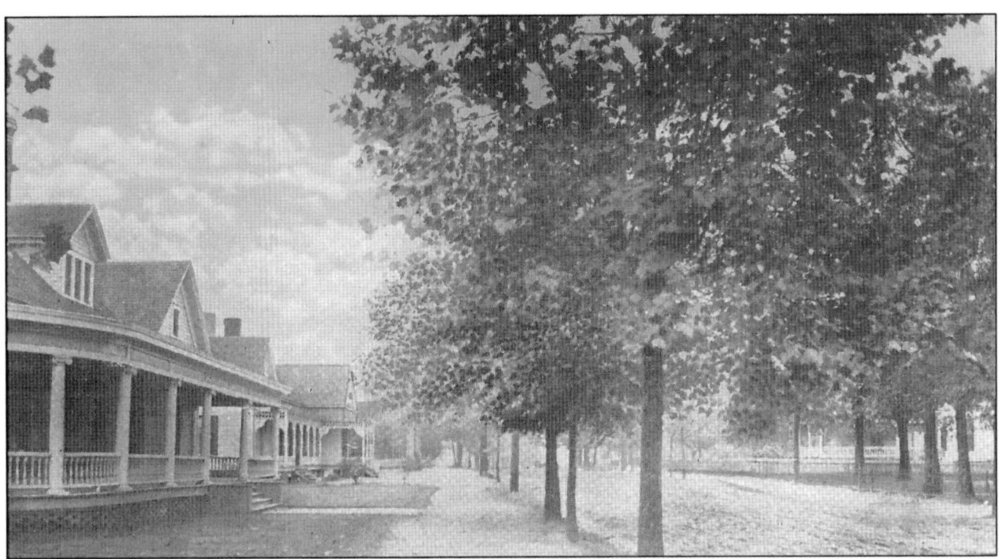

On the opposite North Broad Street corner across Stephens Street, the North Broad residential district stretched closer to downtown Winder than it does today. The houses of prominent citizens occupied property that is now home to commercial and government buildings. This image was taken for a c. 1915 postcard series chronicling the streets and buildings of Winder. Filled with Queen Anne cottages and houses, the Broad Street area between Midland Avenue and Stephens Street was closer to the Gainesville Midland Railroad line and eventually gave way to commercial development during the 1960s. This January 1940 photograph includes, from left to right, Frances Elder Shumake, Bobbie Nell Bentley Cox, and Jack Bentley and shows the diagonal front entry and wraparound porch of Lonie Brooks's house on the corner of the Broad and Stephens Streets intersection. (Above, courtesy of Joe Bowen; below, courtesy of Frances Elder Shumake.)

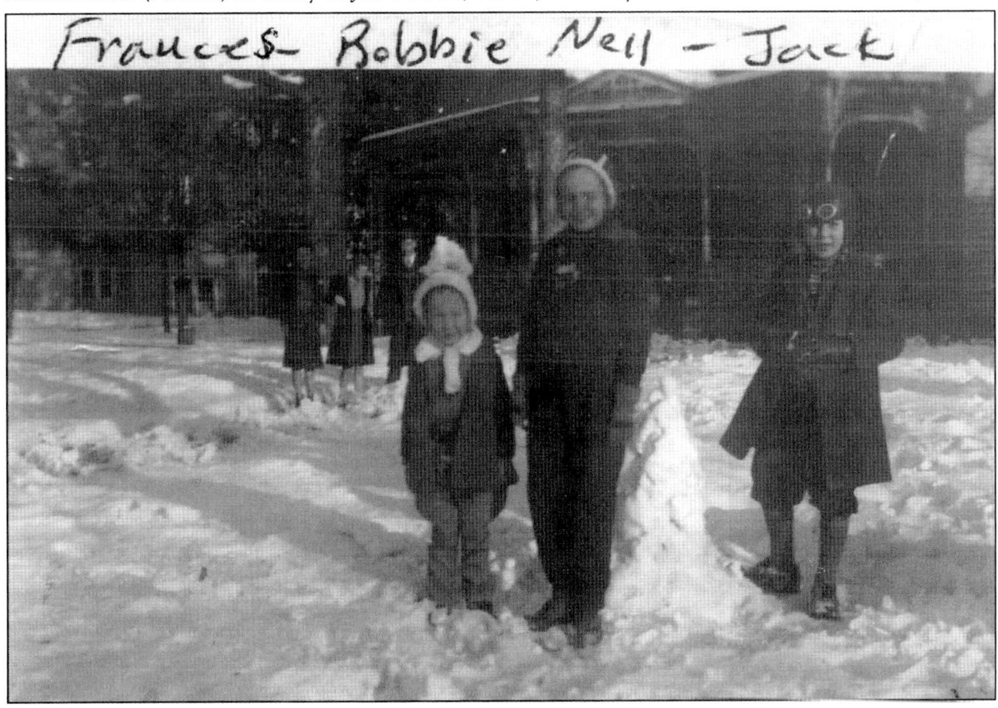

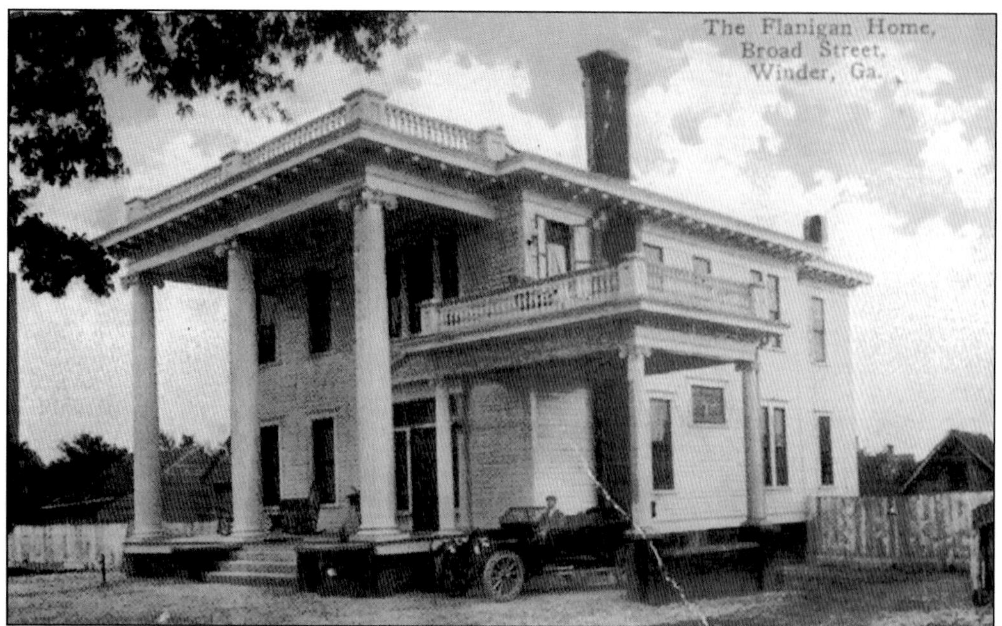

The Flanigan brothers owned one of the leading retail stores in Winder during the early years of the 20th century. This c. 1910 Neoclassical house was built for P.A. "Pink" Flanigan, a partner in Flanigan and Flanigan Pianos, Buggies and Automobiles. Flanigan test-drove the first car in Winder, owned by W.B. McCants; a trip from Winder to Tallulah Falls took over seven hours to complete. (Courtesy of Joe Bowen.)

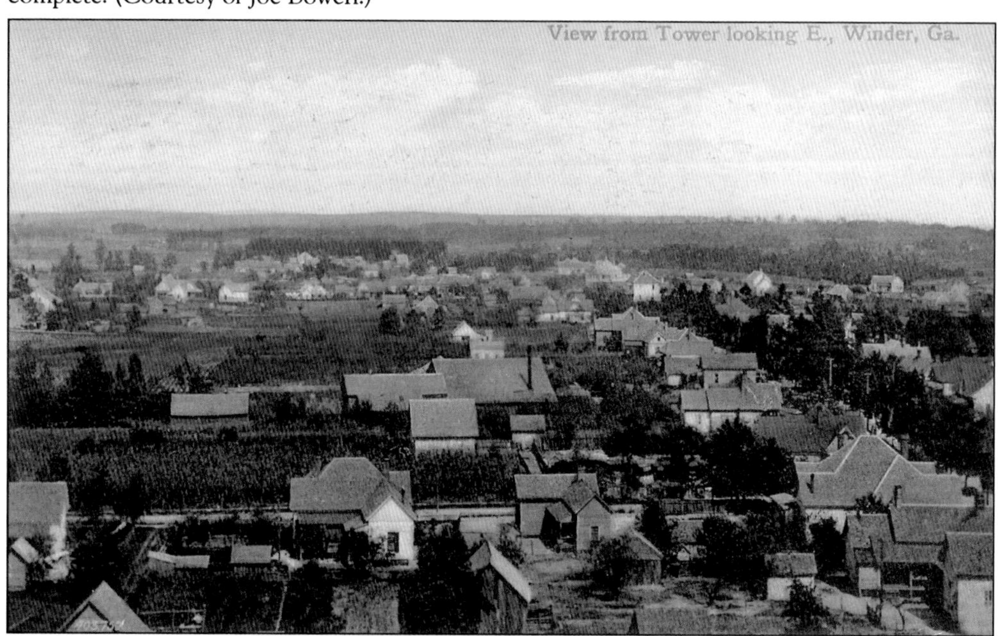

This c. 1912 bird's-eye view of North Broad Street's rooftops reveals the presence of electrical lines strung pole-to-pole on the city's main artery. In the foreground, the residents of Stephens Street had enough room to maintain sizeable gardens. As more people moved into Winder in the 1910s, most gardens were removed to make room for houses. New residents moved to Winder, where manufacturing jobs were plentiful. (Courtesy of Joe Bowen.)

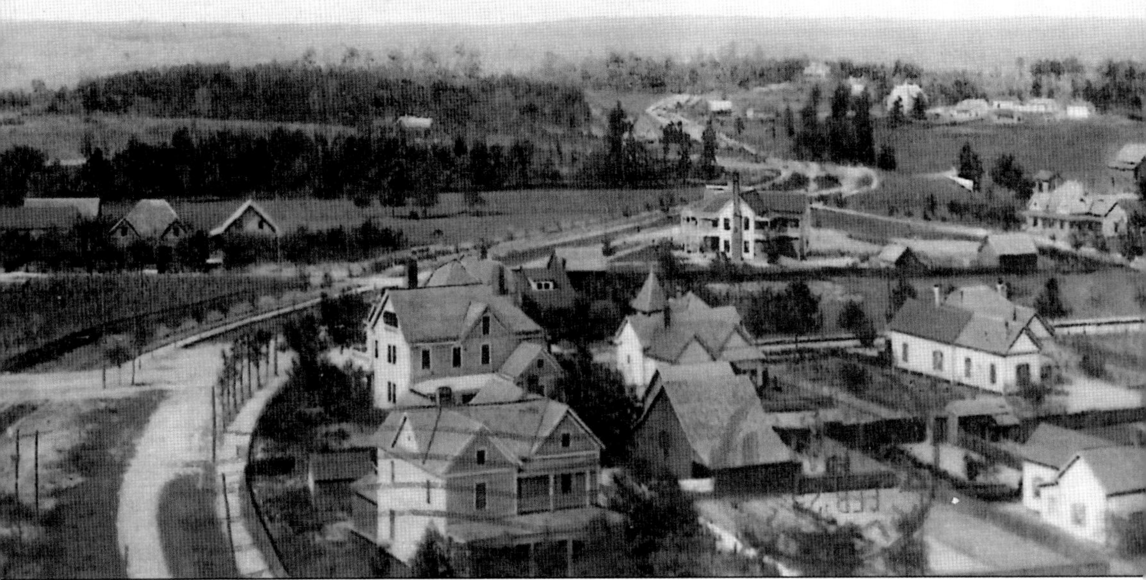

From Broad Street, Midland Avenue to the north was heavily populated with houses in the 1905 Wood Lawn Heights residential development. The houses closest to the rail line were built in the 1890s or before 1905. Predominantly featuring variations of the Queen Anne architectural style for houses and cottages, the Midland Avenue area was home to several of Winder's earliest families, railroad employees, and the First Christian Church manse. (Courtesy of Joe Bowen.)

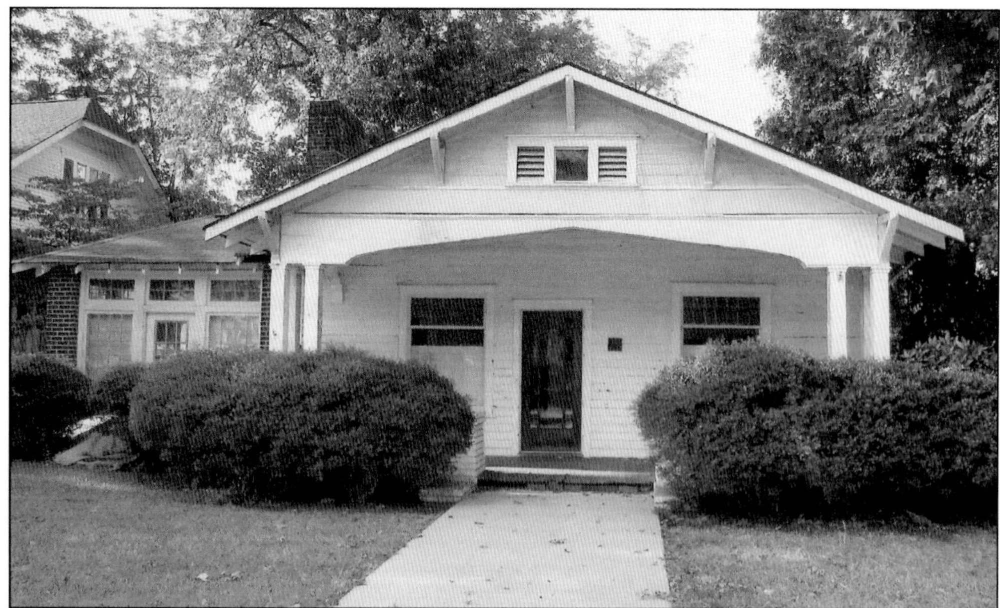

The North Broad Street Residential District, listed in the National Register of Historic Places (NRHP), includes properties along both sides of North Broad, Stephens, and Center Streets and Woodlawn and Midland Avenues. Listed in 1986, the district includes part of the Wood Lawn Heights residential development. The North Broad District is a smorgasbord of house types and styles, with its development occurring primarily from the 1890s through 1945. These side-by-side Craftsman cottages are in the midst of larger houses built in an earlier era. Their neighbors include larger Craftsman houses, the Queen Anne G.W. Smith house (owned and restored by Dee Baxter Russell and Richard B. Russell III), and the brick Colonial Revival house built by Carwood owner W. Clair Harris. Like the Athens-Church-Candler Street District, the North Broad Street District is representative of neighborhood development from the late 19th through early 20th century. (Barrow Preservation Society, Inc., images.)

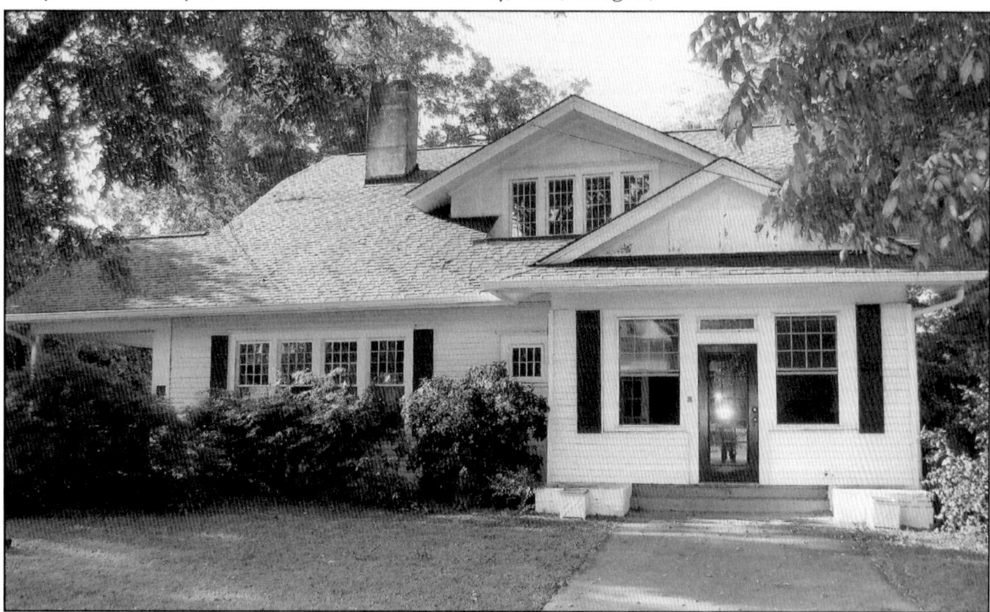

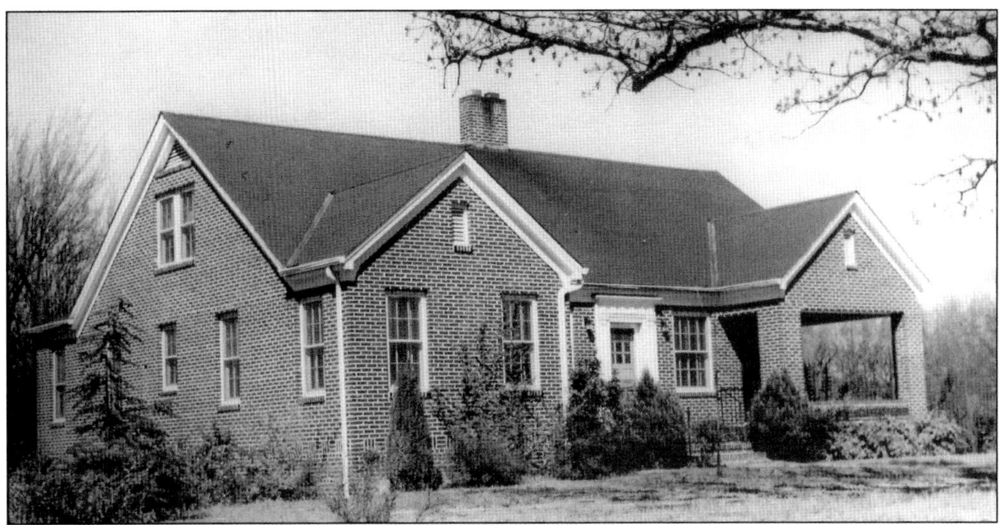

Jesse Bee Robinson and his wife, Pauline Hill Robinson, built this brick house in the Minimal Traditional style in 1941. During the post-Depression years, architectural trends moved toward a compromise of elements from traditional styles and the culture of practicality developed during the lean years of the 1930s. The Robinsons' house incorporated many features of the popular Tudor Revival style while omitting many details identified with earlier styles. (Courtesy of Caroline Robinson Stallings.)

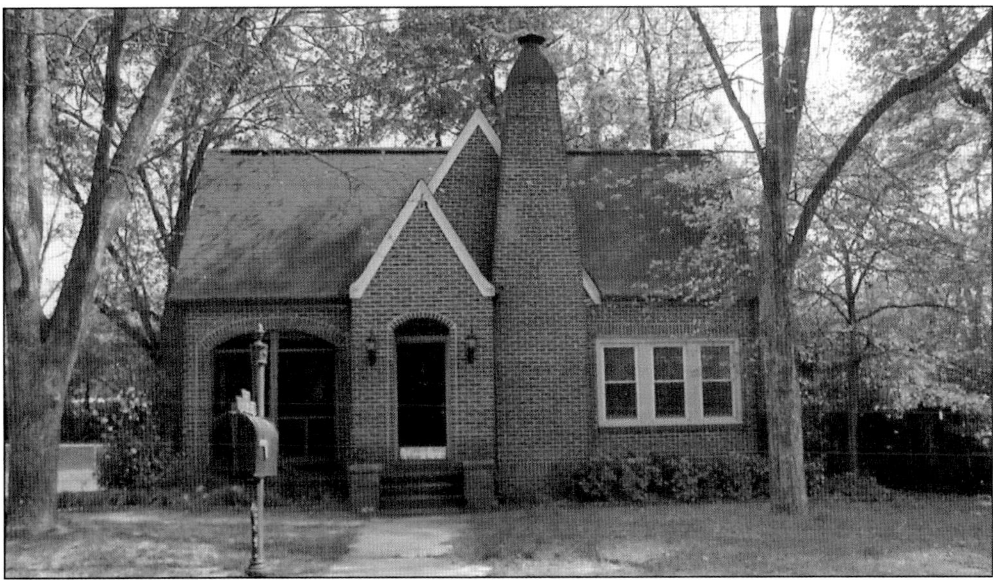

In 1905, Wood Lawn Heights was Winder's first residential development. It stretched from just below the Gainesville Midland Railroad tracks on present-day Midland Avenue to Buena Vista about a mile to the north. Many of the houses were built in the 1930s and 1940s and reflect the influence of the popular Tudor Revival architectural style. A stroll down the streets will take one past houses built for leaders of the community. With bankers, businessmen, and teachers as residents, the houses are a reflection of the stations of their owners. As new streets were cut into established but undeveloped blocks, the original lots for Wood Lawn Heights were redrawn in the 1930s to accommodate demand for larger lot sizes. The neighborhood was an eclectic blend of bankers, attorneys, judges, teachers, railroad employees, merchants, and professionals. The development evolved until the early 1960s. (Courtesy Barrow Preservation Society, Inc.)

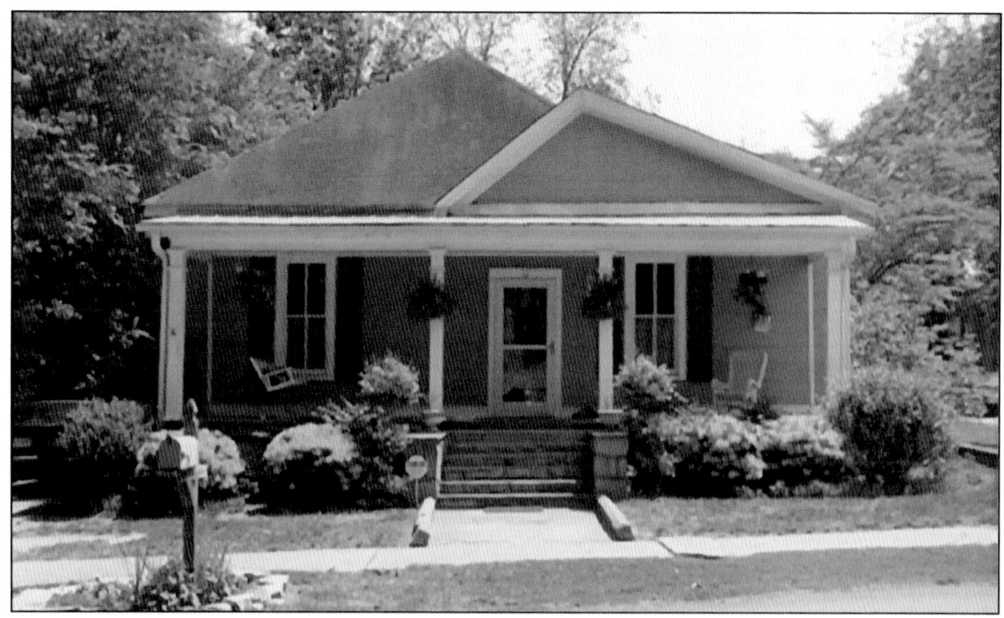

The development of speculative housing did not take hold in Winder until many years after the Wood Lawn Heights development. Consequently, house types and styles were varied, as opposed to the several templates contemporary developers use to direct neighborhood aesthetics and character. Because the Wood Lawn Heights development evolved over a 55-year period, architectural design trends determined the houses represented. The vernacular Queen Anne cottage above was built in 1917. It is most closely associated with Judge Joseph D. Quillian, whose family lived in the house for most of the 20th century. A wraparound porch was later incorporated into the front parlor, hence the asymmetrical front gable above the porch. The house pictured below was built in 1940 in the midst of the Tudor Revival craze driven in part by the popularity of Walt Disney's animated stories featuring Tudor cottages. (Barrow Preservation Society images.)

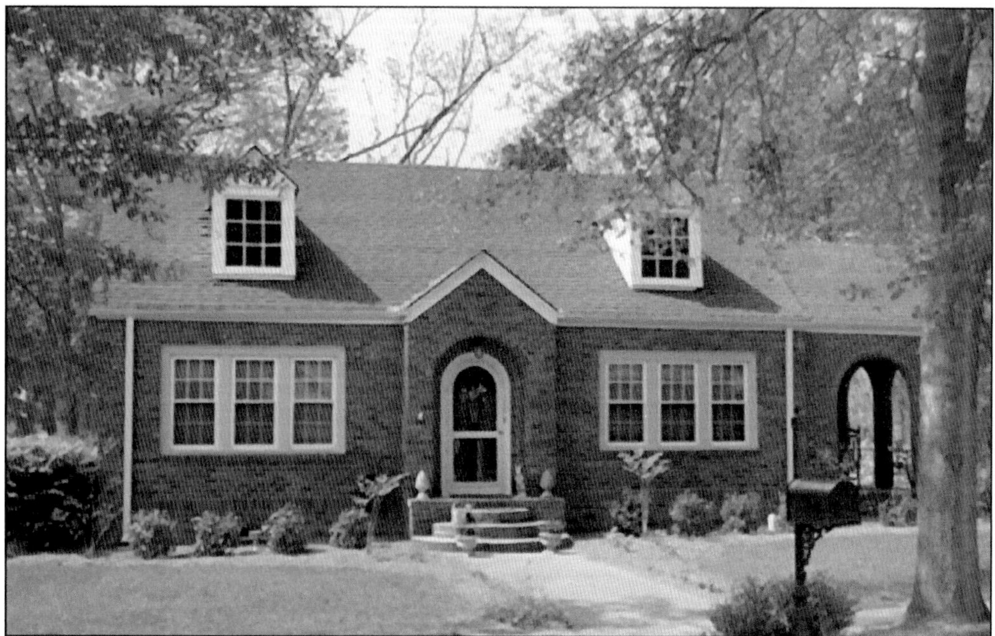

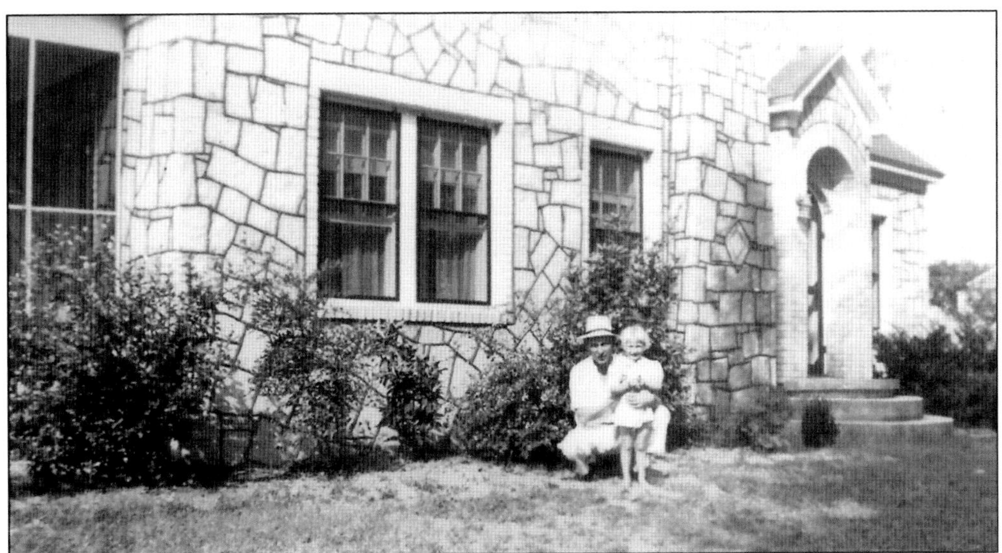

Houses built with granite quarried from Charles Madison "C.M." Ferguson's Flat Rock Quarry, located south of downtown, were scarce in Winder. Most buildings with granite facades were commercial in design and function. Several buildings in Winder were constructed similarly to Bee and Pauline Robinson's granite house. The granite is part of the massive Elberton granite outcropping that permeates the southeastern United States. Sited on Wright Street east of North Broad Street, the house is part of a large middle-class neighborhood that evolved between the early 1900s and 1965, though small pockets of development in this area have continued into the present day. A crew led by Robert Lee Maddox constructed this house, built in the popular Tudor Revival style, for Jesse Bee Robinson in 1938. Pictured in the front yard are Robinson and his young daughter Caroline. (Courtesy of Caroline Robinson Stallings.)

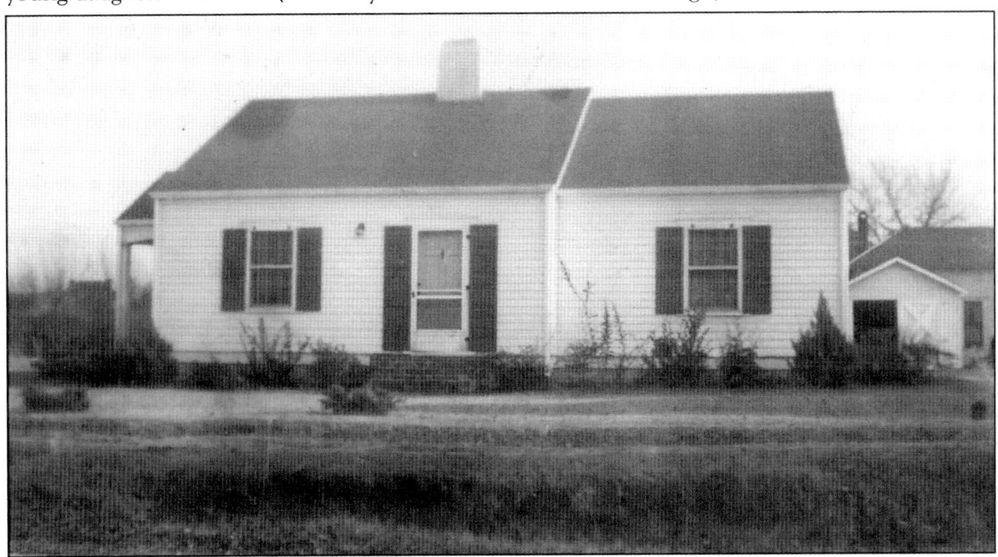

The Great Depression was still fresh when World War II made a global sweep, further changing fortunes for Americans. After his return from service as a Navy flyer, Robert A. Hill and his wife, Reba Garner Hill, made their first home in this folk-style Minimal Traditional house on Walker Street off North Broad Street. Folk-style houses are simple designs including elements from an academic style. (Courtesy of Bob Hill.)

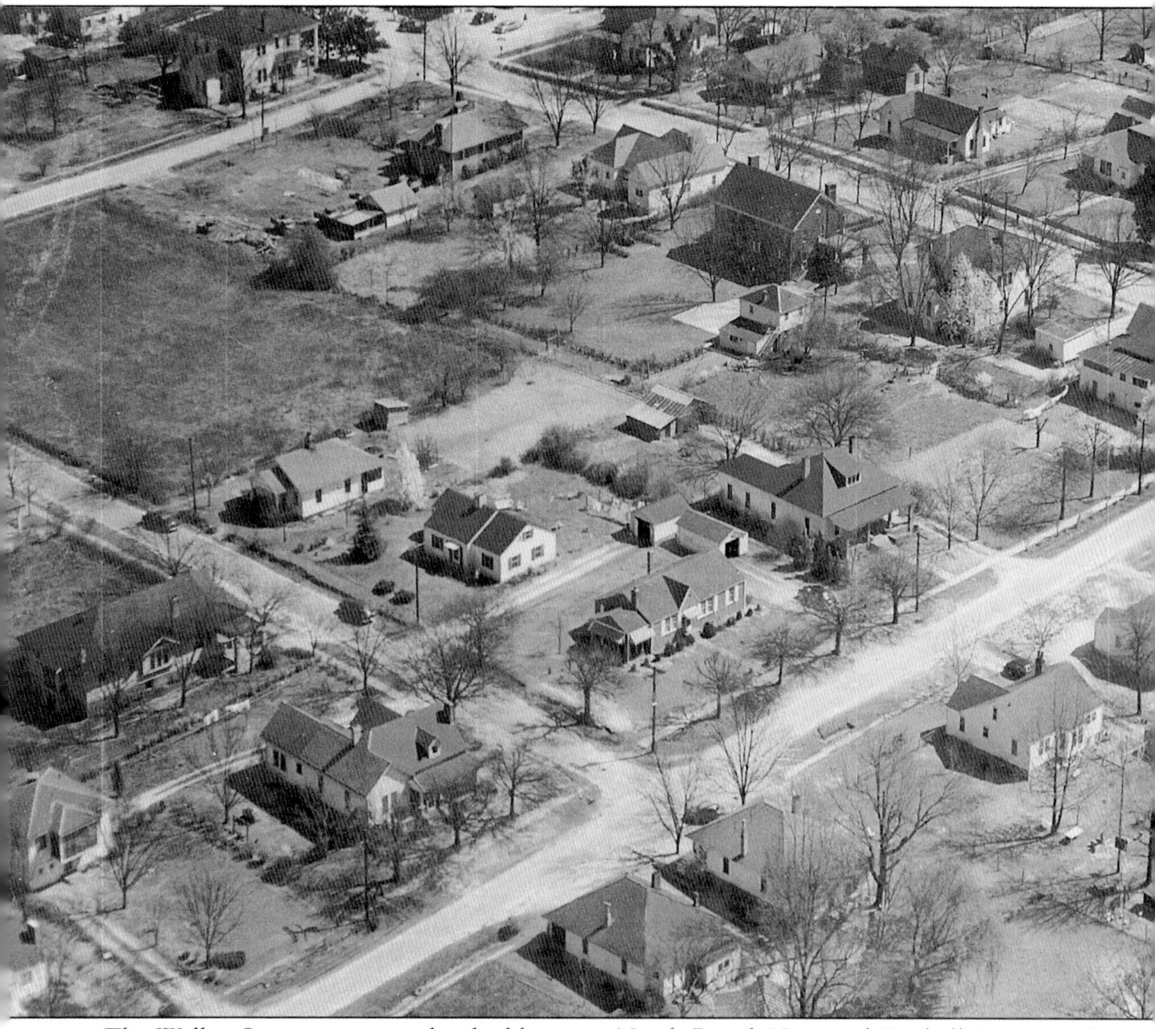

The Walker Street area is sandwiched between North Broad, New, and Kimball Streets and bordered to the west by Woodlawn Avenue. As Winder spread from its central business and residential districts, new development resulted in the construction of a neighborhood of modest houses. (Courtesy of Bob Hill.)

Four
PUBLIC LIFE

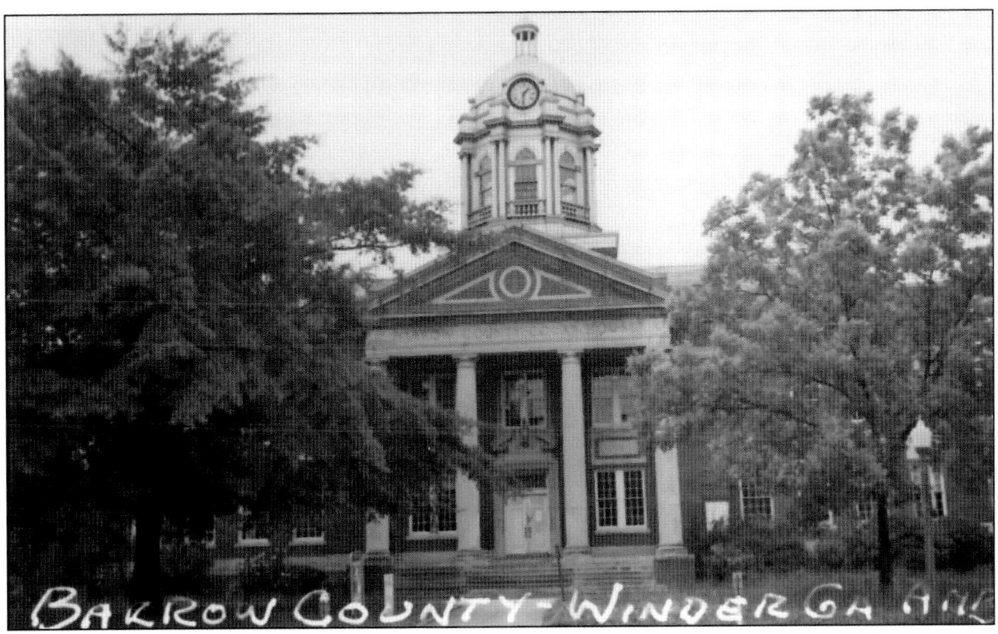

Once Barrow County became a reality, Wiley Harrison Bush moved his house from the corner of Broad and Athens Streets to make way for the new courthouse. The obelisk that once marked the apex of the three counties from which Barrow County was birthed was moved to the traditional site of Snodon, located on the site of the Jug Tavern Institute and Winder School; the site is now a parking lot. (Courtesy of Joe Bowen.)

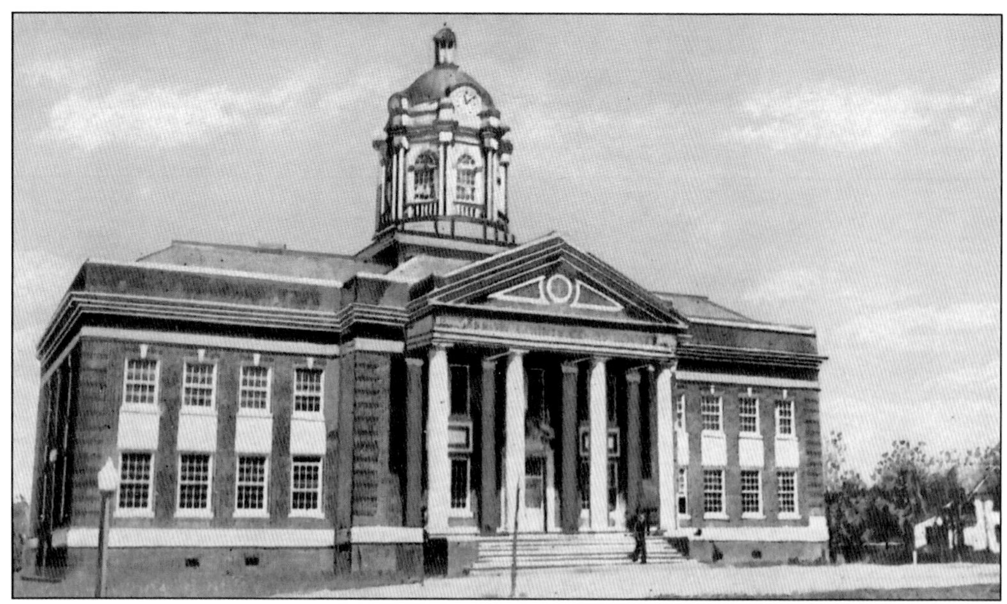

Completed in 1920, the Neoclassical Barrow County Courthouse was designed by noted courthouse architect James J. Baldwin and built by Savannah contractor R.W. Wimbish for $133,400. Baldwin also designed the 1915 Barrow County Jail on the northwest corner of the courthouse block. The Gothic Revival architectural style was often employed for incarceration facilities due to the style's association with sacred architecture. The facility's crenellated towers, elaborate brick corbelling, and polychromatic color scheme brought an air of sophistication to the community. The 1915 building was rehabilitated in 1993 and reopened as the Barrow County Historical Society Museum. Among the exhibits are three original jail cells and the hanging room. A new Barrow County Courthouse and Detention Center was constructed three miles west of downtown in 2009. The historic courthouse is being restored for occupancy by county offices scheduled to be moved back into downtown Winder. (Both images courtesy of Joe Bowen.)

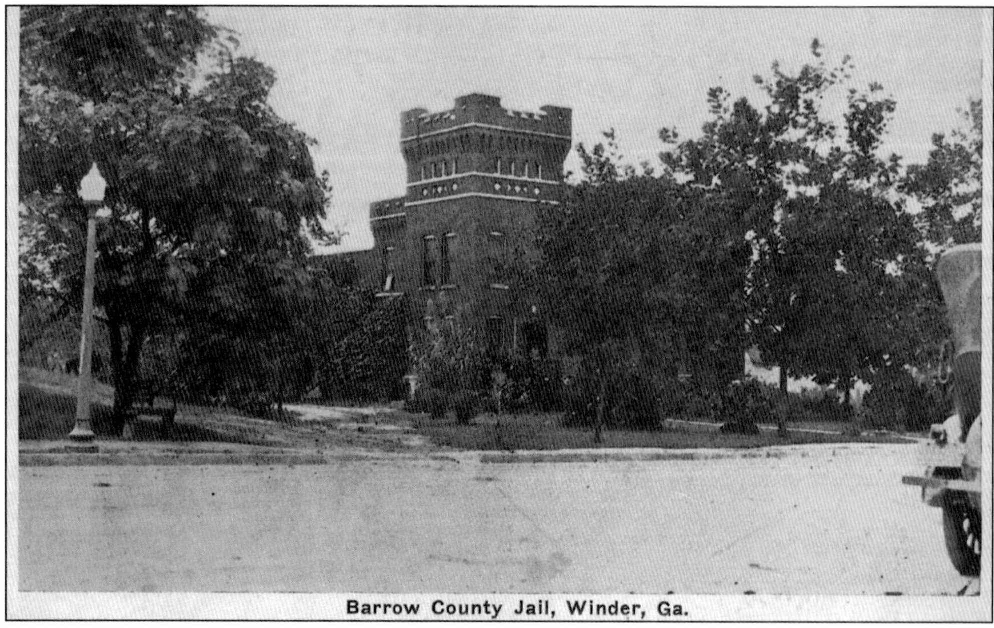

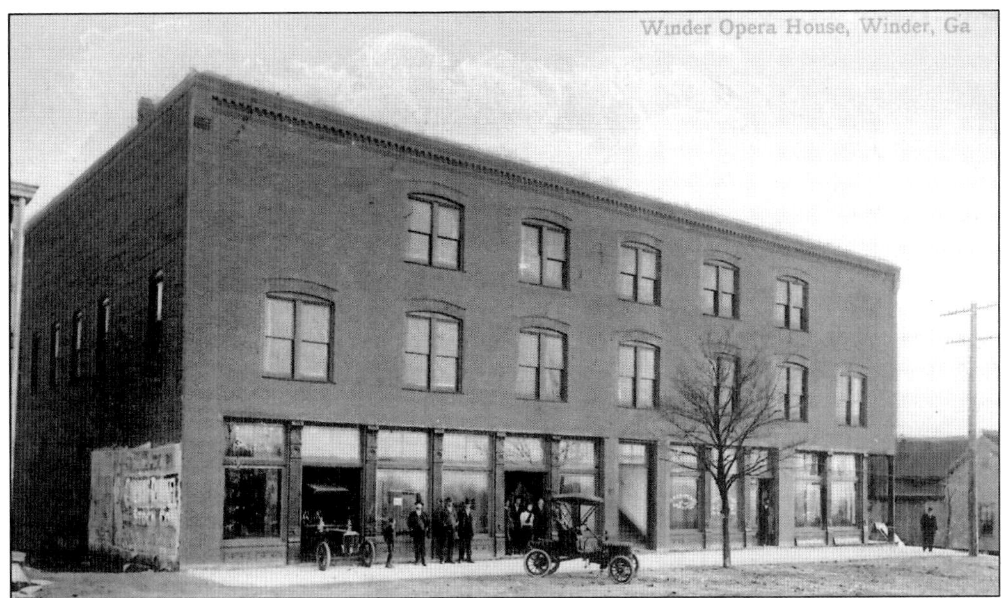

Across Broad Street, near its intersection with Athens Street, the Sharpton Opera House was used as a temporary courthouse by the newly formed Barrow County from 1914 to 1920. With the decreasing frequency of traveling stage shows and the opening of the new Art Deco Strand Theatre across Broad Street, the Sharpton Opera House commenced a new career of being the facility for the conducting of county business. (Courtesy of Joe Bowen.)

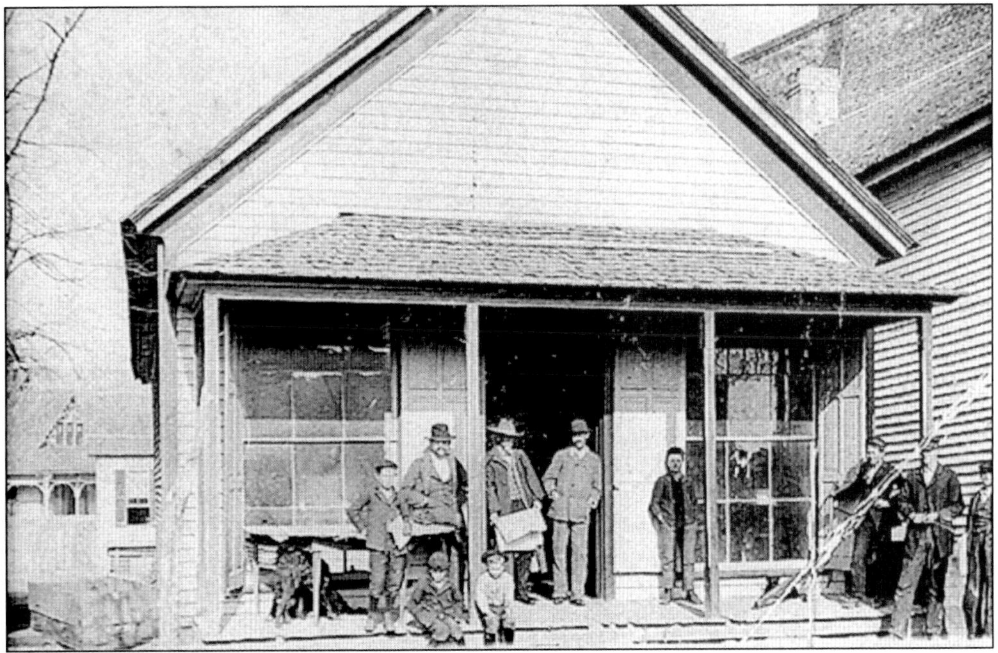

The city of Jug Tavern received its own postal route in 1876. With city founders looking to erect permanent buildings befitting an up-and-coming municipality, the first Jug Tavern Post Office was built to be replaced. This Folk Greek Revival one-room building served the city's early needs for the handling of correspondence to and from the residents and businesspeople of Jug Tavern. (Courtesy of Joe Bowen.)

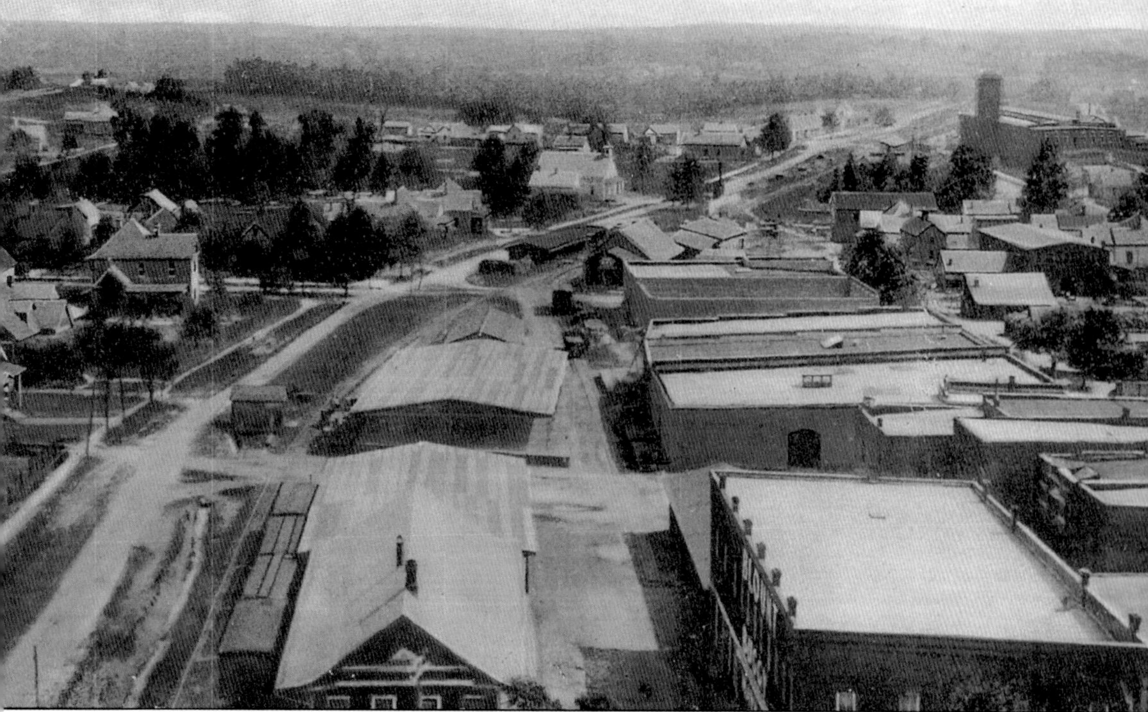

The Gainesville Midland Railroad served mainly as a freight transporter. It ran from Gainesville to Monroe and a few points south. The south side of the curved tracks ran concurrently with Midland Avenue, and the Gainesville Midland served as a dividing line between commercial downtown and the residents who lived as close to downtown as possible without building their houses on the tracks. The Gainesville Midland Railroad utilized covered loading platforms that provided shelter for both freight and the employees unloading it. As a result of its proximity to the railroad, East Candler Street became an industrial district, with clothing factories and retail stores specializing in building materials, farm equipment, feed and seed, paint, and other household building supplies. (Courtesy of Joe Bowen.)

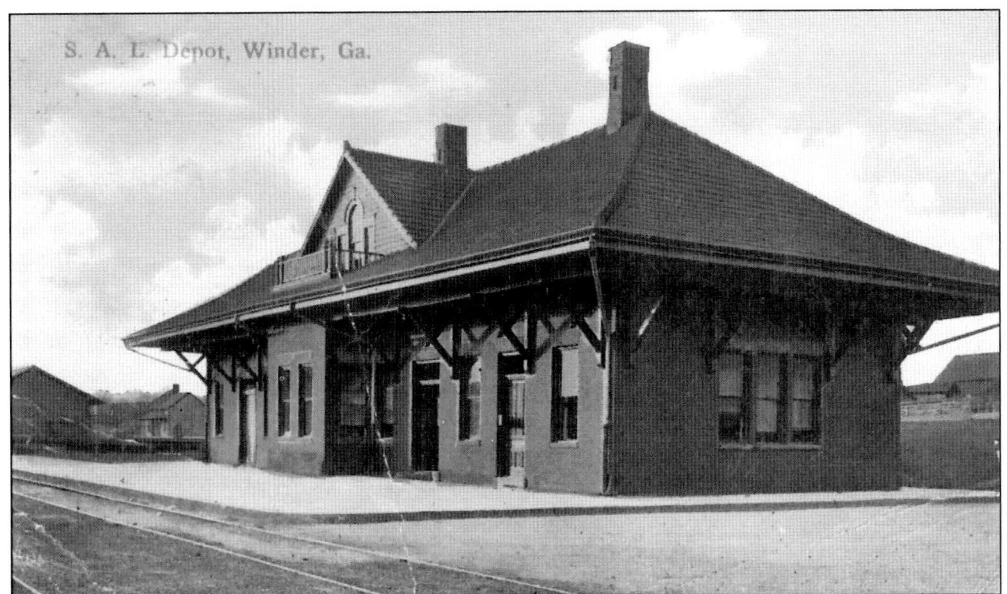

On the other end of Broad Street, Seaboard Air Line Railroad provided service for human passengers. With the evident need for a depot, Seaboard constructed this beautiful Queen Anne transportation building in 1908. Seaboard had a portfolio of six to eight depot models from which it selected a design to fit the host community's needs. The Winder Depot, similar in design to those of many other cities in Georgia, incorporates upgrades in building materials and design. (Courtesy of Joe Bowen.)

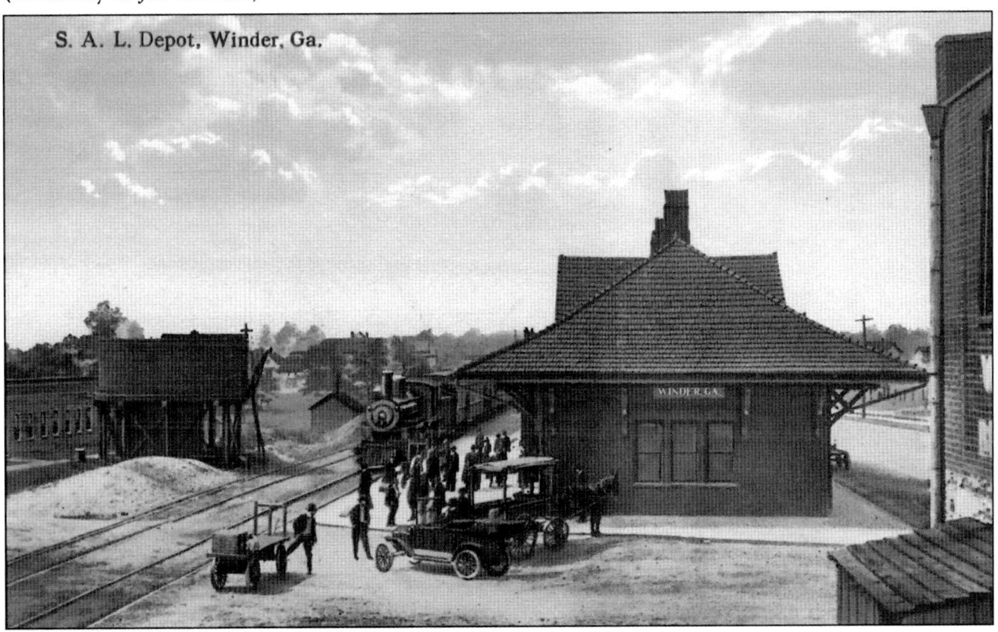

This c. 1910 image is a study of early 20th century transportation modes. Horse-drawn vehicles, a human-powered baggage cart, a motorcar, and the approaching train represent the varied ways in which Americans got around during that era. To the left of the tracks is the water tower, which provided a water supply to the trains. At far left is the Bell Manufacturing Company. (Courtesy of Joe Bowen.)

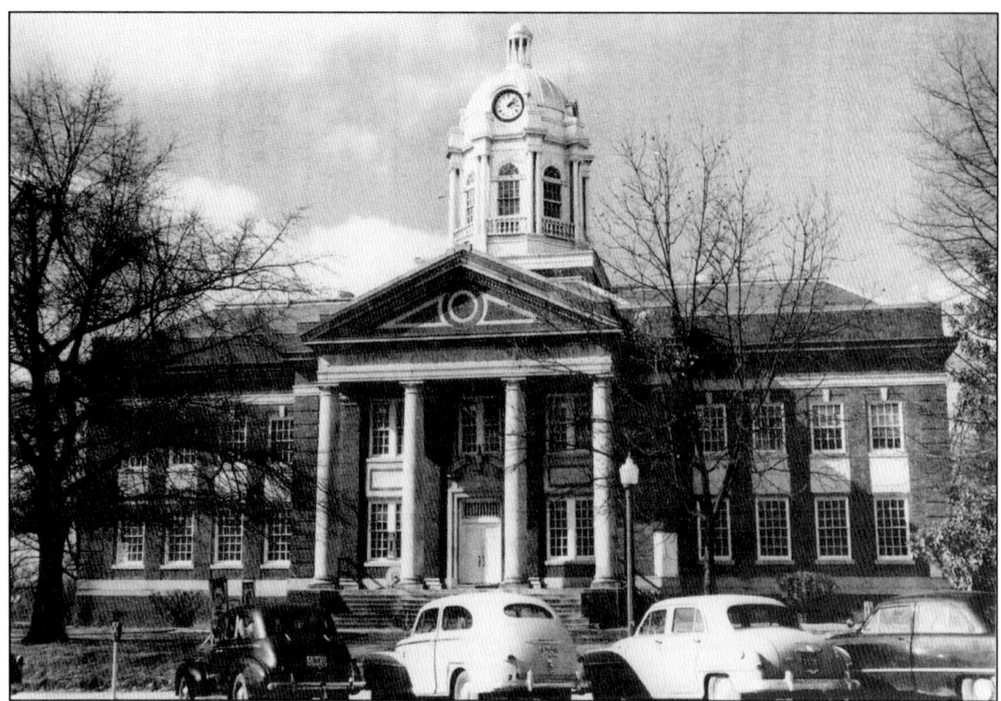

By the 1940s, the Barrow County Courthouse had settled into its place of prominence in the Winder streetscape. Mature trees framed the superb lines of the Neoclassical building, and automobile travel made the courthouse easier to access than early opponents of the formation of Barrow County had considered. Courthouse employees and visitors contributed to the economy of downtown Winder by shopping with local merchants. (Courtesy of Joe Bowen.)

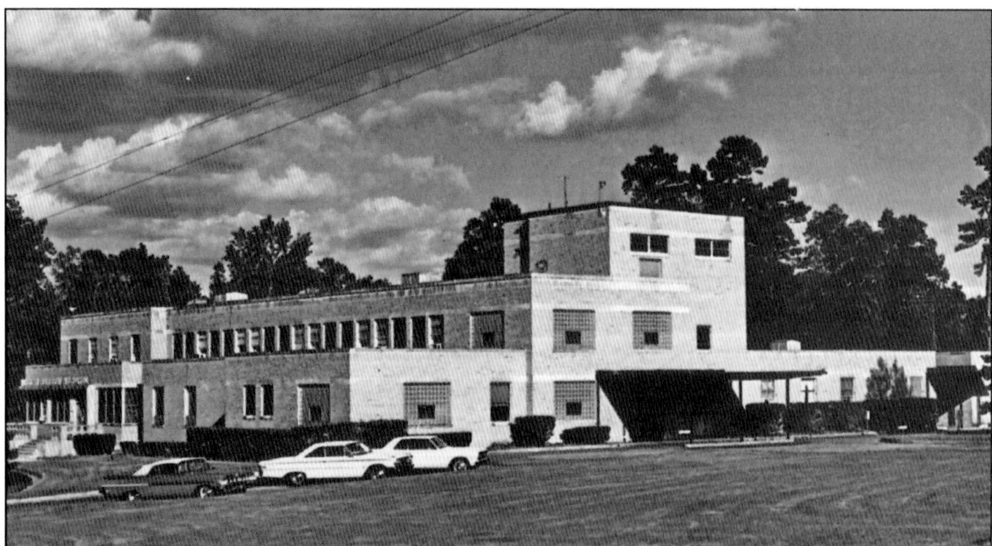

Until construction of the Winder-Barrow Hospital on land donated by the family of Nancy Hill Williams, there were no hospital facilities in the county. This Art Moderne–style building was completed in 1952, offering patients an opportunity for clinical medical care in their hometown. The glass block window treatment allowed natural light in while providing both security and privacy for patients and medical personnel inside. (Courtesy of Joe Bowen.)

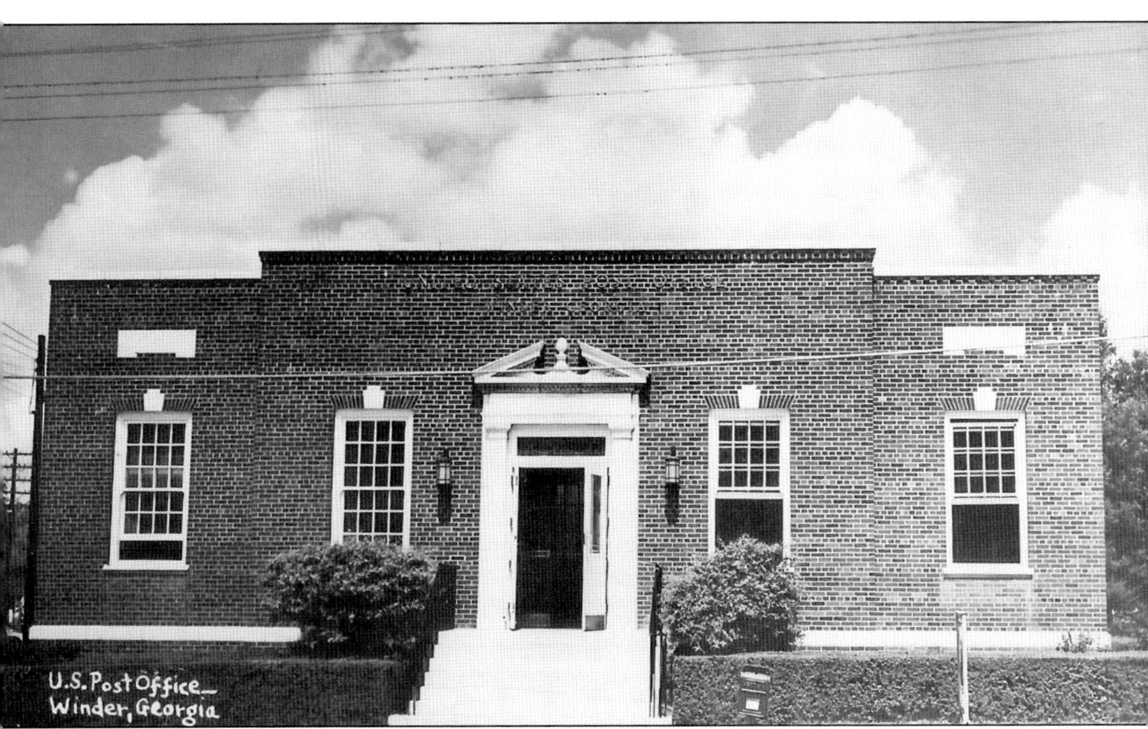

By 1903, the Winder Post Office was housed in the southeast corner of the Granite Hotel. Over the next 50 years, it would move from one storefront to another in downtown Winder in an effort to fulfill the requirements of providing mail service to the people of Winder and Barrow County. In 1935, this commercial variation of the Adam architectural style, with Colonial Revival influence, was built on the corner of North Broad Street and Midland Avenue. The style of this practical, yet dignified, government building of the mid-20th century hearkened back to the founding principles of the United States by inspiring recollection of colonial buildings. The Gainesville Midland Railroad had ceased operation, automobile traffic was steadily increasing in downtown Winder, and this facility provided an outdoor depository box for letters and small packages. After serving as the post office and Winder City Hall, this building is now the headquarters for the Winder Fire Department. (Courtesy of Joe Bowen.)

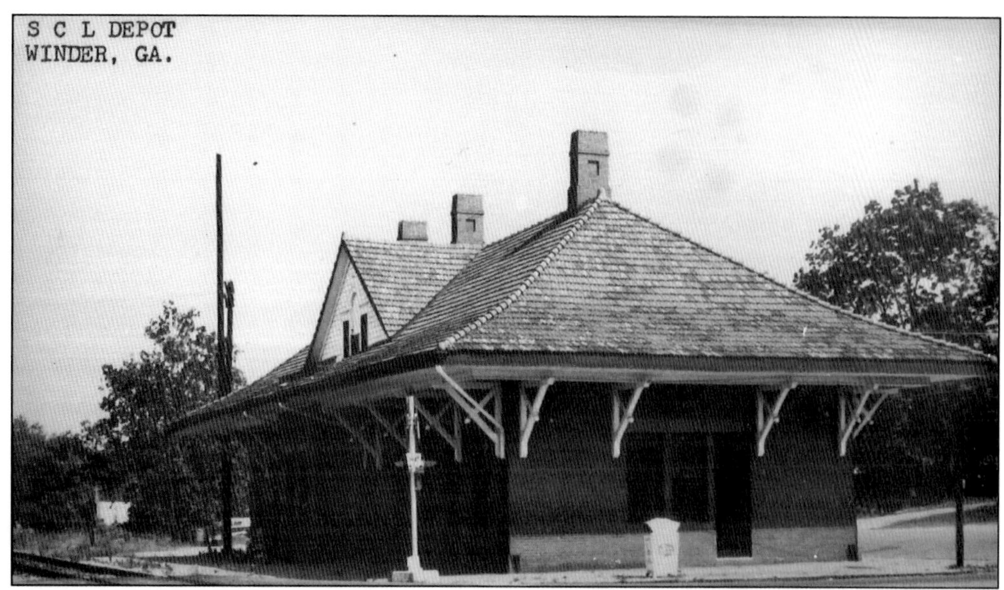

Winder's relationship with the railroad was strong as the 1960s arrived and motor vehicle traffic increased. Passenger travel around the Eastern Seaboard was available on the Silver Comet, while freight trains serviced the many manufacturing plants in the area. By 1970, desegregation meant no more separate passenger waiting areas. Furnishings in Seaboard Air Line depots were comfortable while serving as tools for advertising. The railroad's initials, from its earlier time as Seaboard Air Line, reminded passengers which rail service they were using. The pew-like waiting room benches offered group seating with separate armrests, allowing individual space for busy times. The Seaboard Coast Line depot in Winder boasts beautiful detailing with classic Queen Anne decorative stained-glass transom windows, roof braces, and Palladian windows. Its Ludowici tile roof and corbelled chimneys complete the look of sophistication so sought after by city leaders. (Above, courtesy of Joe Bowen; below, courtesy of Helen Person.)

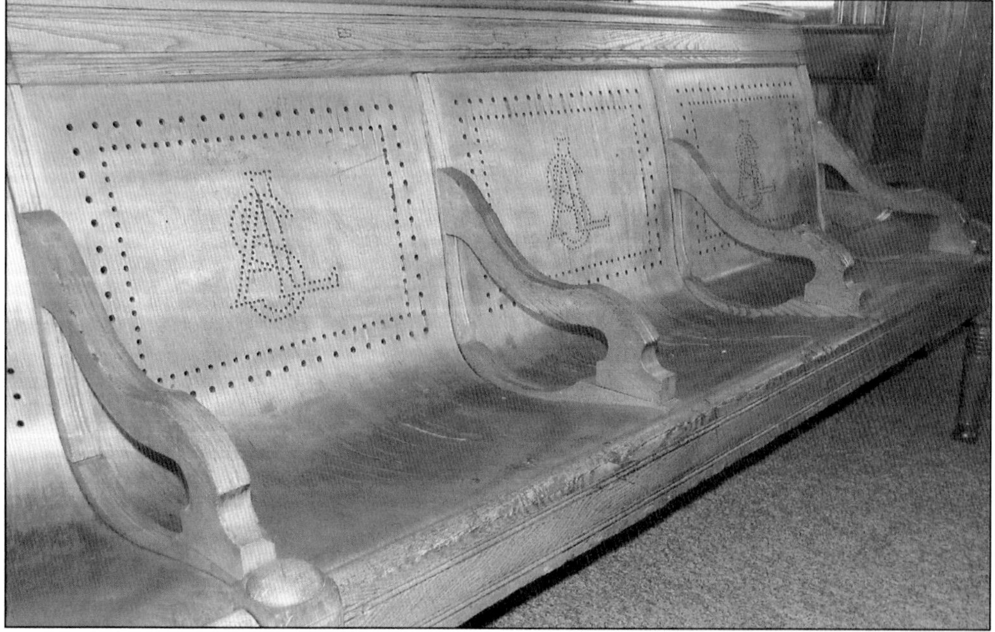

After the Gainesville Midland Railroad ceased operation, the No. 208 engine was gifted to the City of Winder for use as a museum piece. In this photograph, Mayor John Kelley (right) accepts the gift from Gainesville Midland representatives. No. 208 is permanently installed under a car shed beside the Winder Depot. Today, the engine is available for tours via the Barrow County Historical Society Museum. (Courtesy of Caroline Robinson Stallings.)

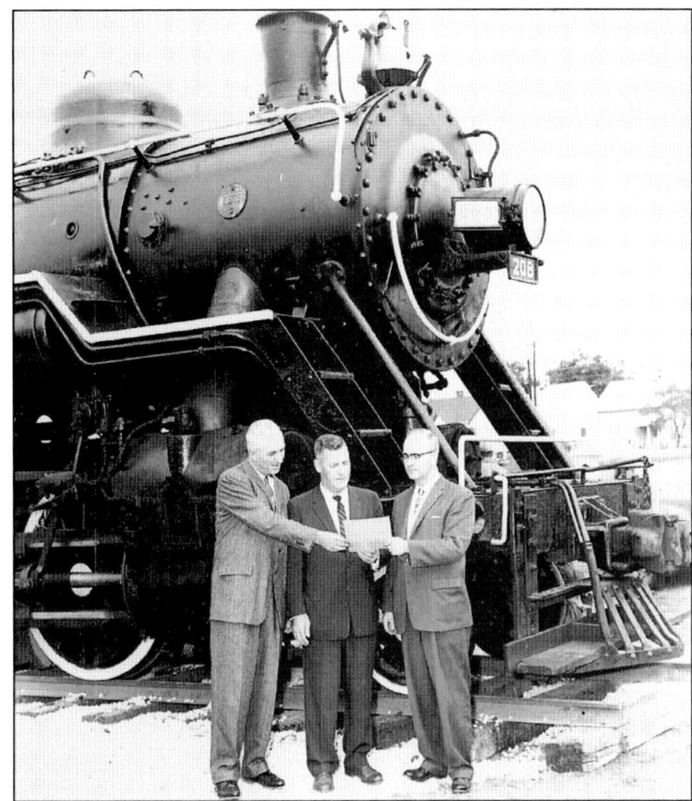

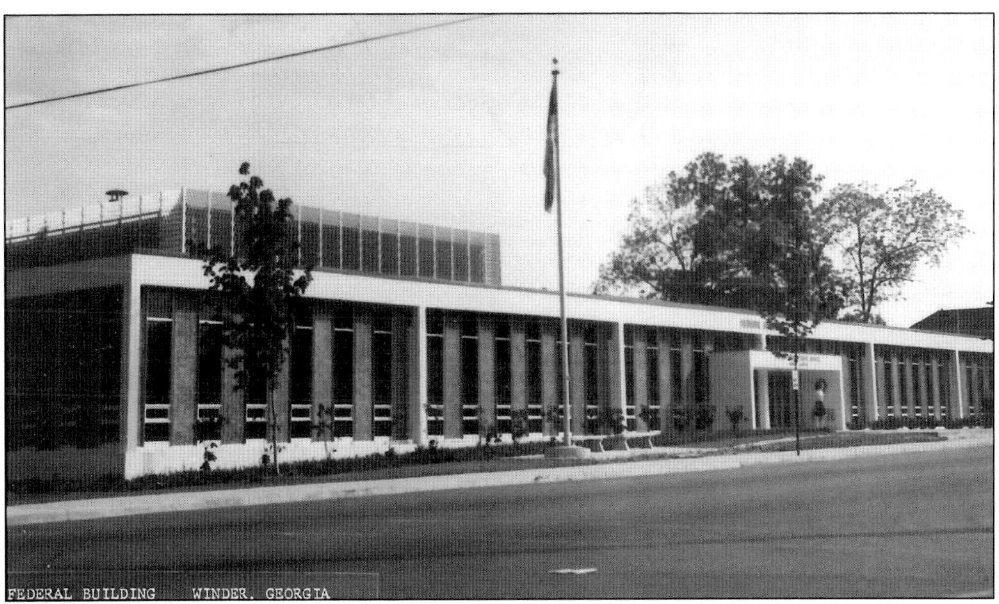

In the mid-1960s, the Winder Post Office moved to the new Federal Building on the corner of Broad and Stephens Streets. Government offices occupied the north end of the building, while the south side of the building was dedicated to the postal service. Parking and a loading dock at the rear of the building on Jackson Street provided accessibility for postal workers and visitors to the facility. (Courtesy of Joe Bowen.)

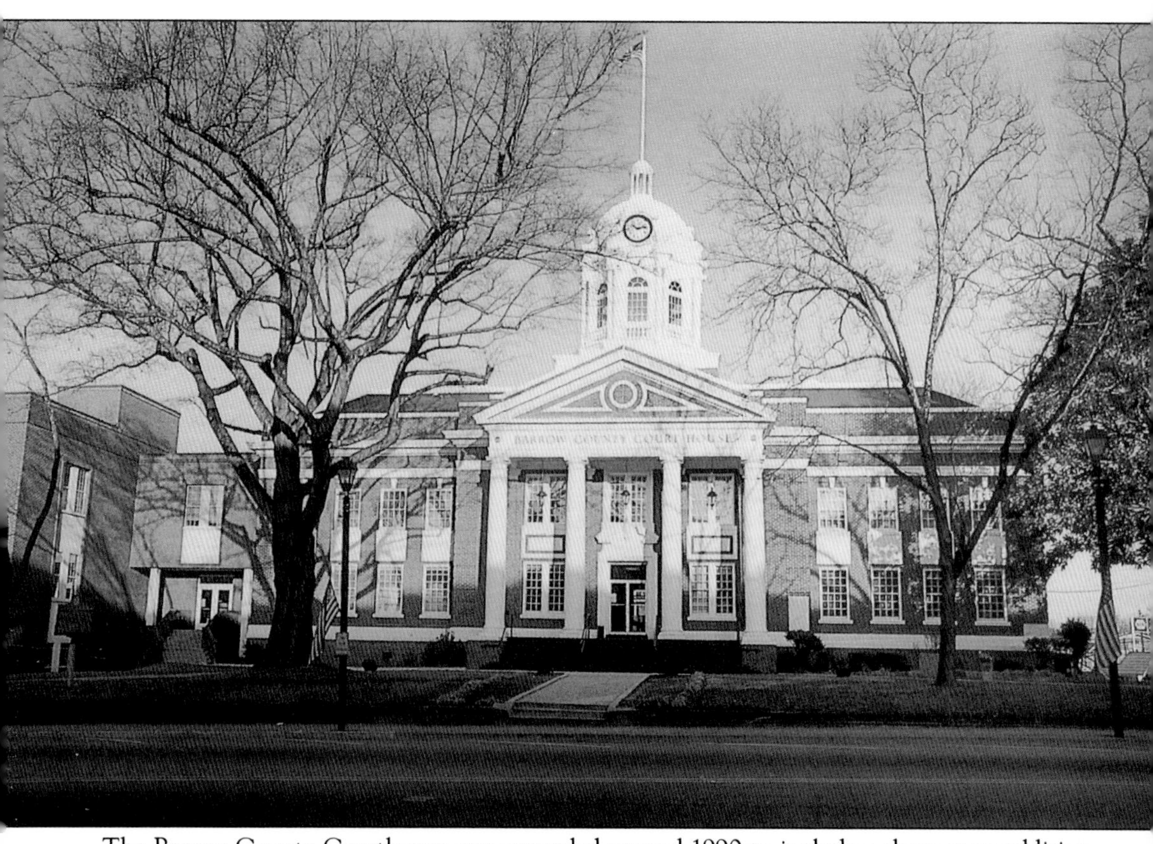

The Barrow County Courthouse was expanded around 1990 to include a three-story addition with a basement. Built to accommodate the many courts servicing greater numbers of people, the addition allowed more space for real estate records and judge's chambers for several courts. As part of a commercial block building, the addition incorporated the scale and some design elements from the 1920 courthouse without attempting to replicate the Neoclassical style. (Courtesy of Joe Bowen.)

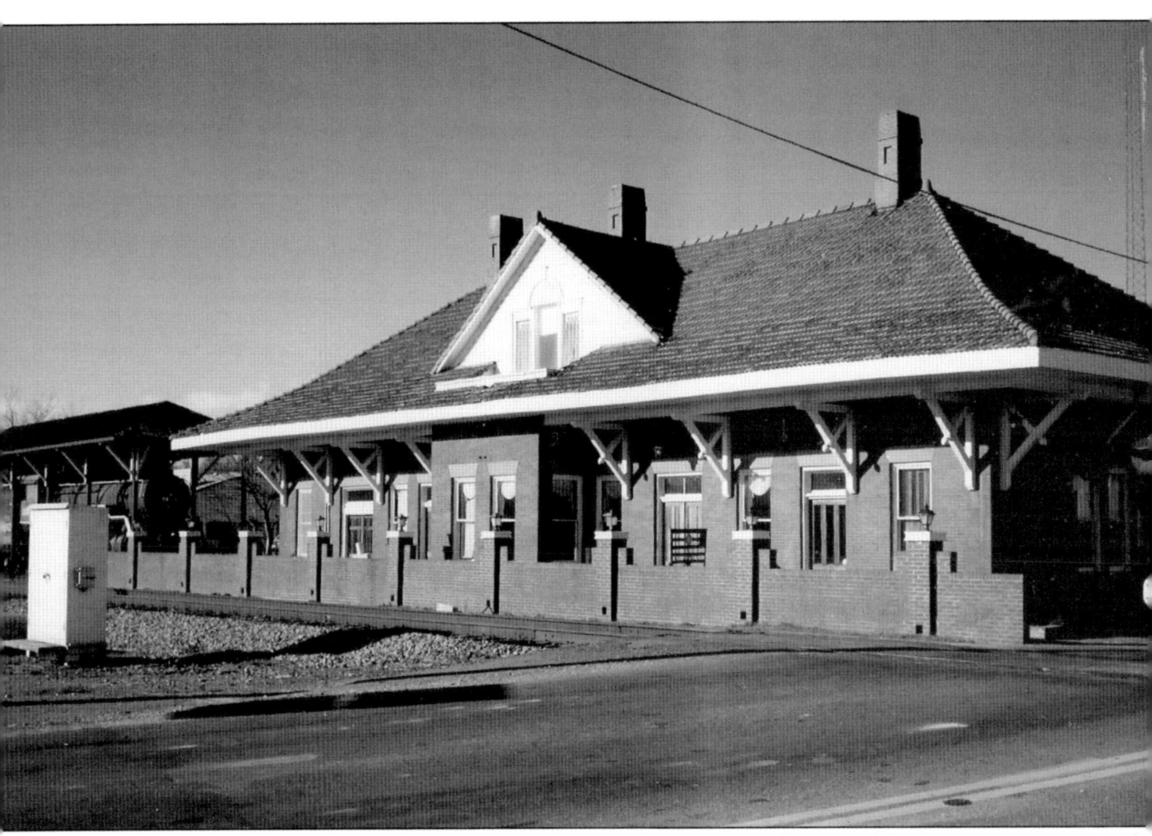

Seaboard Coast Line suspended passenger rail service in the 1970s. With no need for the passenger depot, the railroad gifted the Winder Depot to the city it had served for so many years. The Barrow County Chamber of Commerce offices were moved to the building to continue the depot's long-standing service to the community as a welcome center. (Courtesy of Joe Bowen.)

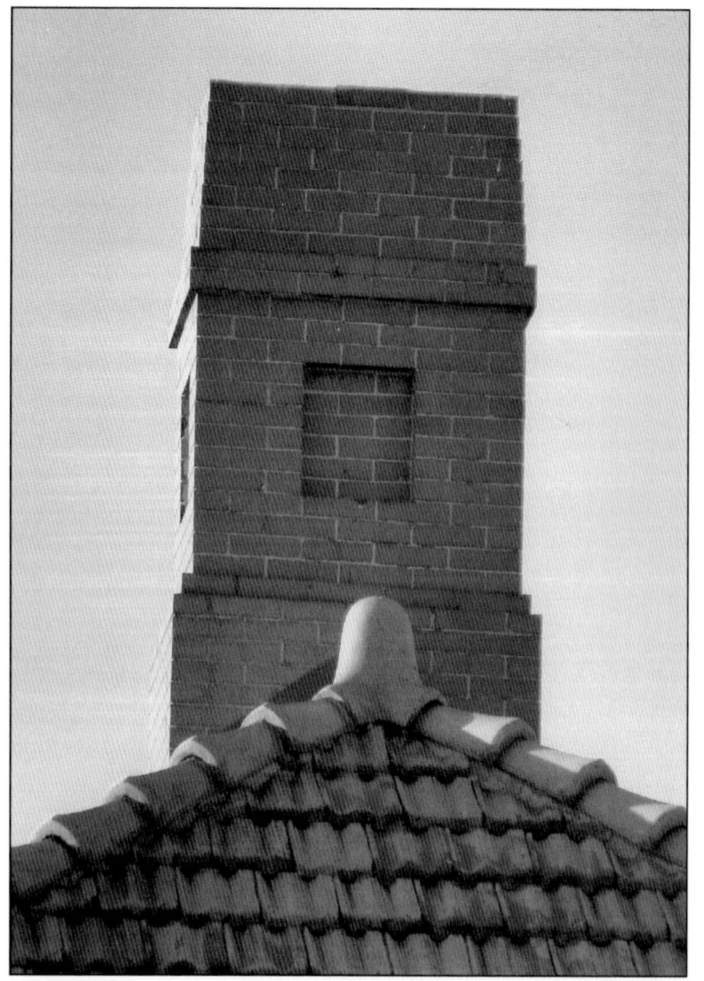

The terra-cotta Ludowici tile and intricate corbelling of one of the three chimneys at the Winder Depot serve as constant reminders of the detail and craftsmanship incorporated into older buildings. Ludowici roof tiles were manufactured in the Long County town of Ludowici, where the major employer was the Ludowici Brick and Tile Company. The roof and chimneys are only a few of the grand architectural details of the Winder Depot. Stained-glass cottage transoms were hallmarks of the Queen Anne style. Their inclusion in the depot reflected America's love affair with this Victorian style. Architectural detail is a hallmark of classically designed buildings. (Barrow Preservation Society.)

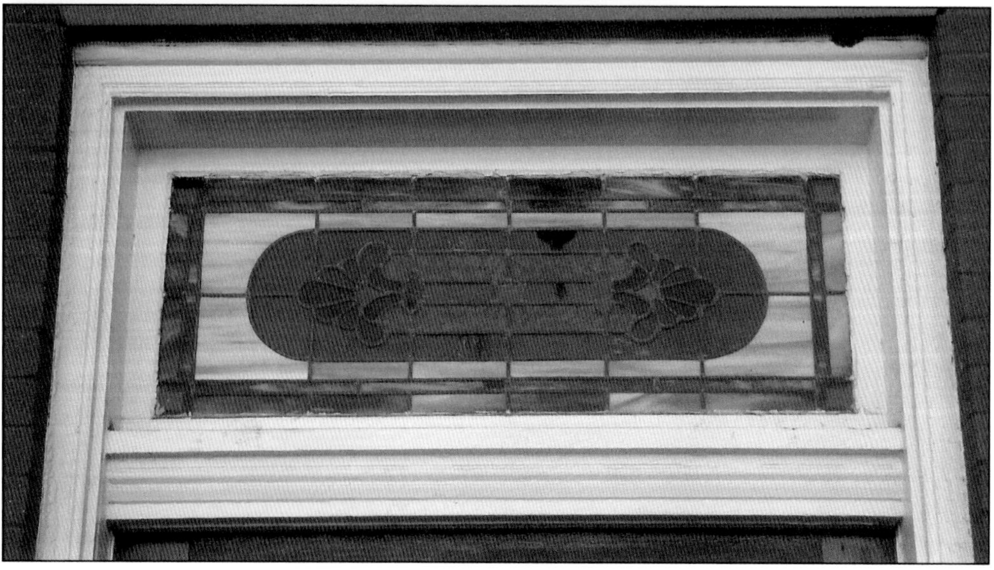

Five

LEARNING

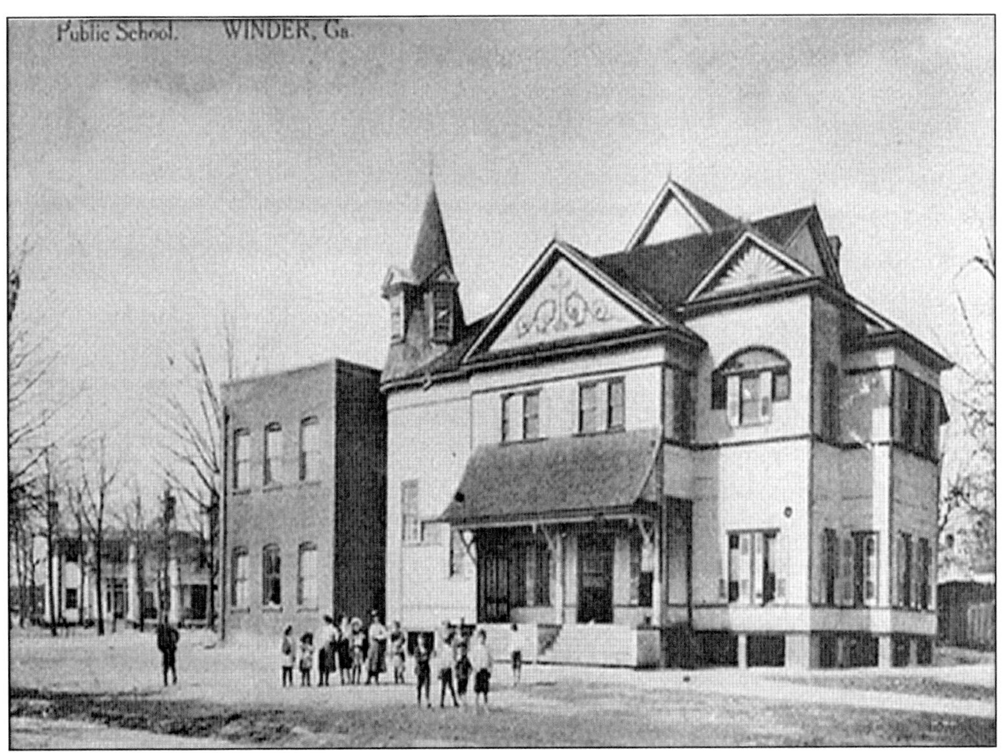

Ensuring that young people could prepare to pursue their chosen professions provided the catalyst for the organization of the Jug Tavern Institute in the late 1800s. This Queen Anne–style building was constructed on the corner of Hog Mountain Road and Church Street around 1885. Spacious classrooms and a "playroom" offered area students their first formal learning environment. The c. 1907 two-story brick addition served grades one through four. (Courtesy of Joe Bowen.)

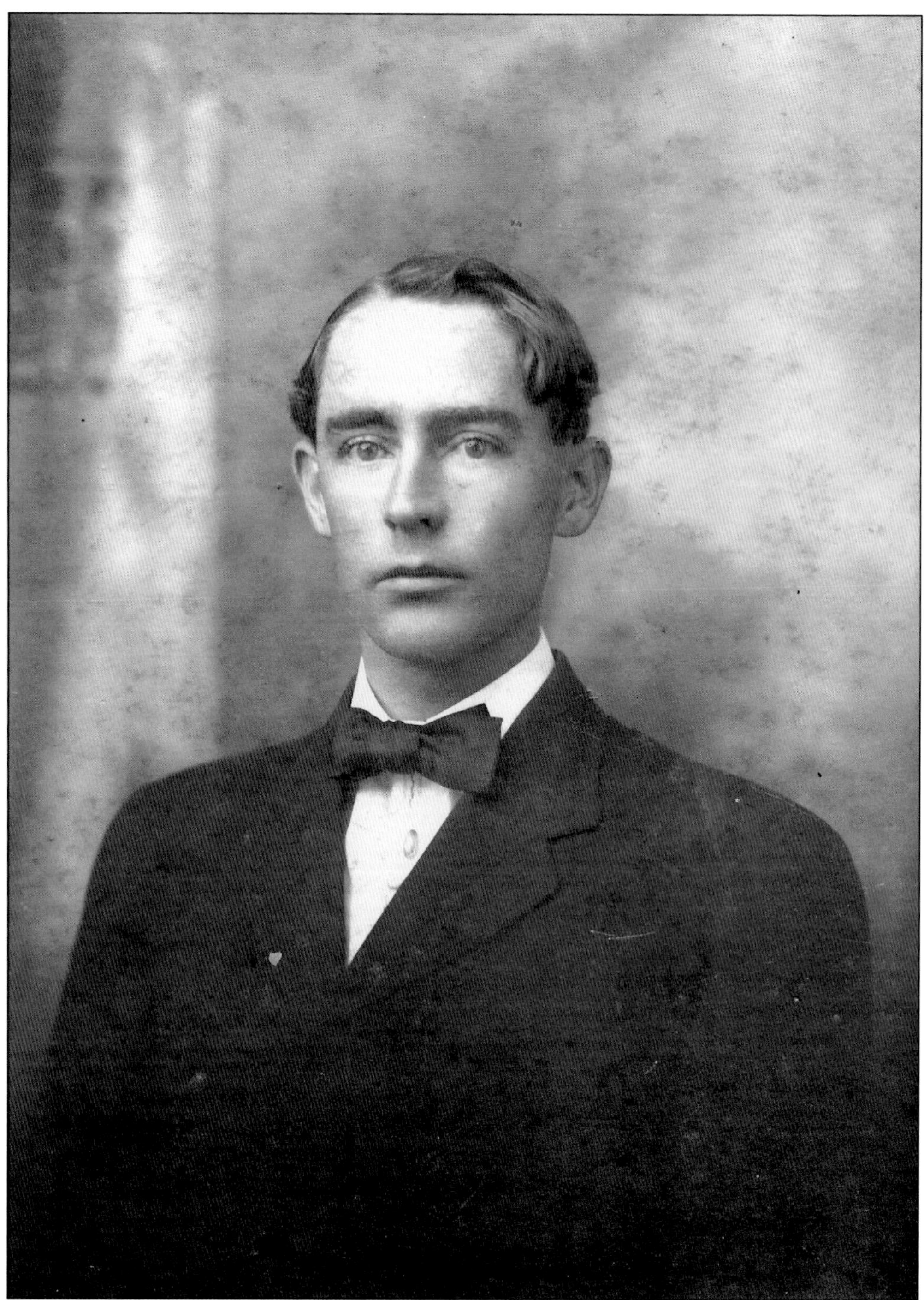

With the formation of Barrow County in 1914, county leaders set about the task of placing all of the county's schools under one structure. W.M. Holsenbeck, superintendent of the Barber's Creek School near Statham, became the first superintendent of the newly formed Barrow County School System in 1915, a position he held until 1920. He also taught and served as principal at Winder High School. (Courtesy of Bill Summerour.)

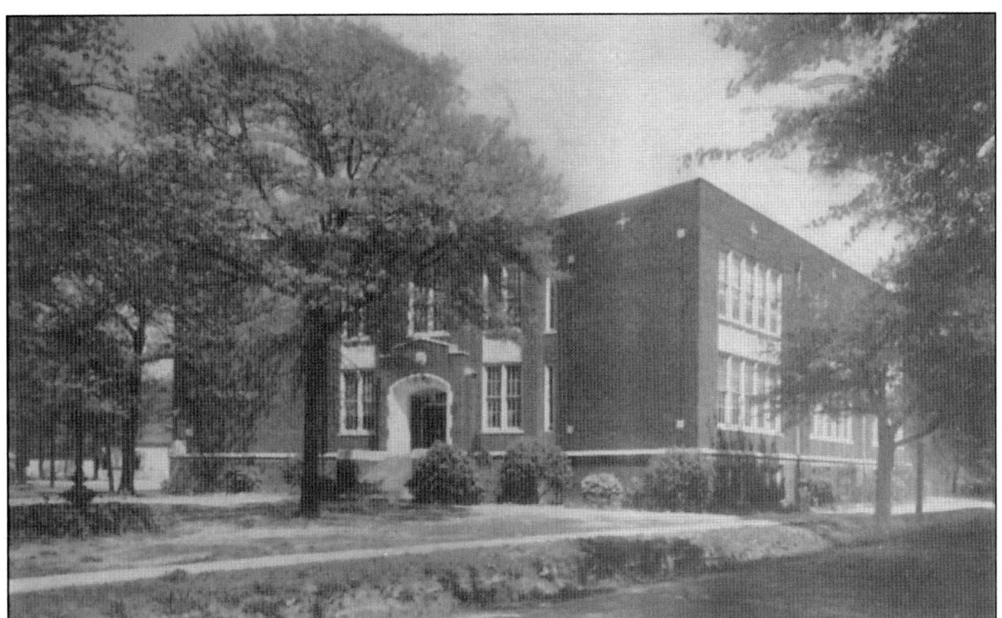

The year 1915 was monumental for the new Winder School System. With Holsenbeck at the helm, the community began the task of replacing the former Winder Institute building with a modern brick structure. Students met in nearby churches until the new school building was completed in 1916. Reflecting the new Art Moderne trend with touches of Art Deco styling, the Winder School cost $40,000 to build. (Courtesy of Joe Bowen.)

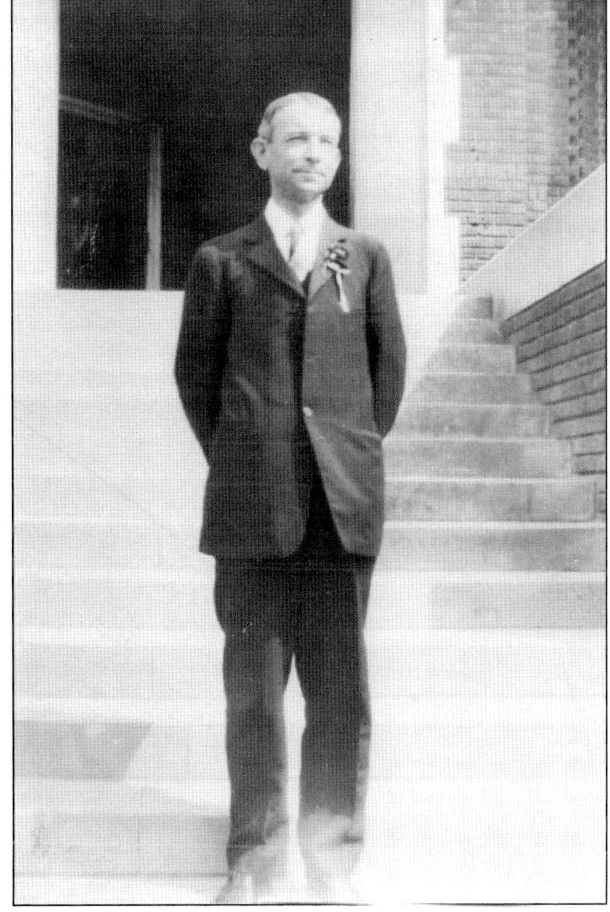

Holsenbeck served his community on the County Council of Defense during World War I and as an Oconee River Soil and Water Conservation District supervisor in the 1930s, as well as being a teacher and the first principal for the new Mathews School. In 1945, Holsenbeck was elected as the 27th District state senator. He donated the land in east Barrow County for the elementary school that bears his name. (Courtesy of Bill Summerour.)

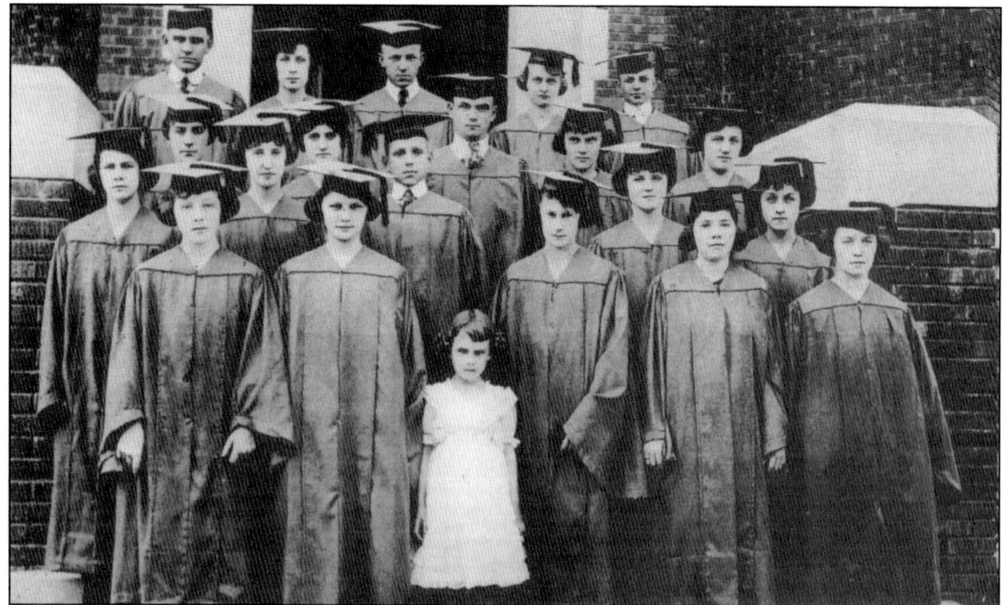

The Winder School class of 1920 included mascot Ruth Love, as well as offspring of some of the area's founding citizens. This photograph was taken on the steps of the Winder School. These students were among the last to attend classes in both the Jug Tavern Institute building and the new Winder School building. W.M. Holsenbeck was both teacher and superintendent for these students. (Courtesy of John C. Jackson.)

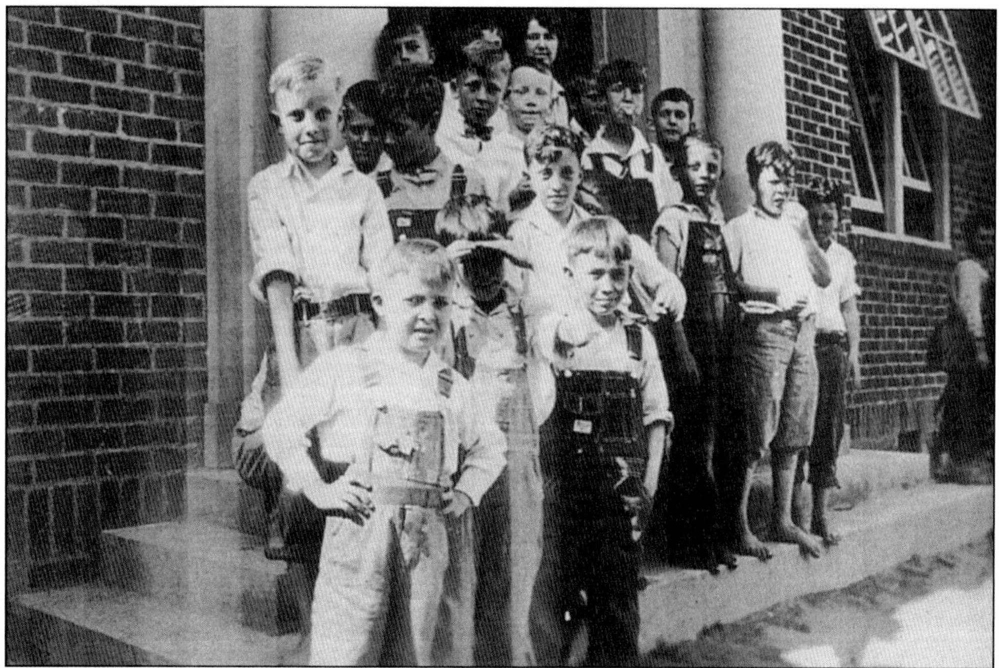

In 1929, the new Winder Elementary School, which housed first through fourth grades, was completed with its innovative cloakrooms. Pauline Hill's 1929 third-grade class took a break from studies to pose for this photograph. Hill parked her pony cart next to the school while she instructed her students. (Courtesy of Caroline Robinson Stallings.)

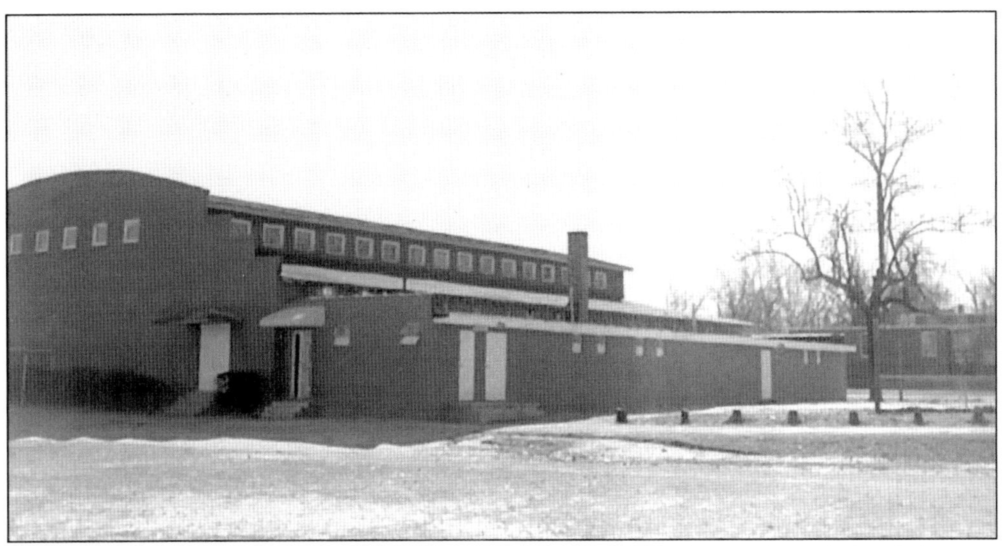

A redbrick gymnasium—affectionately termed "the Red Barn"—was built behind the new elementary school and opened about the same time (1929). Natural lighting from the ribbons of windows beneath the roof provided additional illumination for indoor sports. The one-story field house was added in the 1940s. (Courtesy of Caroline Robinson Stallings.)

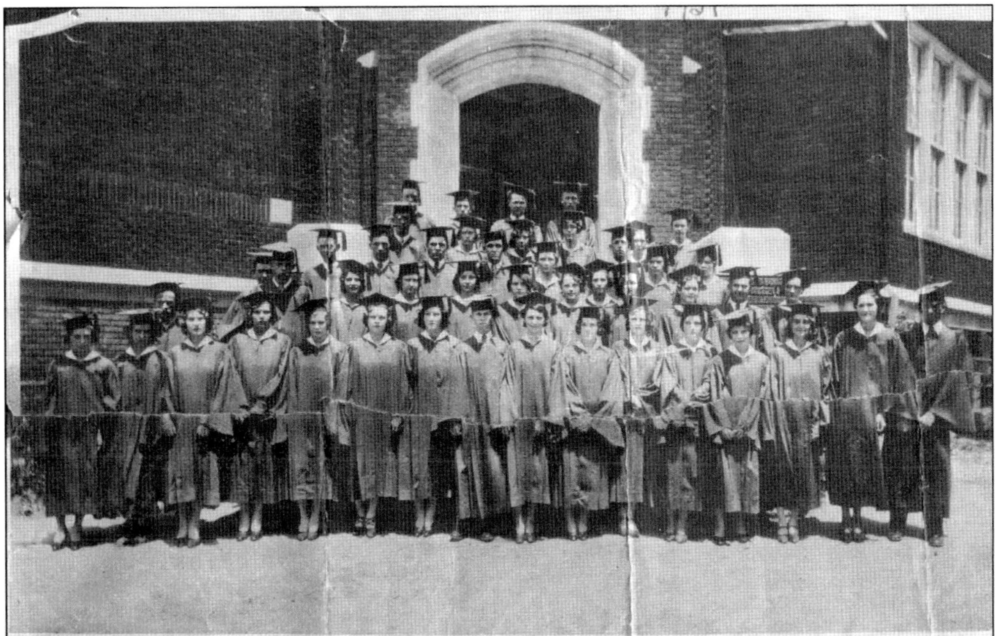

GRADUATING CLASS OF THE WINDER HIGH SCHOOL, WINDER, GA. First row, left to right: Willie D. Stovall, Henrietta McDonald, Geneva Flanagan, Anne Bickum, Emma Collier, Reba Garner, Beatrice Watson, Oran Roberts, Hazel Shelnutt, Annelle Hammond, Nell Elrod, Carrie Lou McCain, Emma Ola Perry, Olivea Kesler, Sara Jack McDonald, Richard McDonald. Second row: Robert Adams, Hubert Henson, Eloise Fullibright, Cathryn Hargrove, Birnice Poole, Helen Wills, Anne Elder, Ruth Hall, Gladys Hardigree, W. C. Sharpton, Hazel Church. Third row: Gartrell Elliott, Gordon Wages, M. C. Harrison, Dorough Cronic, Ralph McEver, Annie Ried Hancock, Mildred Eley, Emmie McCain, Virginia Crisp. Fourth row: Clarence Segars, Betty Lou Harrison, Lois Dillard, Agnes Elliott, Bill Jones, Beatrice Healor, Ora Belle Shedd. Fifth row: Clyde Patrick, James Harrison, Tom Henry Ridgeway, Royce McDonald, Juiette Saunders.

—Photo by Leonord & Co.

Enrollment in the Winder Schools had more than doubled by 1931, as evidenced by this photograph of the 48 graduating seniors of the class of 1931. Despite the new elementary school and gymnasium, space in the schools was at a premium. (Courtesy of Bob Hill.)

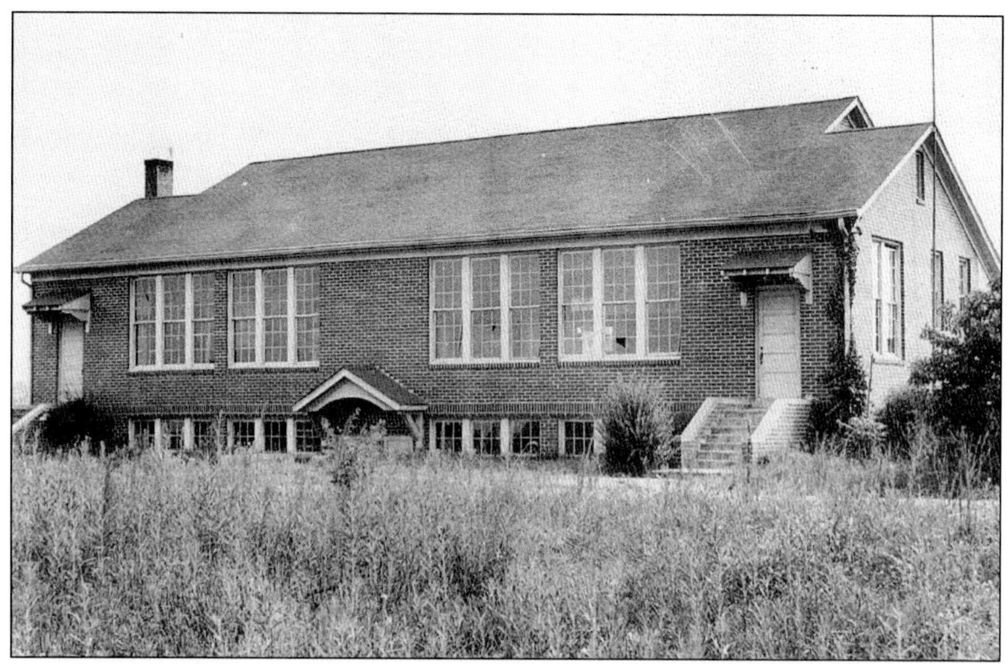

Black students in Winder attended school at the Winder School located in the Glenwood section of east Winder. This building served students in the Glenwood area from around 1935 until a new school was built in the late 1950s. The two-story building served all grade levels. With consolidation of the city and county school systems in 1958, the Winder School in Glenwood became known as Glenwood School. (Courtesy of Barrow County Historical Society.)

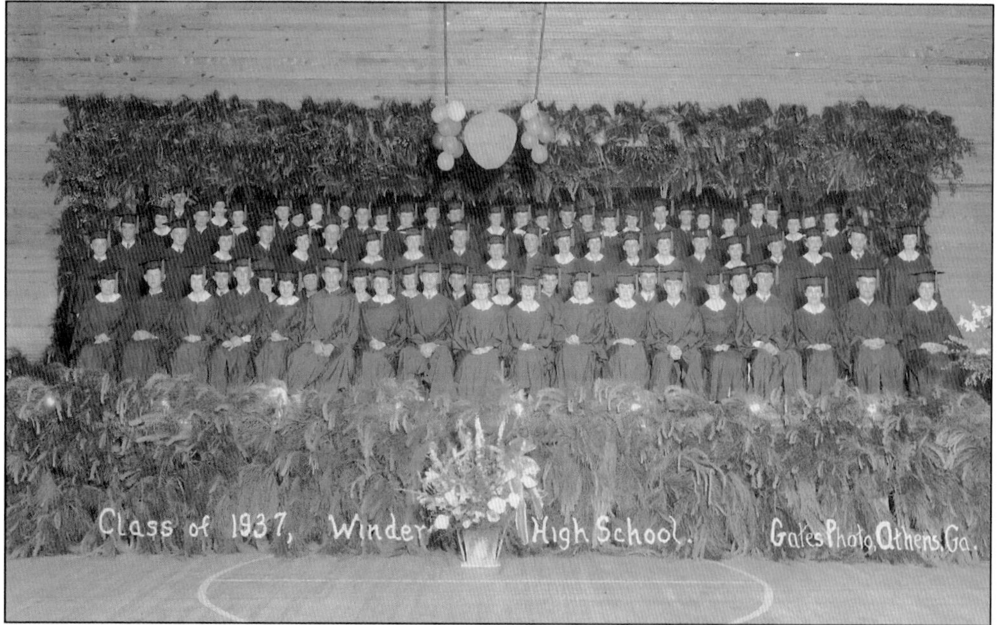

The Winder High School class of 1937 is pictured during graduation ceremonies in the "Red Barn." The gymnasium's polished hardwood floor (for basketball) was complemented by its knotty pine beaded wallboard. The gymnasium served the Winder City Schools for over 50 years until its demolition in the late 1970s. (Courtesy of Evelyn Arnold.)

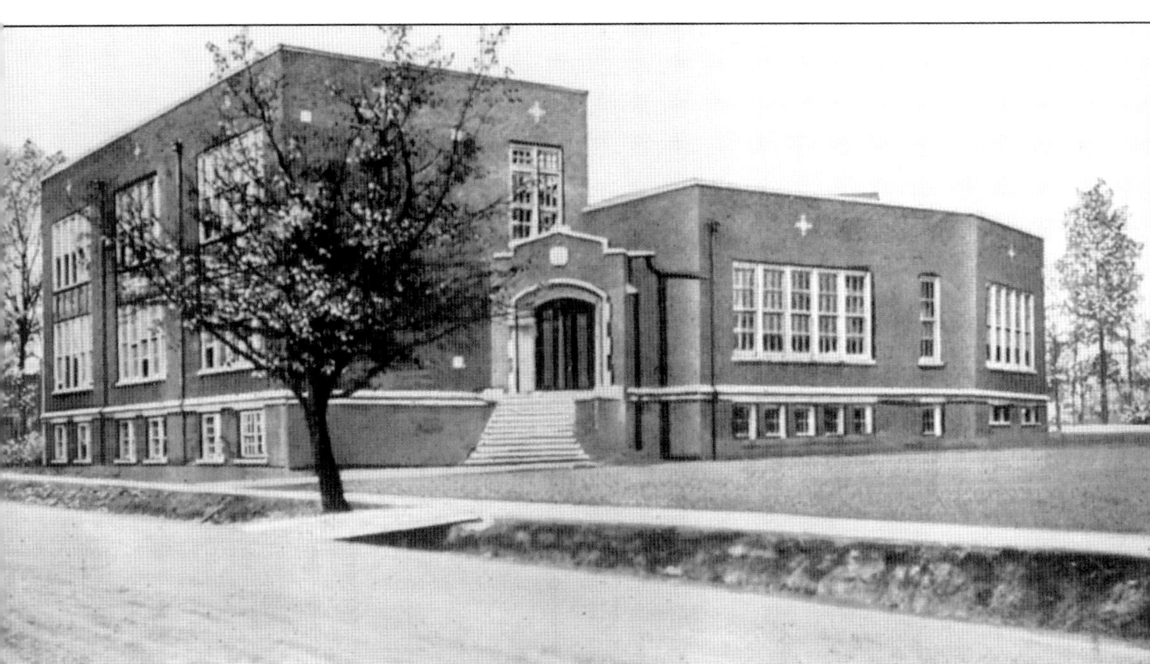

The Church Street side of the 1916 Winder School showed its three-story classroom building and curved auditorium. Just as churches served as schools when fire and construction caused children to be without classrooms, the school furnished churches and the community with a meeting place. This school burned down in 1938 and was never replaced. A new high school was completed on Bellview Street in 1940. Constructed on the former Arch Perry estate, the high school and 1929 elementary school were joined by the gymnasium, and in 1958, a new addition connected the two school buildings. The addition accommodated vocational, music, cafeteria, and band facilities. (Courtesy of Joe Bowen.)

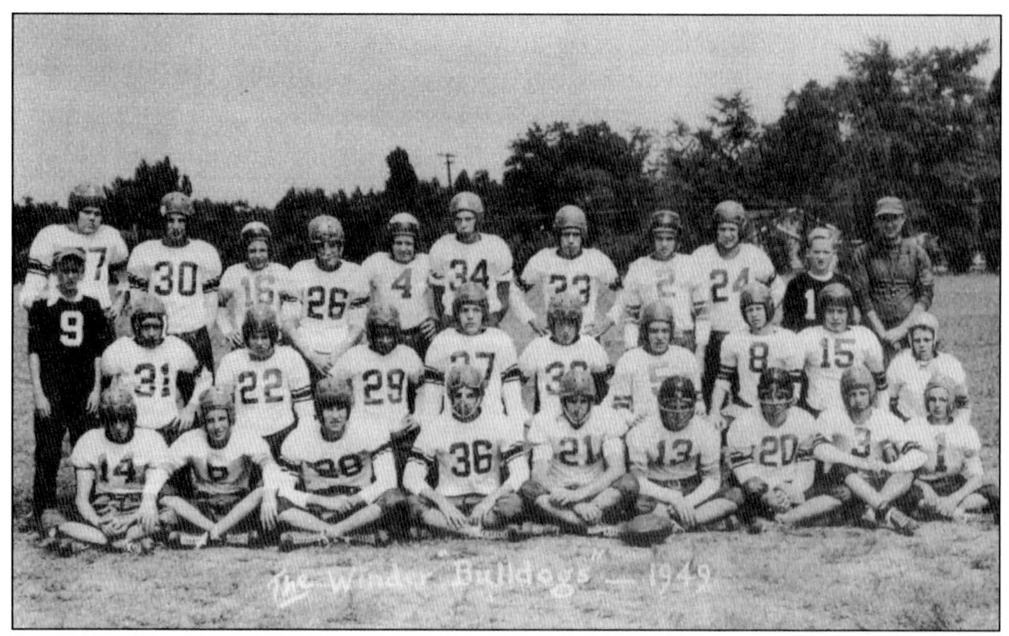

Football and band became synonymous with academics after World War II. Though both programs had existed much earlier than 1942, their integration into the life of the community did not become commonplace until the late 1940s. The Winder High School football team and the new Winder High School Marching Band of 1949 were photographed for the high school yearbook, the *Panorama*. The addition of majorettes to the marching band was a new phenomenon courtesy of director William H. Robison. A Winder native and veteran of the US Marines, Robison coordinated band programs throughout the schools until his 1969 retirement. (Both images courtesy of Caroline Robinson Stallings.)

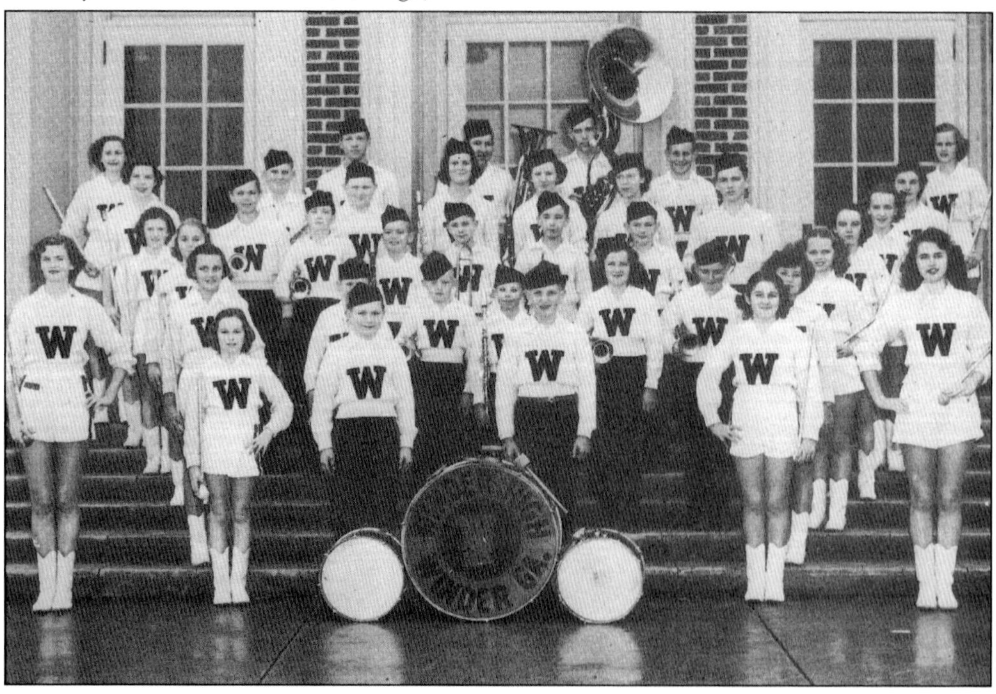

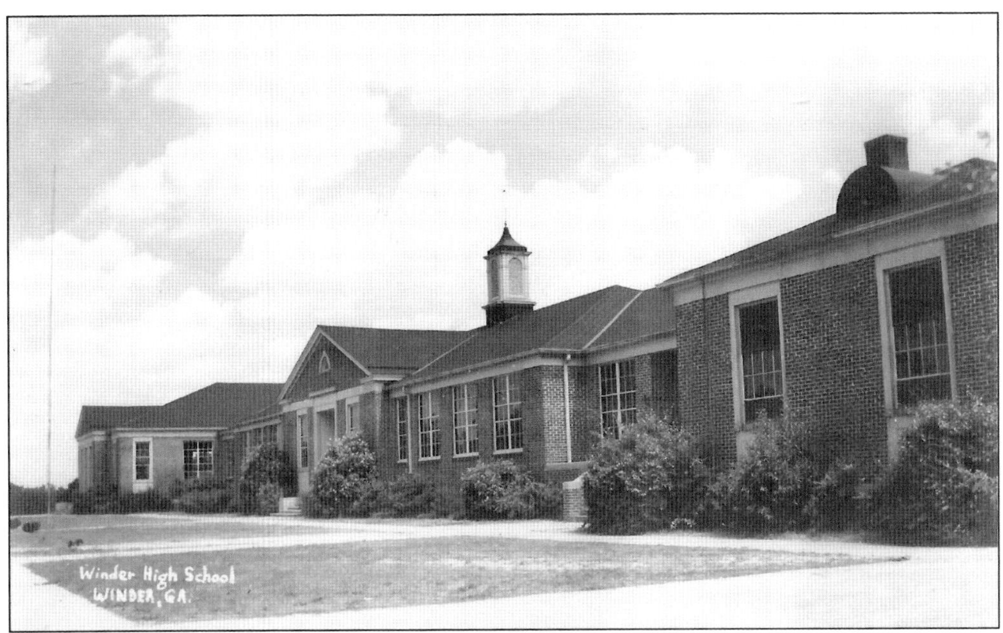

Rapid enrollment increases in the Winder School Systems and the destruction of the high school building in 1938 spurred the construction of a new high school (pictured above) on Bellview Street. Completed in 1940, this brick Greek Revival structure included a state-of-the-art auditorium, science and home economics labs, offices, and spacious classrooms. This building served the Winder School system through its consolidation with the county schools. In 1970, desegregation brought all of the high school students in the county together under one roof for the first time in the school system's history. The 1956 eighth-grade class is pictured below on the stage of the auditorium, the site of numerous community events. A late 1960s remodeling of the auditorium did not include new wiring, and a fire in the auditorium's wiring ignited the blaze that engulfed the building in December 1972. (Above, courtesy of Joe Bowen; below, courtesy of Evelyn Arnold.)

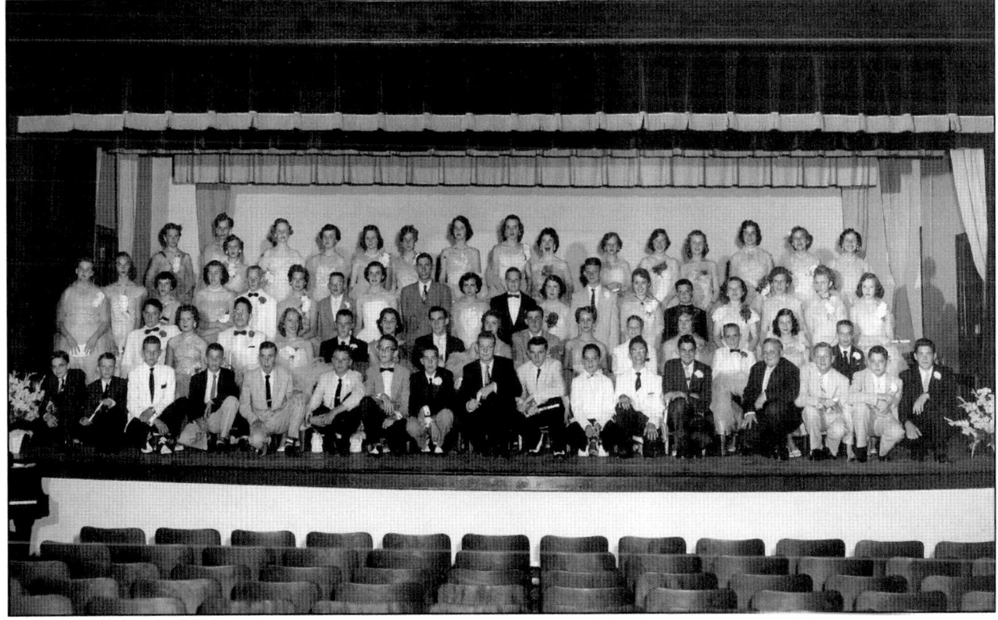

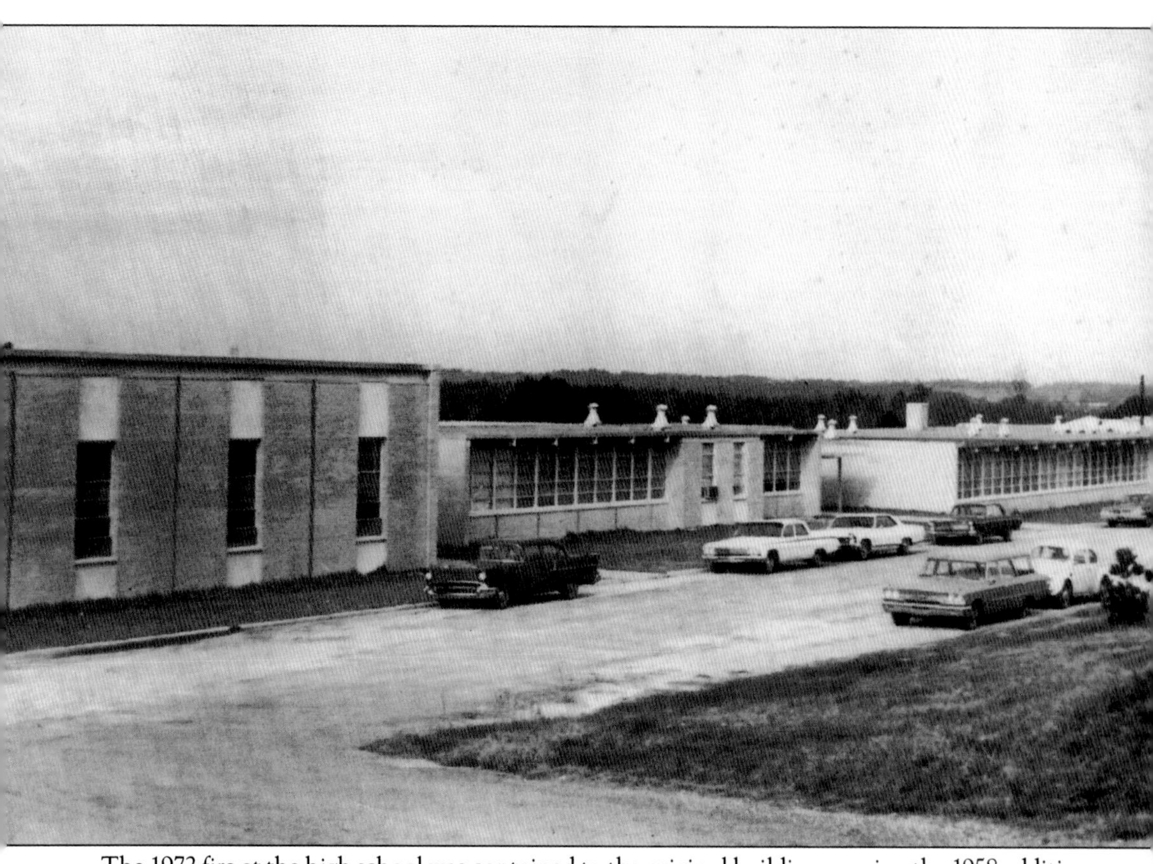

The 1972 fire at the high school was contained to the original building, sparing the 1958 addition and 1929 elementary school. Instruction continued at the elementary school, with displaced classes meeting in other sections of the building. The high school was gradually moved to the 1964 Winder Middle School on Fifth Avenue in north Winder. Building expansions including a new gymnasium, the W. Clair Harris Stadium (1966), and a sports complex serve the Winder-Barrow High School community today. This building was demolished in 2005. (Courtesy of Caroline Robinson Stallings.)

Six
WORSHIPPING

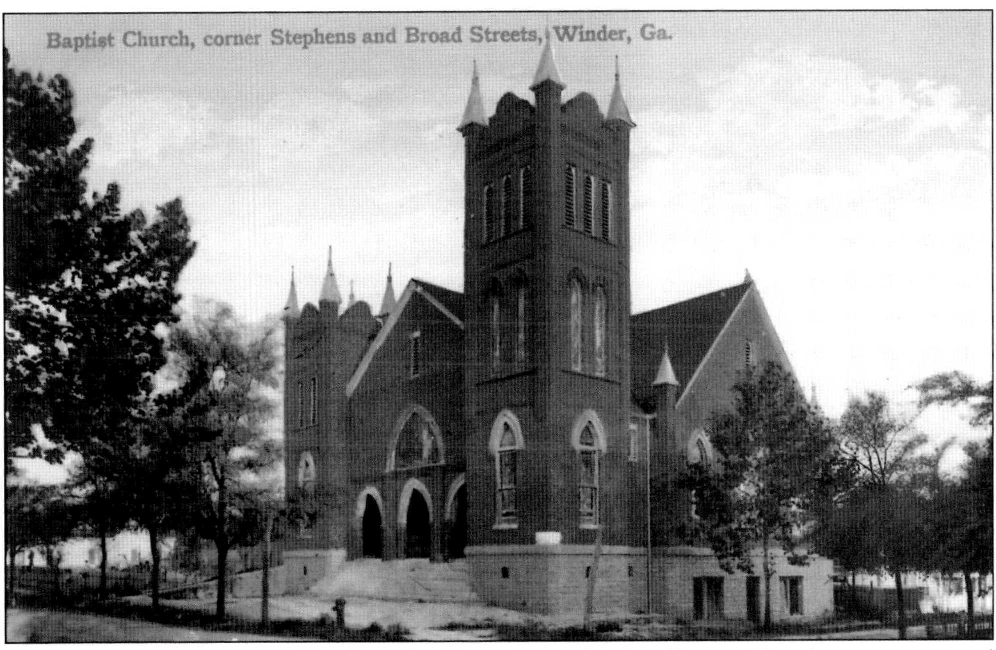

Begun in 1907, the stone-and-brick Gothic Revival Winder First Baptist Church was constructed for $20,000. The 500-seat sanctuary was dedicated on May 10, 1914. The North Broad Street church is an example of high style architectural design. The building features Gothic arched windows and doors, elegantly corbelled twin towers, and breathtaking stained-glass windows. When built, it was part of a residential neighborhood. (Courtesy of Joe Bowen.)

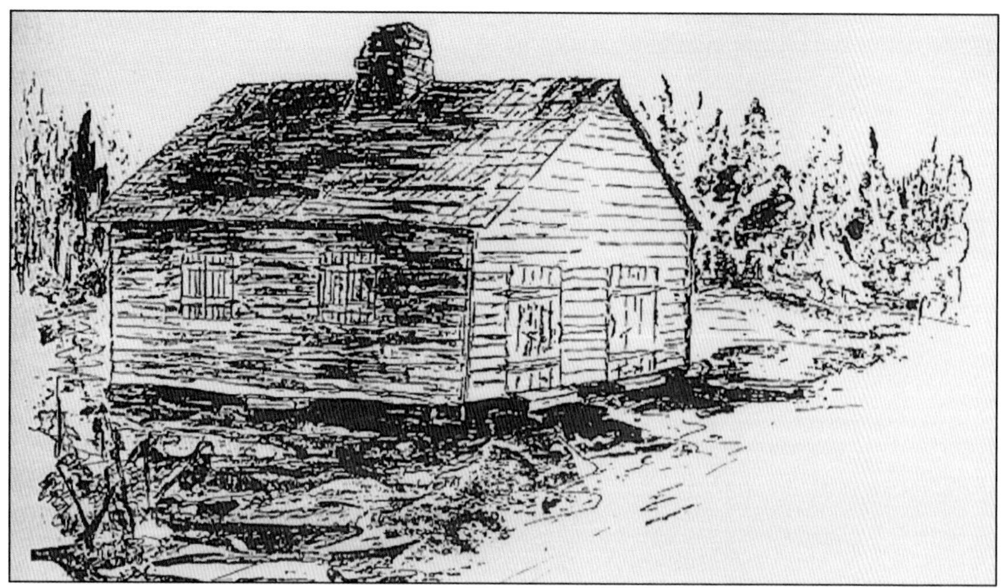

As Jug Tavern and Winder grew, so did its churches. The Concord Methodist Church was established in 1836 in a rough log cabin built by church members on Hog Mountain Road just west of the Jug Tavern Community. It was located on present-day Athens Street, west of downtown Winder, near a spring just north of Concord Cemetery. (Courtesy of Winder First United Methodist Church.)

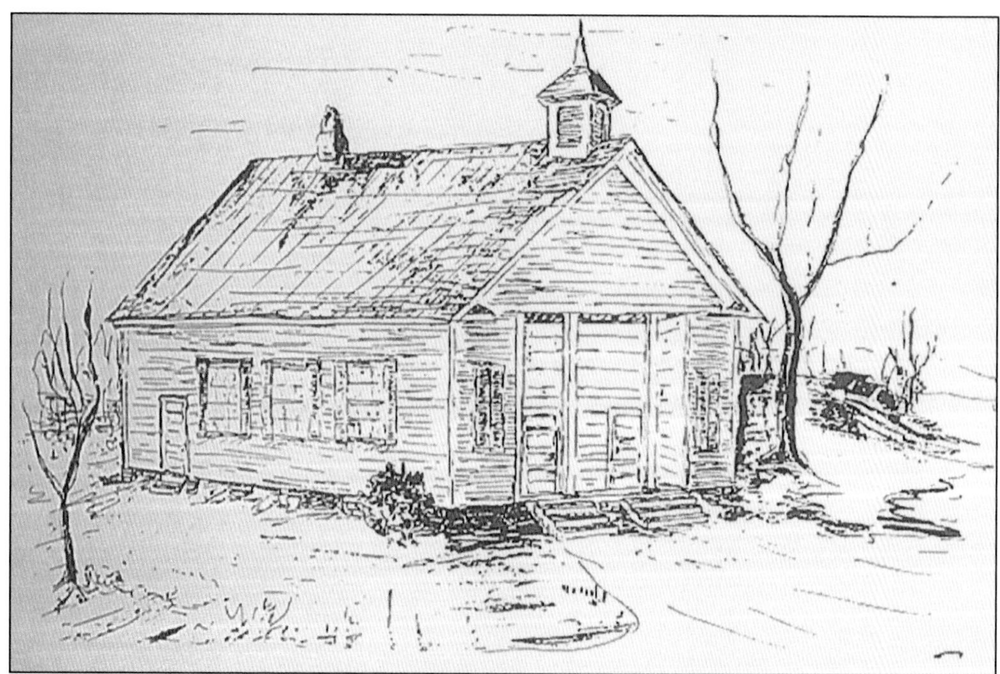

In 1858, Dr. I.J.M. Goss made a gift of 10 acres of land for a Methodist church and burying ground in the Jug Tavern Community. The building was one room with open rafters, rough boards as pews, and a rough lumber floor. The building had exterior doors for separate men's and women's entrances, with segregated seating inside. The church held preaching one Sunday per month. (Courtesy of Winder First United Methodist Church.)

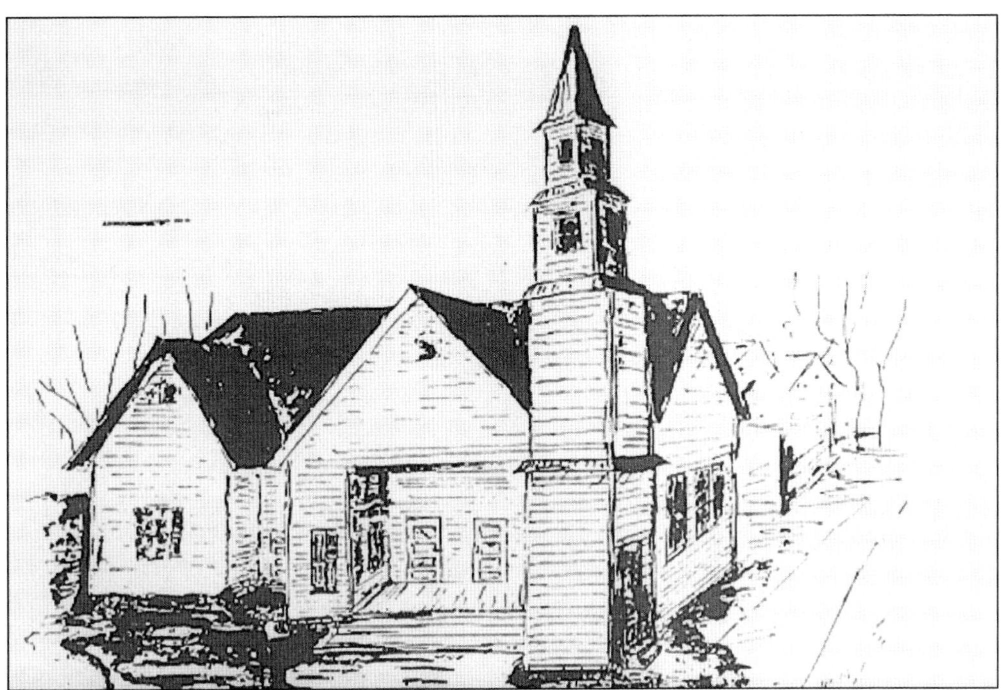

In 1870, the third Methodist church was built on Hog Mountain Road. The second church building was moved across the road so that the new building could be constructed. The third building was a little larger and was constructed of dressed lumber with a ceiling, recessed porch, and columns. Ten years later, it was sold to Mark Whitehead, who rehabilitated it into a dwelling. (Courtesy of Winder First United Methodist Church.)

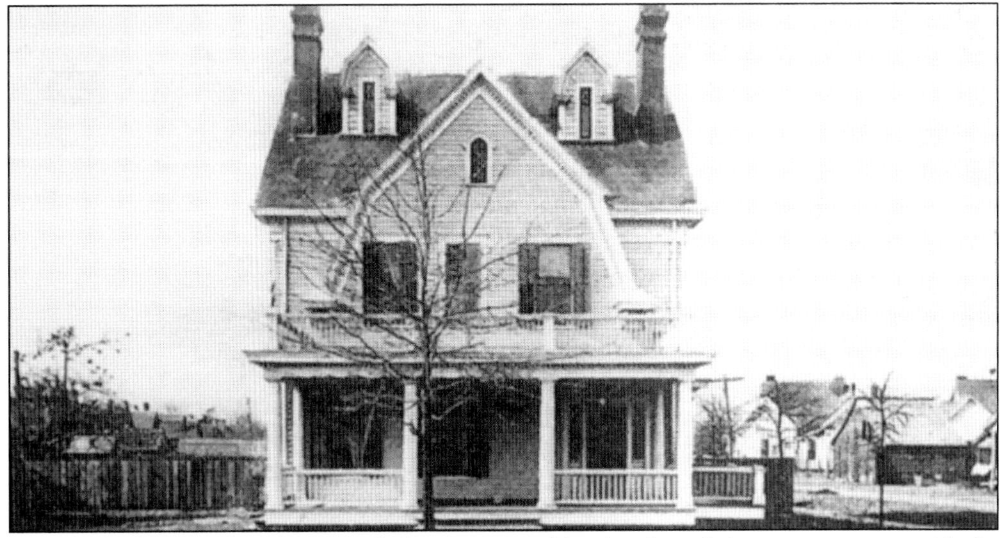

The Methodist congregation provided its pastor and his family with living quarters suitable for raising a family, facilitating counseling sessions, providing hospitality to visitors, and conducting home weddings and baptisms. In 1907, the second parsonage was constructed behind the church building on the corner of Center Street and Kelly Drive. The Dutch Colonial building was demolished in the 1990s. (Courtesy of Winder First United Methodist Church.)

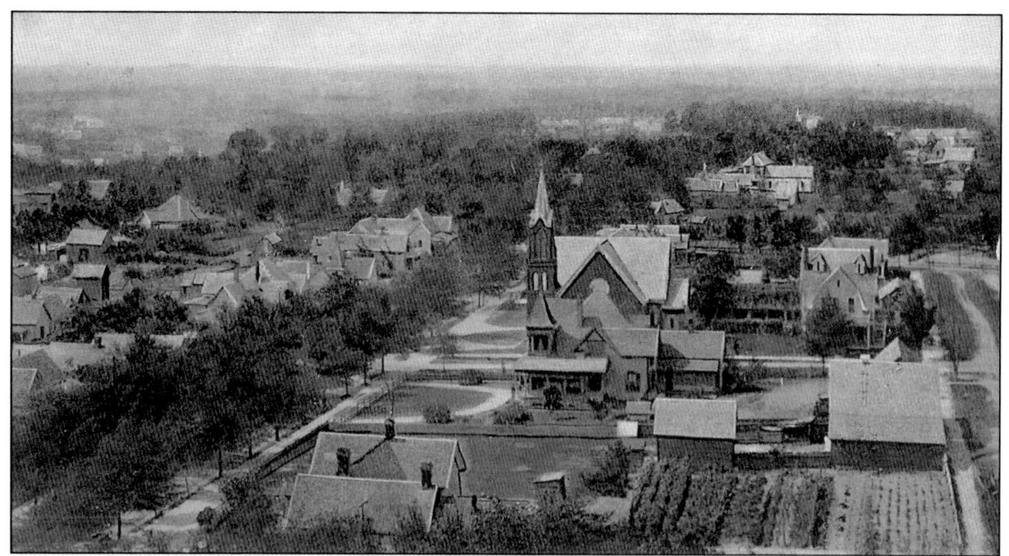

Still more growth in the community required that a larger facility be built for the Methodist congregation. In 1880, Dr. J.C. DeLaPerriere sold the church a lot on the corner of Candler and Center Streets for $65, and the Old Concord Methodist Congregation, South, church was built. In 1884, the church's name was changed to the Jug Tavern Methodist Church, South, and it became head of the new Jug Tavern Circuit. In 1894, the church's name was changed to Winder Methodist Church, South, in keeping with the name of the town having been changed two years prior. The church's membership continued to grow rapidly, Winder's first brick church building was constructed in 1904 on the Candler Street site. A Gothic Revival style building, the sanctuary featured exquisite stained-glass windows and a mahogany tongue-and-groove vaulted ceiling. These 1906 postcards show the church as anchor to the Candler Street neighborhood (above) and the church with its telescoping steeple. (Above, courtesy of Joe Bowen; below, courtesy of Winder First United Methodist Church.)

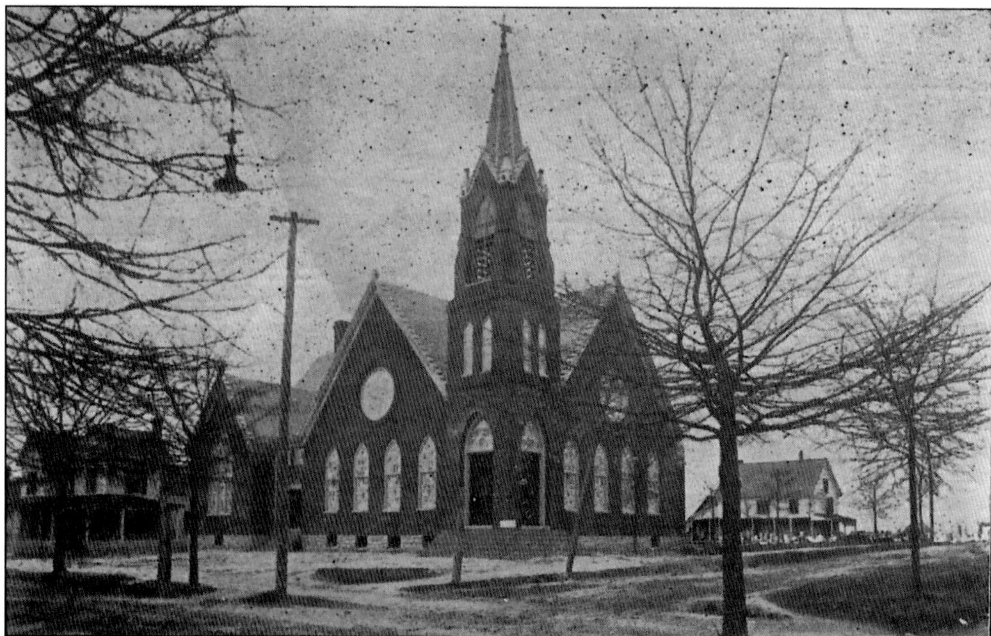

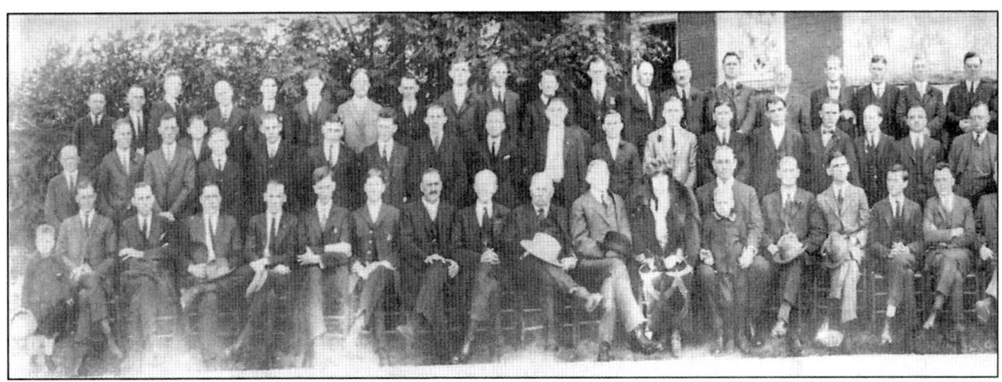

In keeping with tradition, the men and women of the church met in segregated Sunday school. The Baracca Men's Bible Class (above) counted among its members many of Winder's leading citizens. Their wives and single women of the community met in the Philathea Women's Bible Class. The classes met in three Sunday school rooms on the west side of the sanctuary. While the men administered the business of the church, the women supported church efforts through mission work. A board of stewards composed of many of Winder's community leaders led the church in such efforts as construction of a new Sunday school wing, installation of the heating system, and custom-built graduated length pews to fit the sanctuary's configuration. (Both images courtesy of Winder First United Methodist Church.)

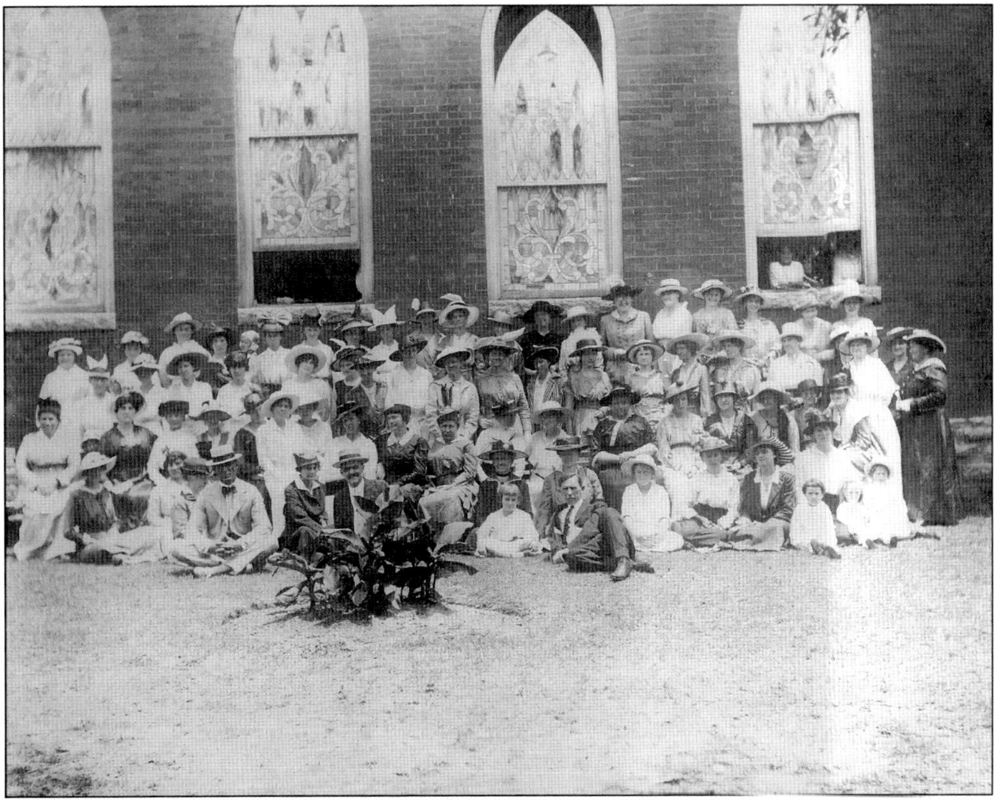

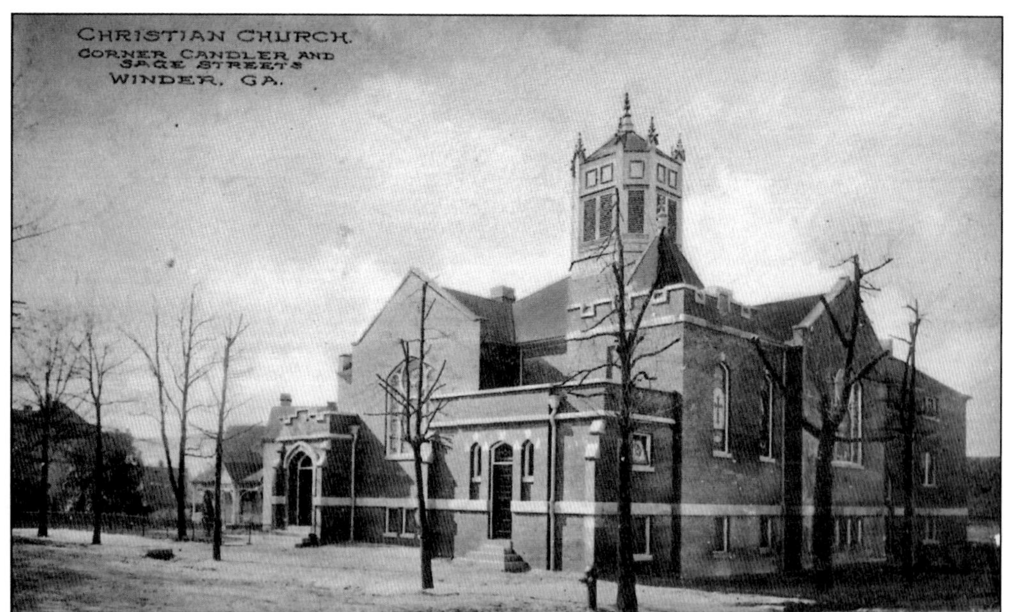

The 1909 First Christian Church was the second brick church in Winder. Constructed on a lot donated by member Hillman D. Jackson, the church commanded the corner of East Candler and Sage Streets. The structure featured a tower-like crenellated pavilion with turret, Gothic arched stained-glass windows, and an ornately spired bell tower. The congregation transferred the stained-glass windows to a new building in 1971. (Courtesy of Joe Bowen.)

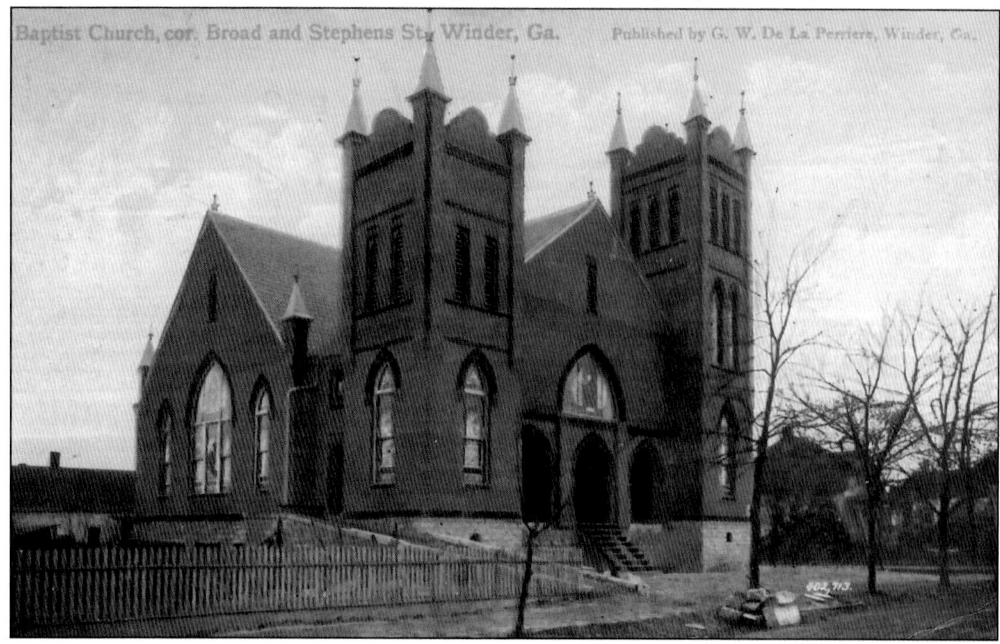

Winder's third brick church was the First Baptist Church, dedicated in 1914. This 1912 postcard shows the church exterior in the latter stages of construction. Temporary wooden steps were replaced by a granite staircase before the church's dedication. Additions of Sunday school and fellowship space in the 1930s and an education building in the 1960s completed the facility. With no more room to expand, the congregation moved to a new building in 2005. (Courtesy of Joe Bowen.)

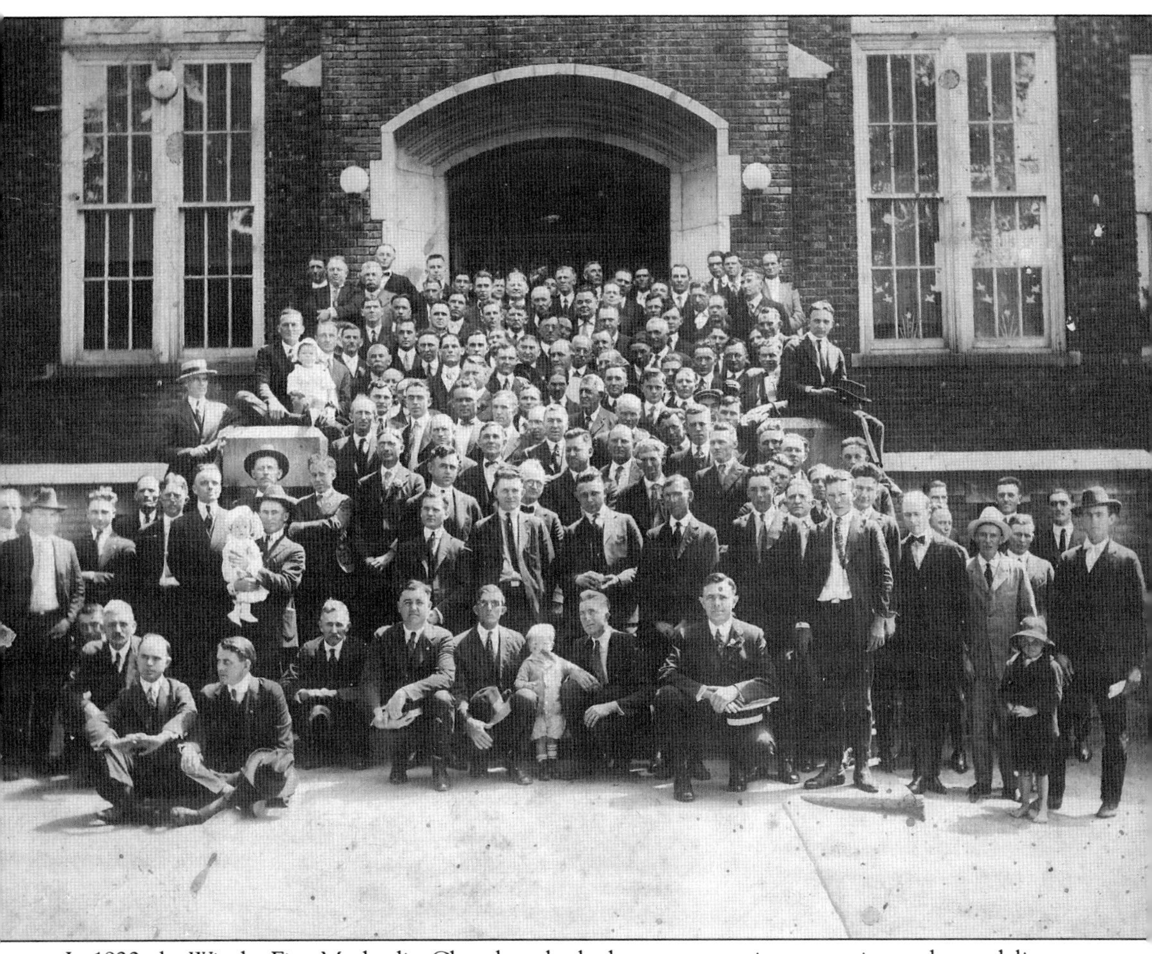

In 1920, the Winder First Methodist Church embarked on an aggressive expansion and remodeling project. During construction, the greatly expanded Men's Baracca Bible Class met at the Winder High School two blocks away. Worship services and other church events took place both at the school building and at the Presbyterian church on the corner of Athens and Beulah Streets. (Courtesy of Bob Hill.)

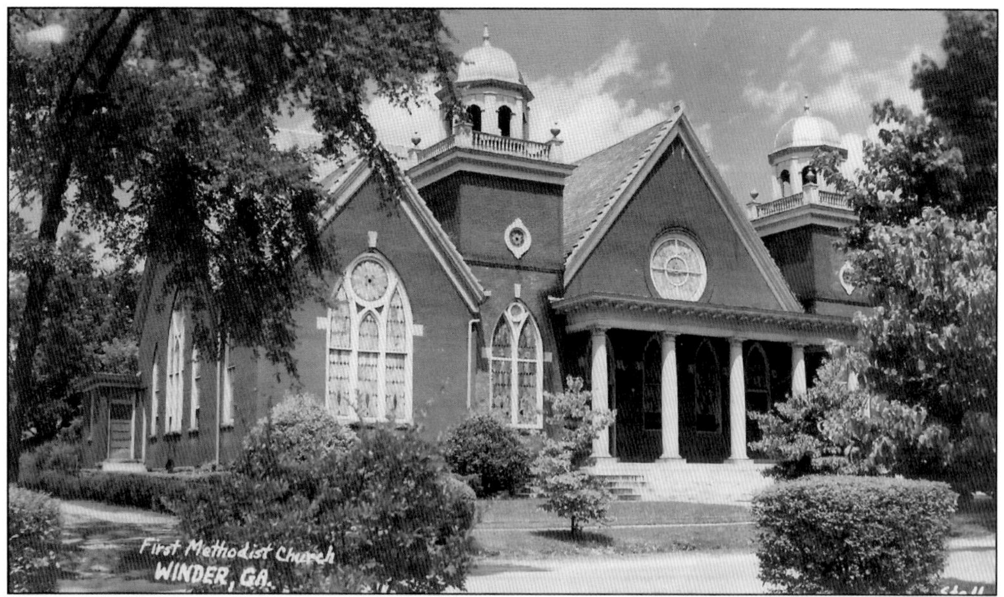

The remodeling of the First Methodist Church added a full-width portico with granite steps, semicircular Sunday school addition with assembly room, and convertible classrooms. The telescoping steeple was modified into a pumpkin-domed bell tower with a twin added where previously there had been a door that accommodated the segregated entrances. The addition modified the Gothic Revival building to incorporate a Neoclassical influence with the portico. Tragically, this building was consumed by fire on July 26, 2012 during a thunderstorm. (Courtesy of Joe Bowen.)

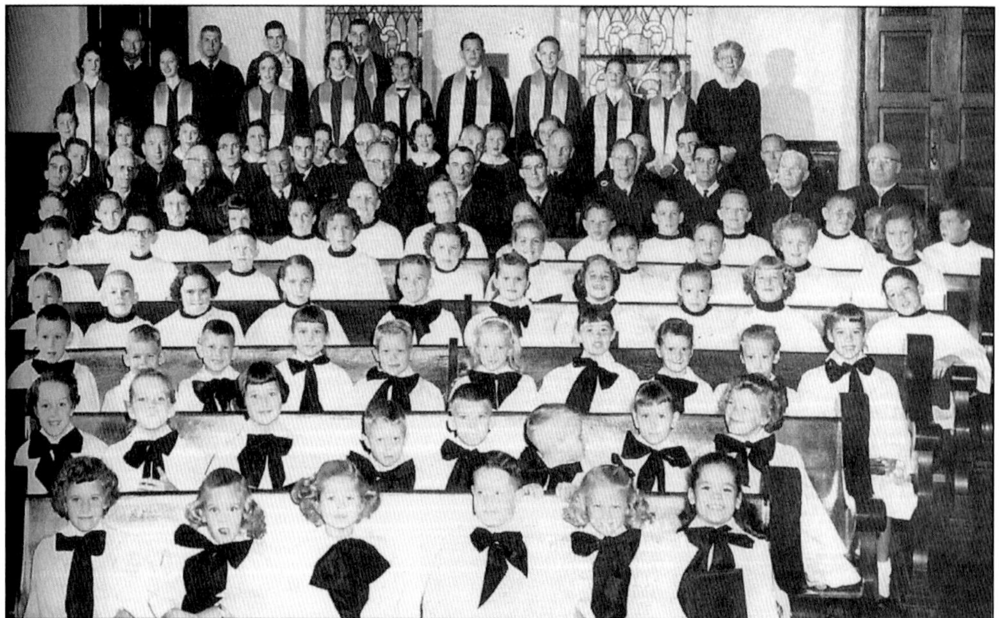

The rapidly growing Winder population translated into a membership boom for the churches in Winder. This 1958 photograph of the five choirs under the direction of Beulah Ferguson Robinson at the Winder Methodist Church illustrates the importance of training young people to follow in the footsteps of their leaders. The Methodist church offered choirs for all members ages four and up. (Courtesy of Bob Hill.)

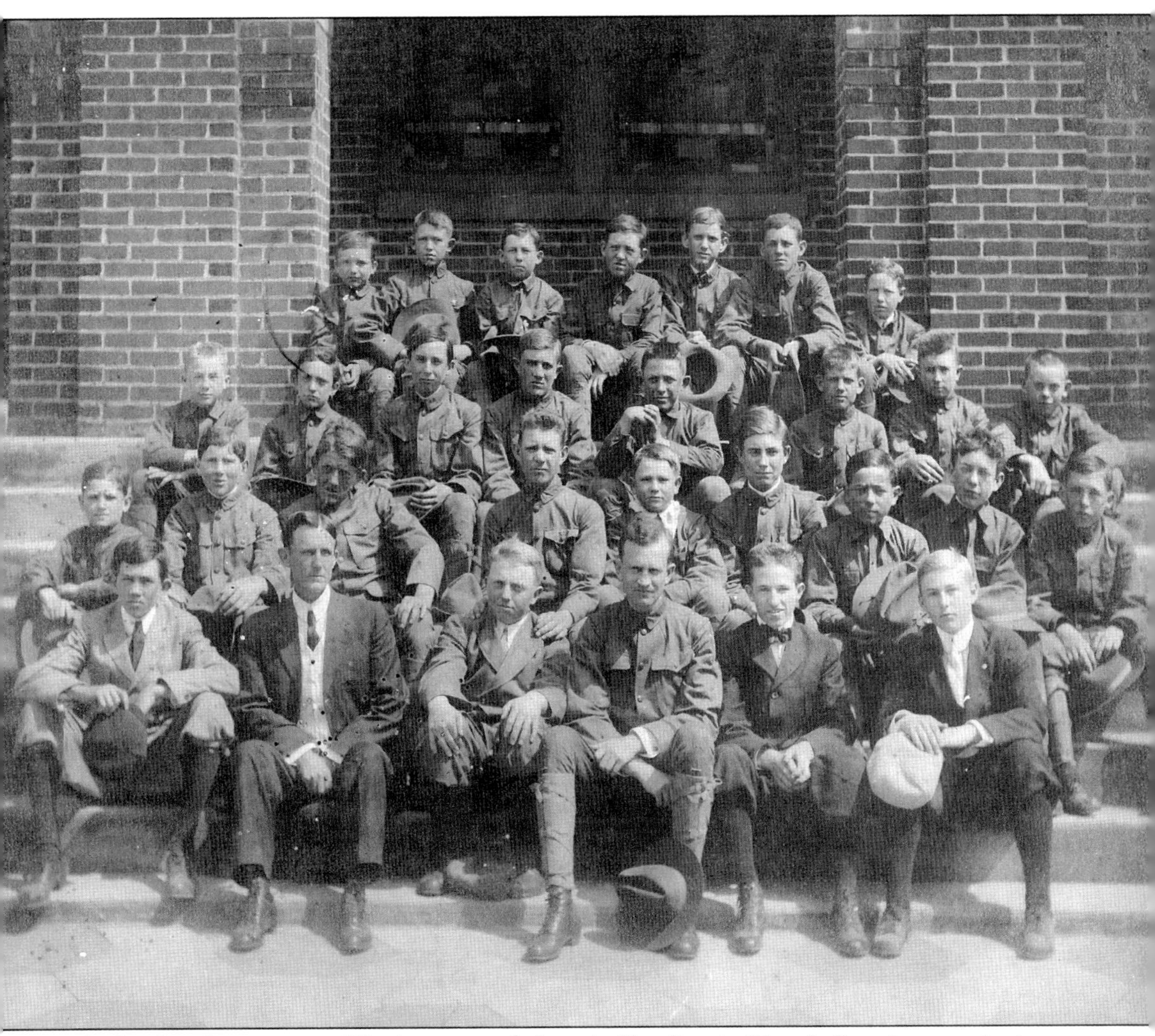

The first Boy Scout troop in Winder met regularly at the First Baptist Church. Scouting organizations have traditionally served their country, church, and community with special projects designed to inform and equip boys and girls to become responsible citizens whose words and deeds honor themselves and those with whom they come in contact. This photograph was taken on the steps of the church in 1912. (Courtesy of John C. Jackson.)

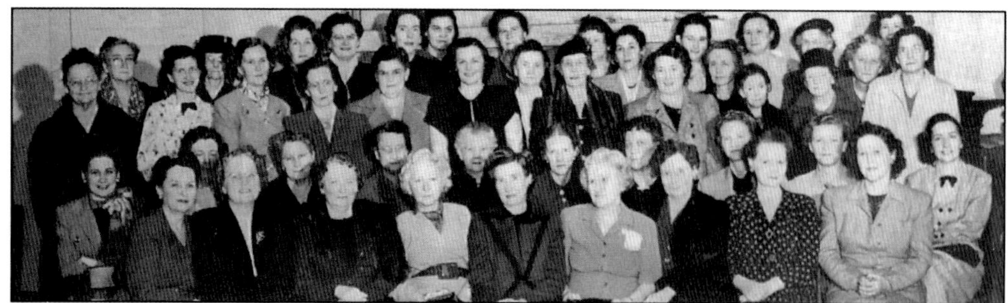

Recognizing that the women of the church often held the key to programs that would drive mission service, Starr Blasingame Carithers spearheaded the formation of the Women's Society of Christian Service in 1940 and, later, its auxiliary unit, the Wesleyan Service Guild. In 1958, the organizations combined into the United Methodist Women. The members formed small groups known as "Circles" that took on additional projects of special interest to the members. (Courtesy of Winder First United Methodist Church.)

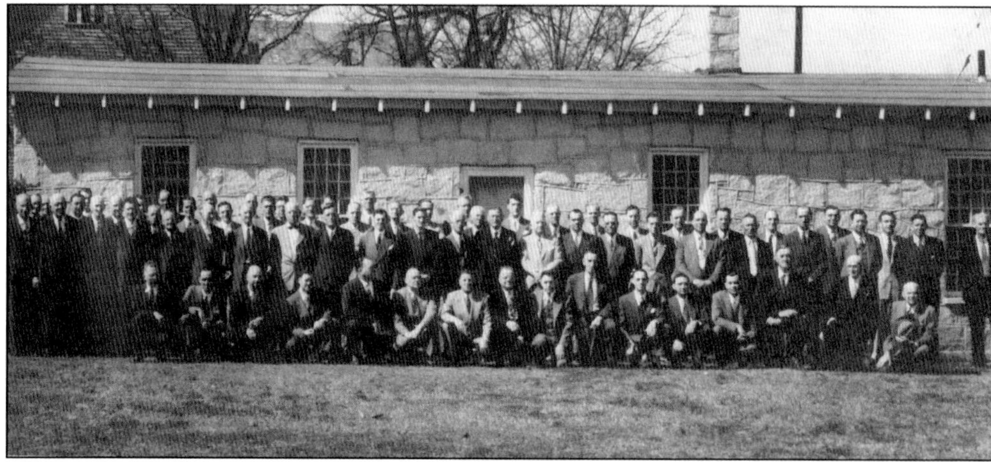

In 1945, the men of the church formed the Winder Methodist Men's Club, dedicated to special projects benefiting the church and community. The organization built an *L*-shaped granite clubhouse across Kelly Drive from the parsonage and added a large barbecue pit for social events and fundraising projects. The Winder Methodist Men's Club was the first such men's organization in the state of Georgia; it is now known as the United Methodist Men. (Courtesy of Bob Hill.)

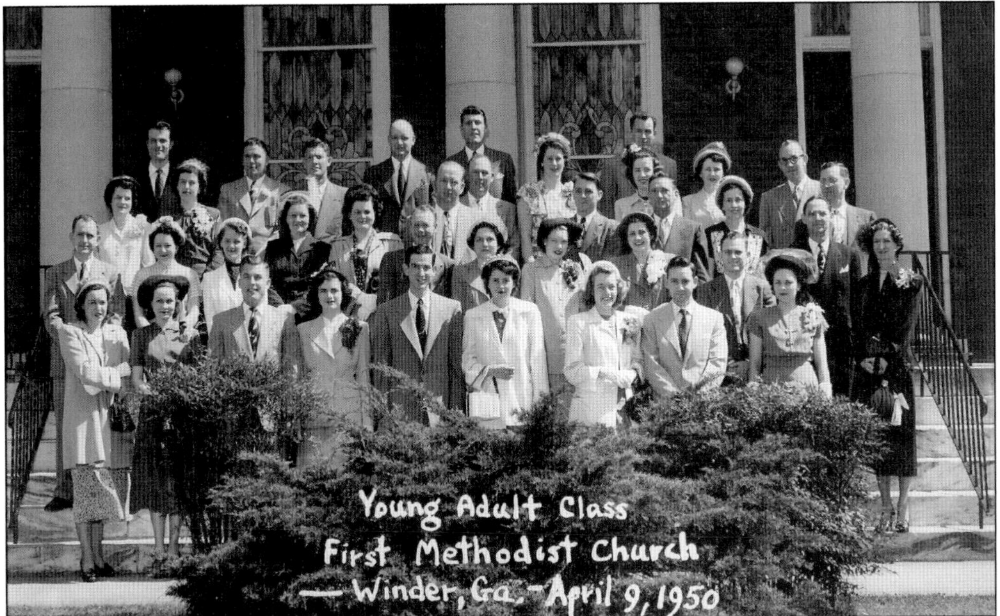

As the churches continued to grow, the men's and women's Sunday school classes began to resemble small congregations. The focus on small-group formation helped to encourage closer relationships among the members. The young adult class was composed of single and married men and women between 20 and 40 years of age. The smaller class sizes were more manageable and fostered closer spiritual mentoring opportunities. (Courtesy of Evelyn Arnold.)

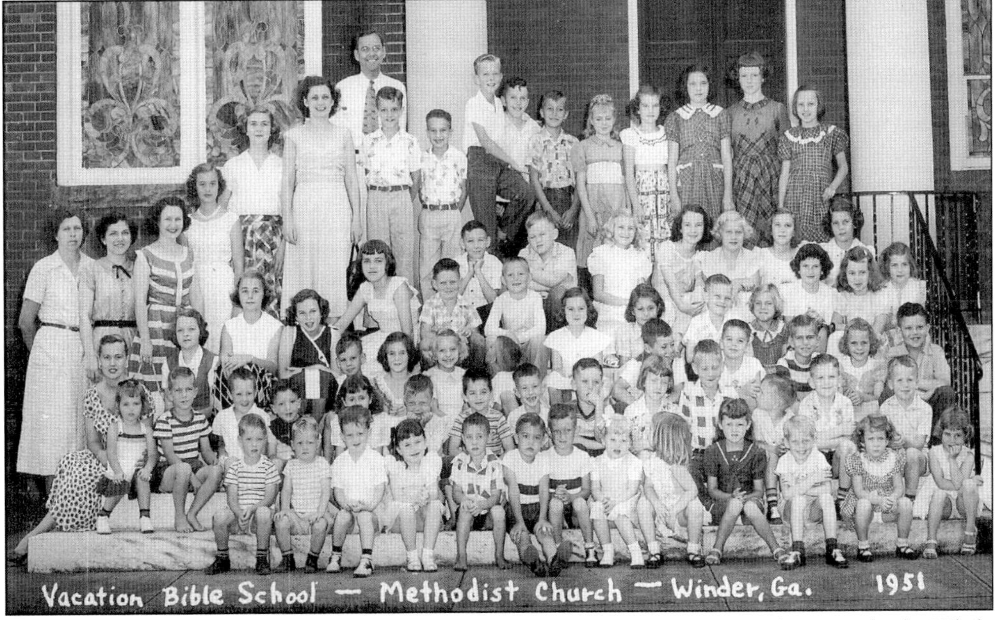

Vacation Bible School was a tradition in Winder long before the brick churches were built. While the churches had previously combined for summer Bible school events, the 1940s and 1950s ushered in an era of church-sponsored Bible school. This photograph from the 1951 Methodist Vacation Bible School features children from age three through eighth grade participating in weeklong activities focusing on spiritual growth and mission service. (Courtesy of Bob Hill.)

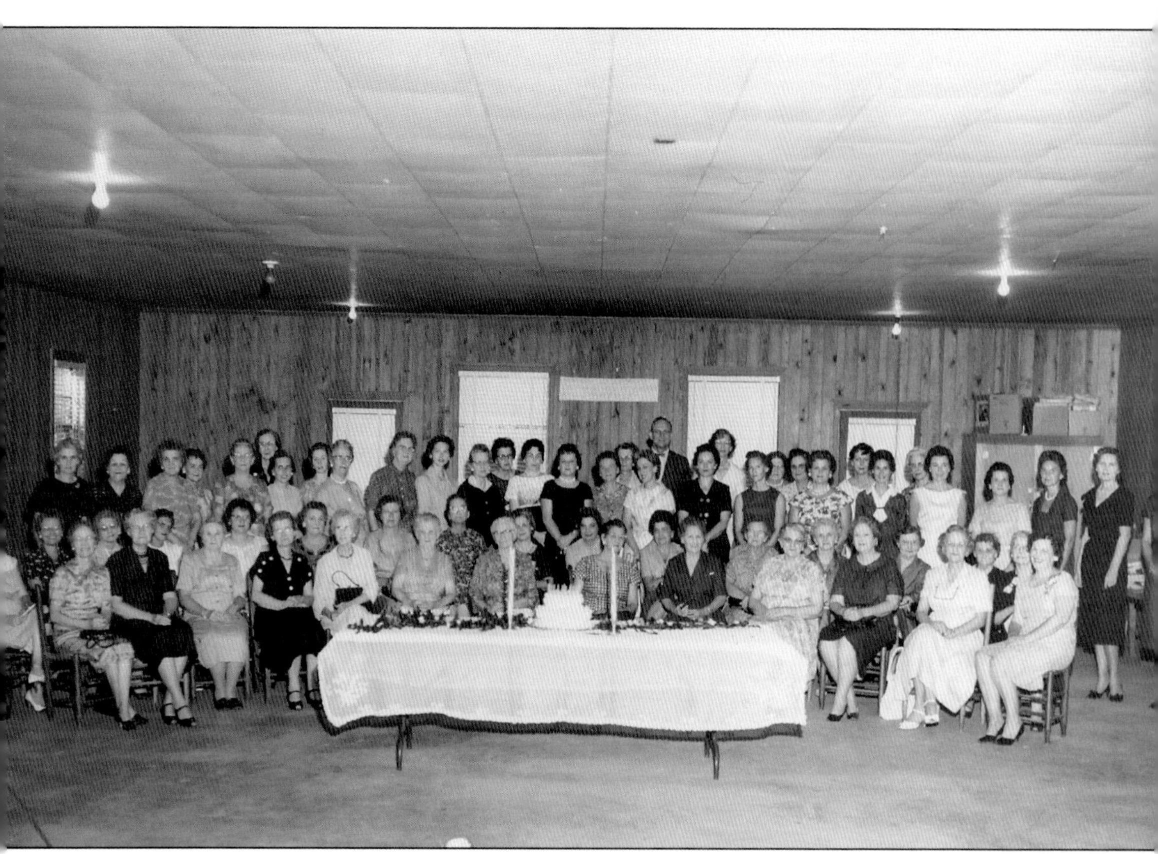

In 1960, the United Methodist Women celebrated their anniversary at the Winder Methodist Men's Club clubhouse. The building's rugged exterior, built in a vernacular Craftsman style, transitioned to a more finished appearance inside. Knotty pine bead board, a practical concrete floor, and a tiled ceiling with flush-mounted lights allowed for streamlined maintenance, versatility for different age groups and meeting types, and offered two meeting rooms with kitchen and bathroom facilities. As culture changes, so do the ways and means of the church in relation to its role in the community. Civic and professional organizations, special interest groups, and community activities now compete with the simplicity of the mid-20th century, when most activities outside of the home involved the church. Still, local churches look ahead to societal trends to help them tailor programs and groups to meet the needs of a modern world. In Winder, active church groups are working to fulfill their calling, and they continue to seek buildings that will assist them in that effort. (Courtesy of Evelyn Arnold.)

Seven

Civic Life

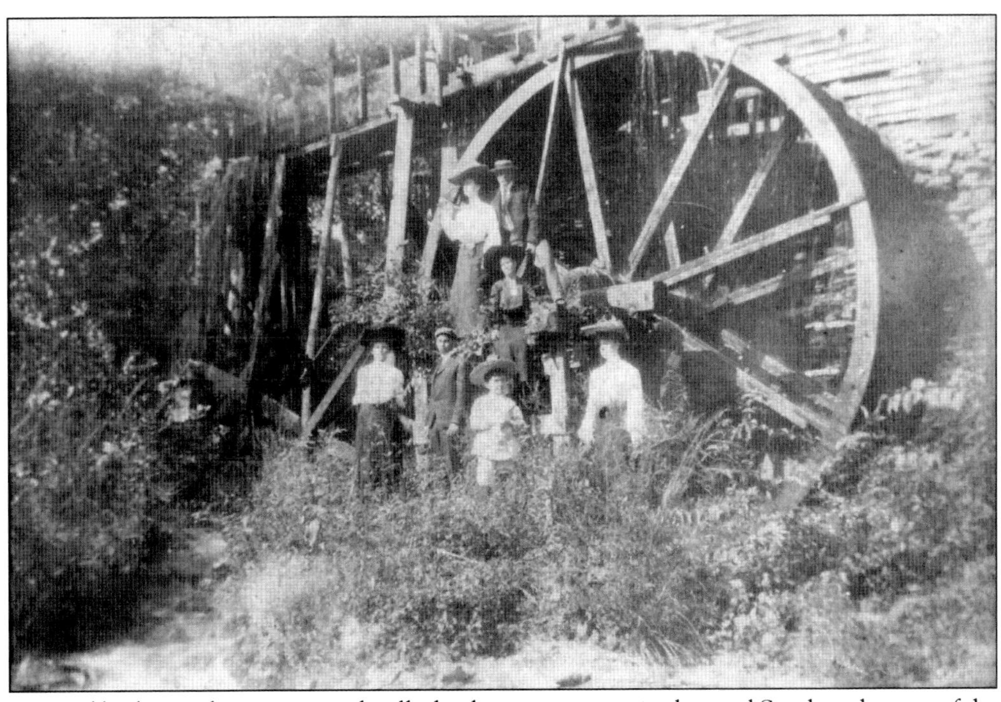

Covered bridges and water-powered mill wheels were common in the rural South at the turn of the 20th century. Because they were located on rivers, grain mills were popular recreational sites for "city folk" wanting to escape the noise and busyness of life in town. This c. 1900 photograph portrays a group of picnickers enjoying the mill wheel on a spring afternoon. (Courtesy of Bob Hill.)

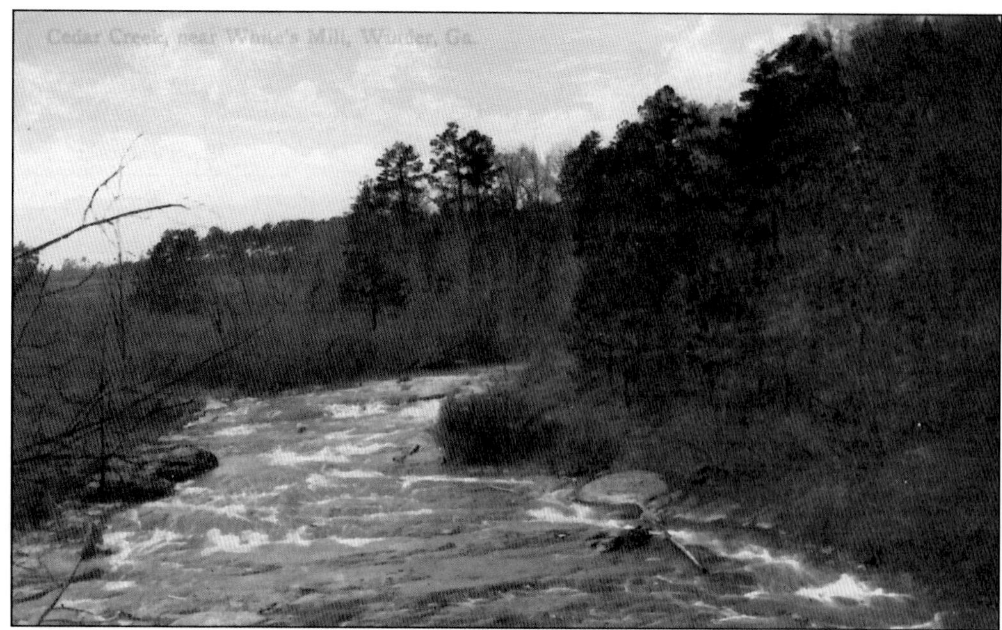

Cedar Creek and its sister tributary, the Mulberry River, are the primary water sources for Winder. Postcard series often highlighted the natural scenery in addition to the signs of progress and prosperity in a community like Winder. This photograph, taken on the outskirts of Winder around 1907, celebrates the cool tranquility of Cedar Creek as it meanders toward White's Mill. (Courtesy of Joe Bowen.)

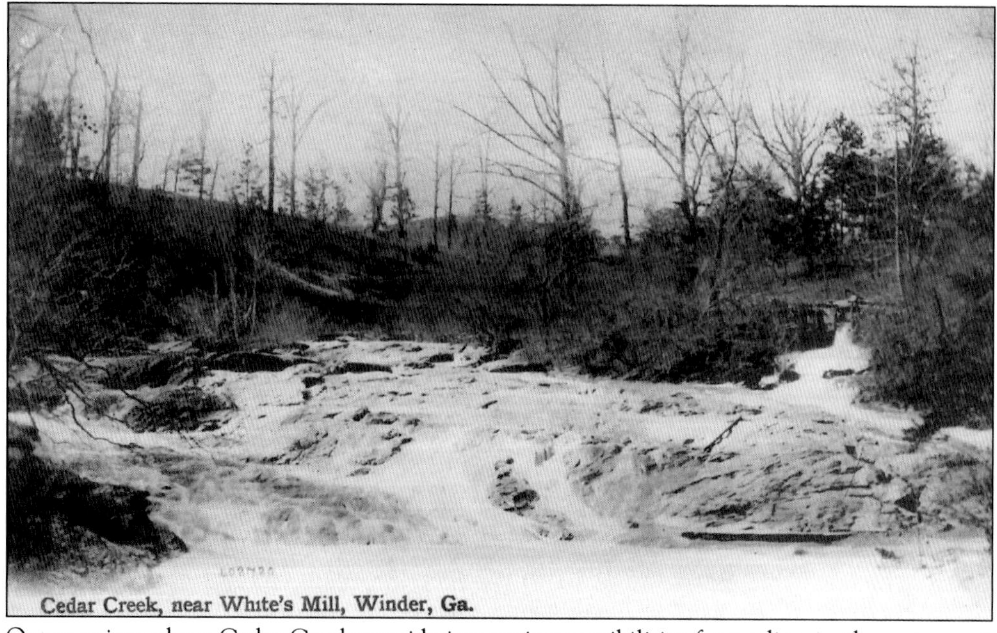

Outcroppings along Cedar Creek provide interesting possibilities for wading in the water as it rushes over the rocks. For many years, daring children and teenagers tried their luck and their balance on the fallen trees stretched to the other side of the creek. Real estate development along Cedar Creek has greatly limited access in recent years, relegating fun afternoons at the creek to distant memory. (Courtesy of Joe Bowen.)

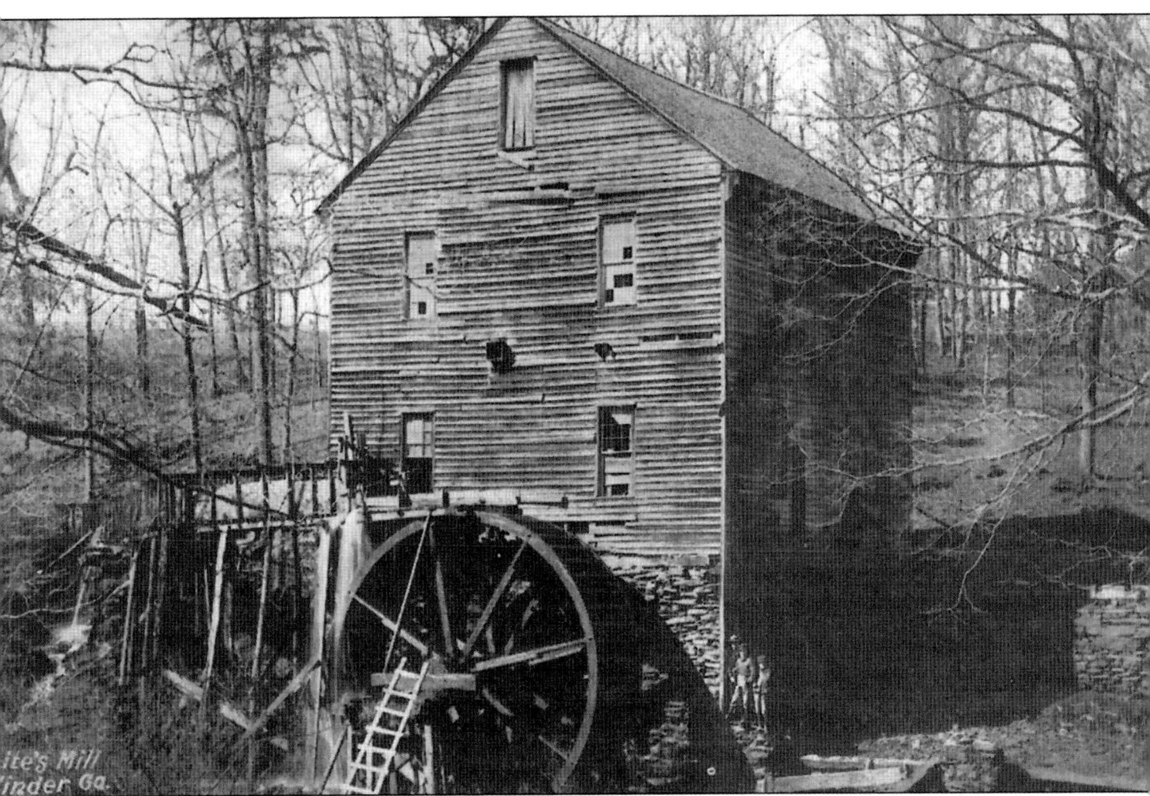

White's Mill was no longer in operation when these postcard images were taken in the early 1900s. Still, the site remained a popular picnic spot for people from Winder. The mill is representative of rural granaries in the South. A simple two-story frame building with side gabled roof, the mill was built strictly to fulfill its purpose rather than to provide a pleasing appearance. Long gone before the end of the 1900s, the White's Mill site is now closed to the public. (Courtesy of Joe Bowen.)

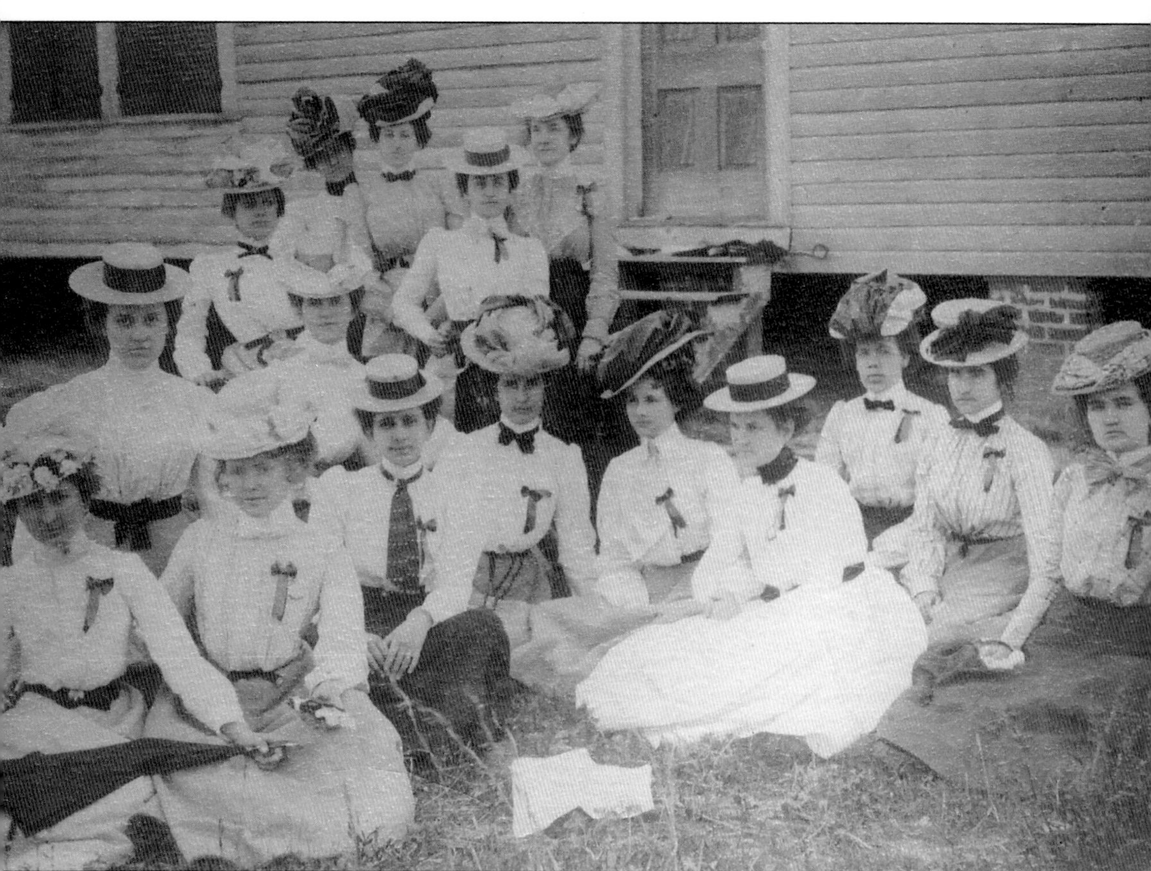

The 20th Century Club, a society of young Winder women, gathered to exchange ideas, make new friends, and become assimilated into the community. A forerunner of the modern civic club, the 20th Century Club was modeled after sister organizations in larger cities. Primarily composed of teachers, the group provided young women with an outlet for socializing and improving oneself at the same time. (Courtesy of Bill Summerour.)

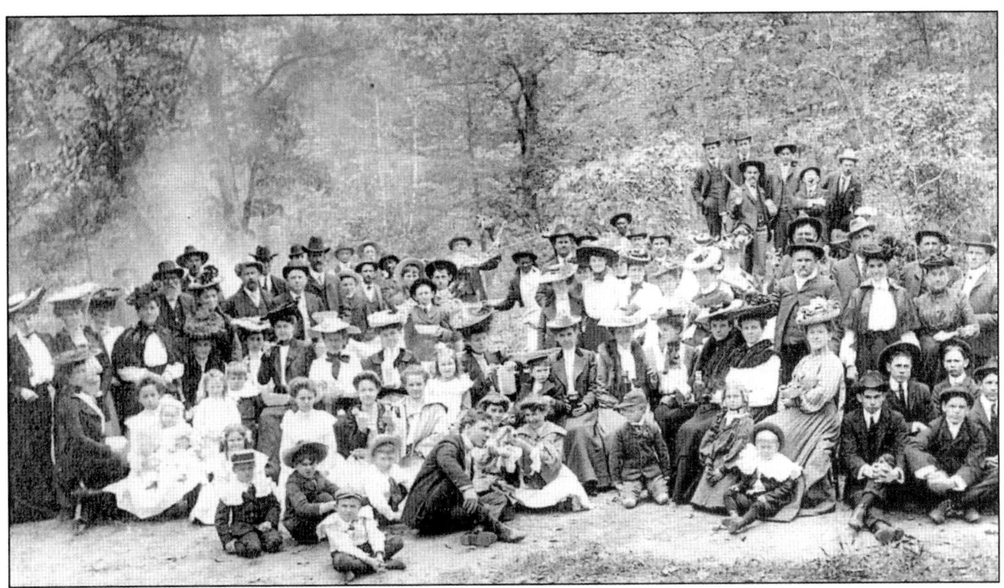

The group in the c. 1900 photograph above included members of Winder's leading families. Transporting a group of this size to the White's Mill picnic site, three miles from town, took a lot of coordination, horsepower, and a determination to gather in the country. These citizens recognized that strong relationships would work to galvanize the community spirit that must undergird any successful civic efforts. (Courtesy of John C. Jackson.)

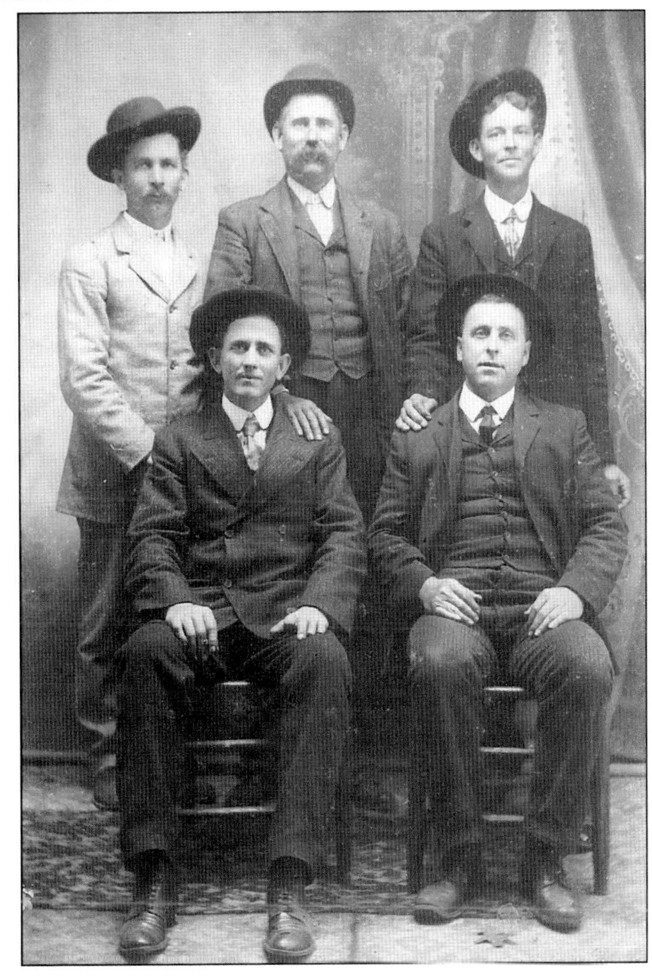

The Ferguson-Coker family (right) contained some of Jug Tavern's leading civic contributors. Offspring of the J.R. Cokers, these five sons absorbed their parents' lesson to take an active interest in their hometown. With eldest son Charles M. Ferguson (upper left) leading the way, this family was involved in every facet of the community and was integral to the city's prosperity. (Courtesy of Bill Summerour.)

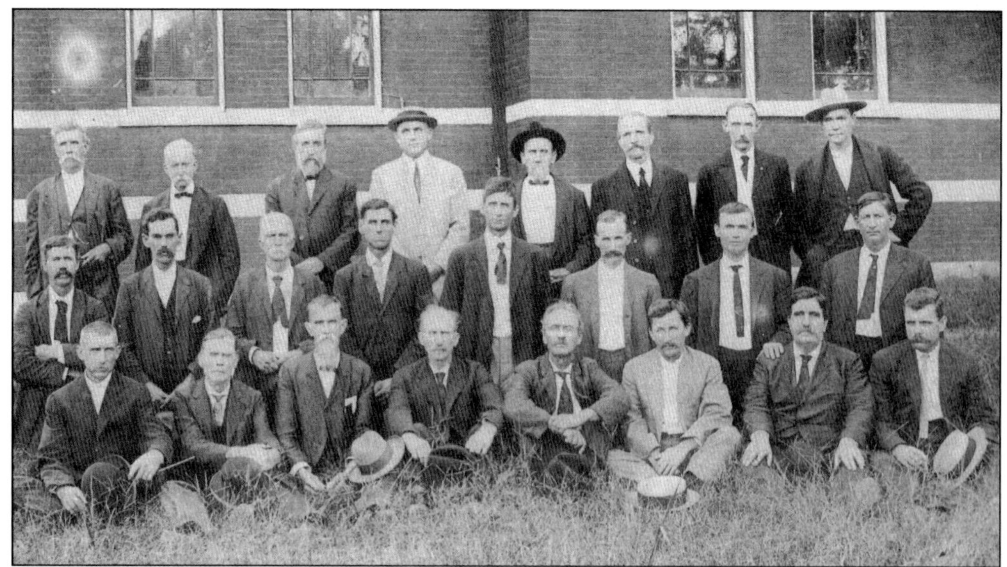

Civic clubs serving the community have been a driving force behind Winder's growth from its beginnings. The Winder Lodge No. 333, Free & Accepted Masons (F&AM), was formed in 1891 as the Jug Tavern Lodge No. 333. The organization's name was changed in 1896. Counting some of the city's most respected leaders among its members, the Winder Lodge was one of the community's first civic organizations and is still active today. (Courtesy of Bob Hill.)

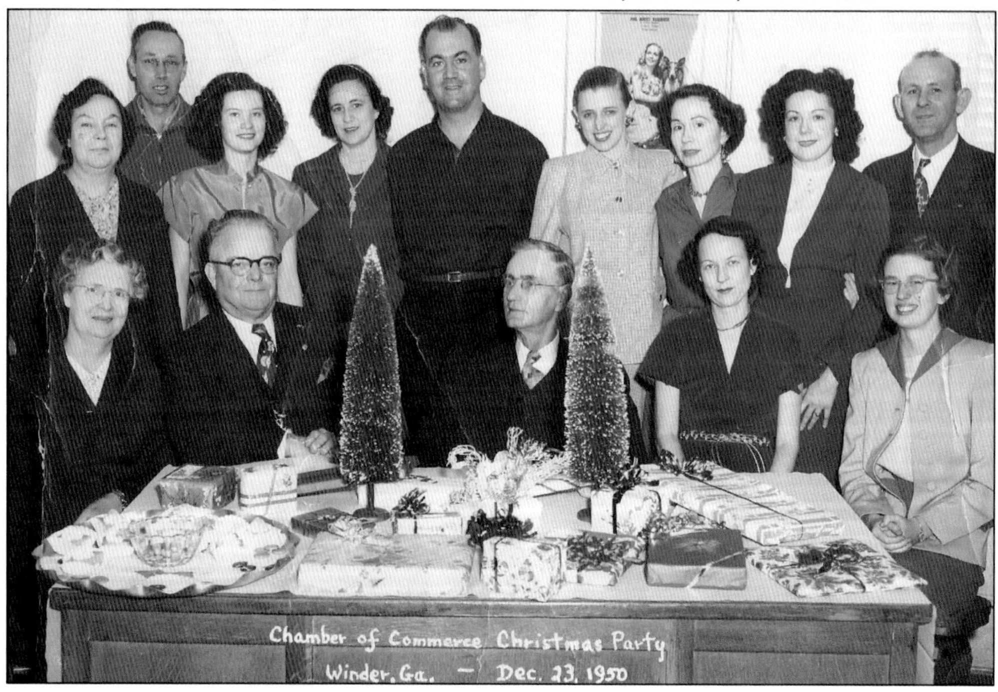

The Winder-Barrow Chamber of Commerce was formed in 1947 to boost jobs throughout Barrow County, recruit new businesses for the area, and address issues such as adequate housing and improvement of athletic and recreational facilities. By harnessing the efforts of businesses throughout the county and its cities, the chamber of commerce provided social and business networking opportunities for the growing community. (Courtesy of Bill Summerour.)

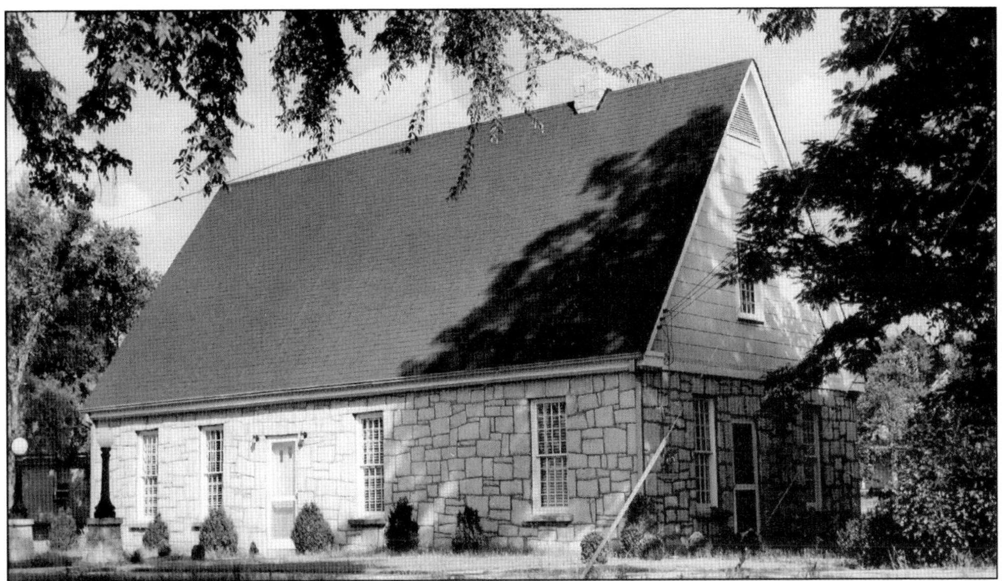

In 1944, Col. Dala Watson built and donated the Federal-style granite building that was named Watson Hall in his honor. The building has served as a meeting place for the Children of the American Revolution (CAR), as well as for its related organizations, the Sons and the Daughters of the American Revolution (SAR and DAR, respectively). A portrait of Colonel Watson was unveiled during the 1954 State Convention of the Children of the American Revolution, which was hosted in Winder by the local chapters. DAR Chapter Regent Mildred Pledger (left) and CAR president Marie Perry (right) looked on as Elaine Smith (second from left) and Carol Thompson (second from right) unveiled the portrait that still hangs in Watson Hall. Watson Hall has served as a meeting place for its associated organizations, as well as serving as a social center for various community groups. (Both images courtesy of Elaine Smith Dickens.)

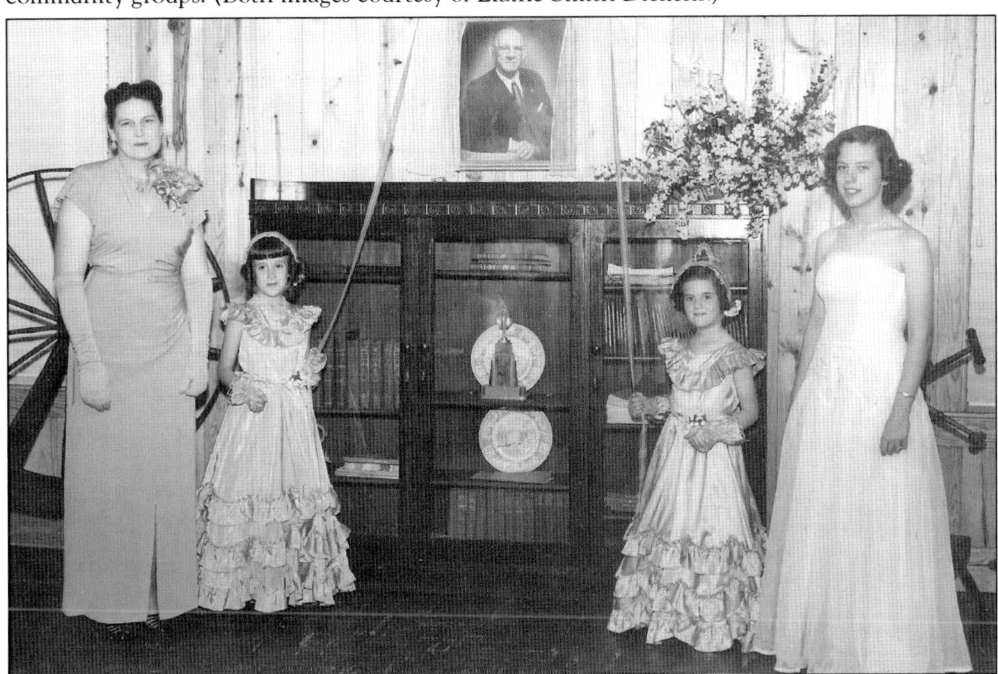

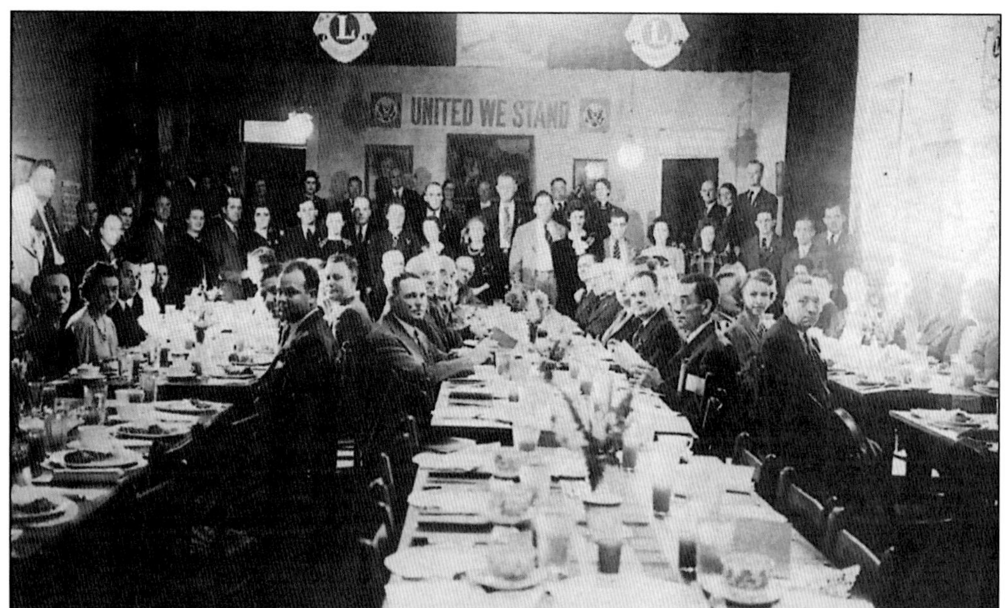

The focus of many civic organizations was to provide opportunities for businessmen to network in an effort to promote their businesses and, ultimately, their community through extended associations with other chapters. The Winder Lions Club was chartered in 1942. The club met in the American Legion Hall for two years before purchasing its first clubhouse on May Street. In 1951, the group purchased its present 13.5-acre property east of downtown and erected a Colonial Revival–style clubhouse. The Winder Lions Club has served the community for over 70 years and is a leader in supporting Little League and Dixie Youth Baseball and programs to benefit the blind and other physically challenged individuals, and it has boosted community involvement for a stronger civic life. The club also sponsored the county fair for more than 25 years. (Above, courtesy of Bob Hill; below, courtesy of Kay Hinton Eddleman.)

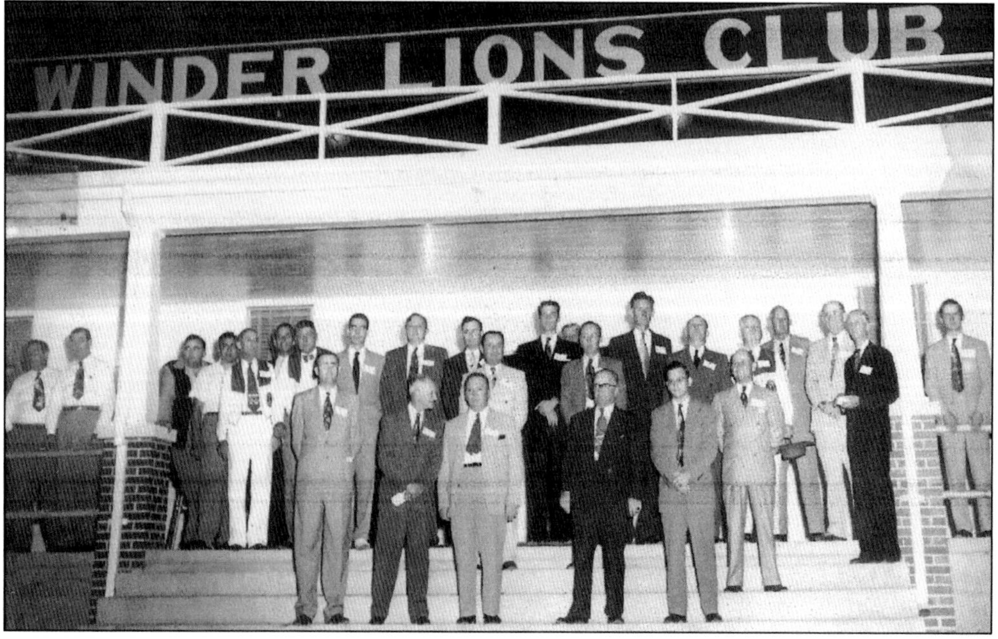

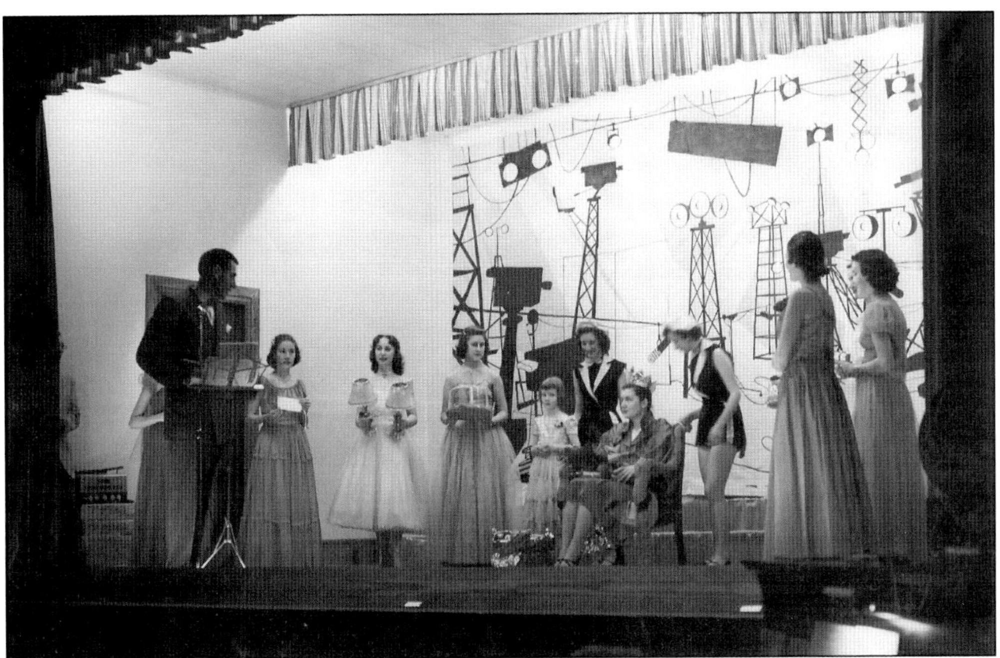

Groups both inside and outside of Winder and Barrow County have benefited from the Winder Lions Club's civic pride. These images depict a 1950s Winder Lions Club Stunt Night that united talent from throughout the city to have fun while raising money to benefit Lions programs. Entertainment, laughter, and good food for a good cause is the recipe the Lions and other organizations have found to be the most successful ally in their efforts. As civic organizations nationwide work to keep community involvement alive, the Winder Lions Club continues its efforts to boost Winder. (Courtesy of Kay Hinton Eddleman.)

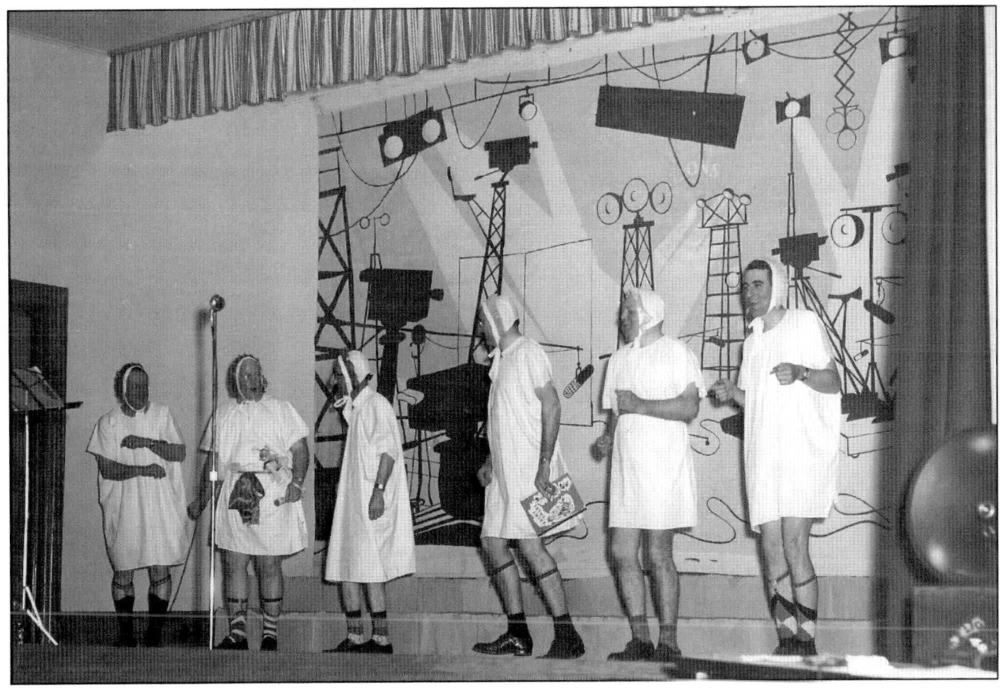

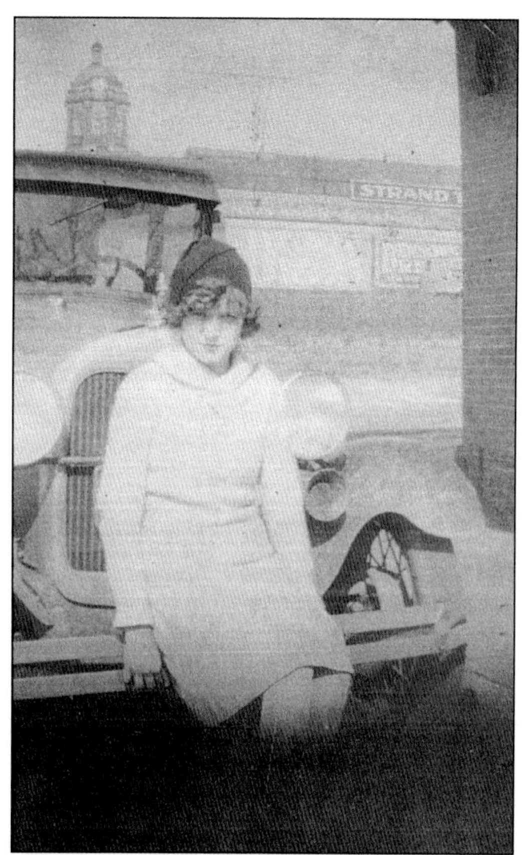

Going to the "picture show" was a social event in Winder from 1916 until the Strand Theatre's marquee was darkened in the late 1970s. With the Barrow County Courthouse and Strand Theatre in the background, a young Reba Garner Hill (pictured at left) waited at the Seaboard Air Line Depot in the early 1930s for her parents to finish their business inside and take her to the movie. Below, five-year-olds Haase Arnold Jr. (left) and Bill Adams saddle up as they excitedly wait for an afternoon with Roy Rogers and Trigger on the big screen. Movie advertisements at the Strand often included live stage performances, sidewalk promotions, and lots of signage to catch the attention of passersby and their eagle-eyed children. (Left, courtesy of Bob Hill; below, courtesy of Evelyn Arnold.)

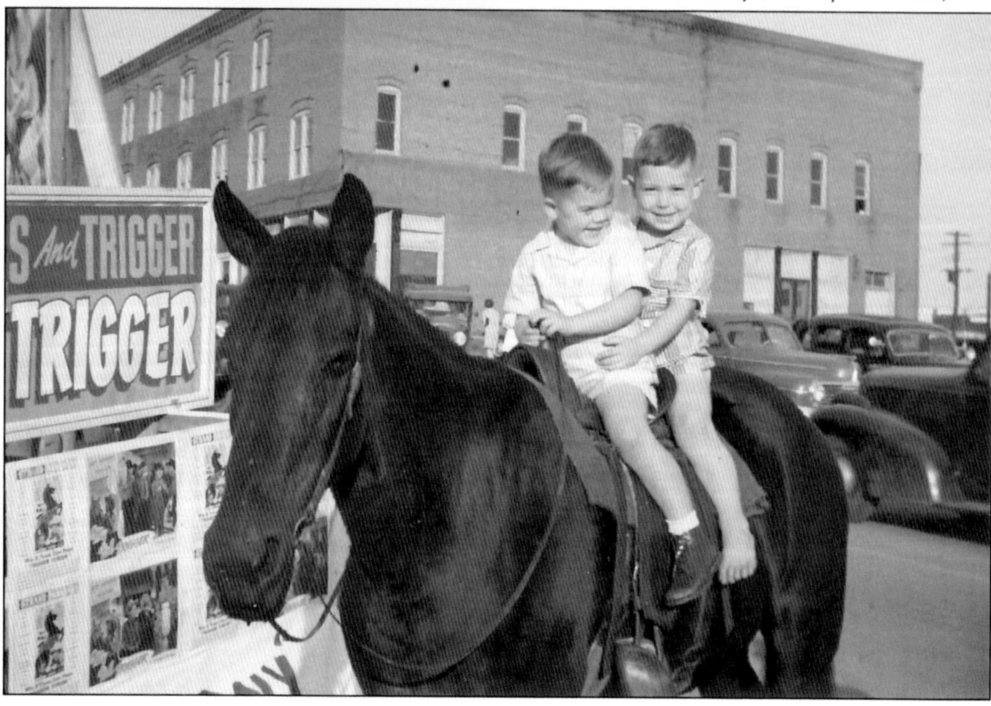

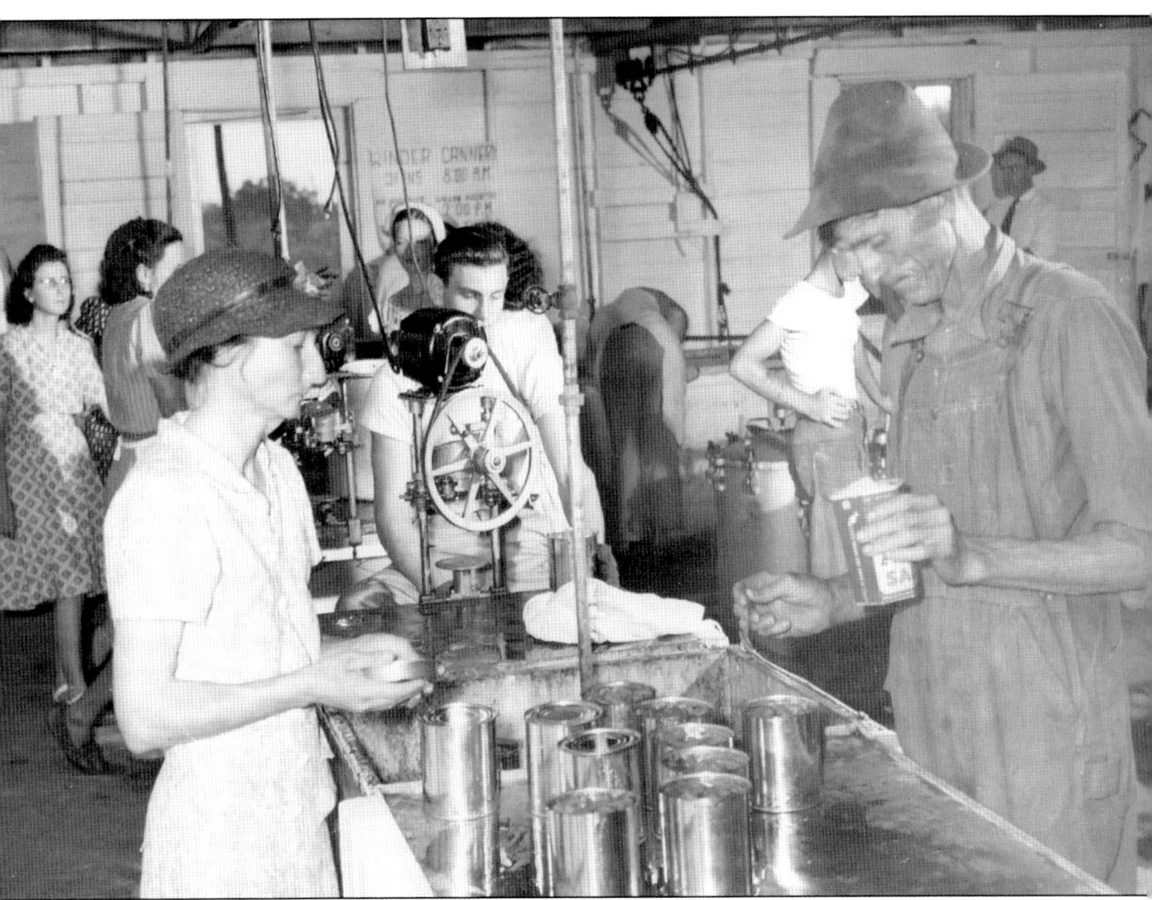

For some people, social involvement took place at the Cannery from the 1930s through the 1950s. The facility, located on West Candler Street near Rose Hill Cemetery, provided local gardeners with the tools and machinery needed to adequately can fruits and vegetables for long-term storage. Going to the Cannery for the afternoon often resulted in learning about different cooking methods, picking up some recipes to try, or making new acquaintances.

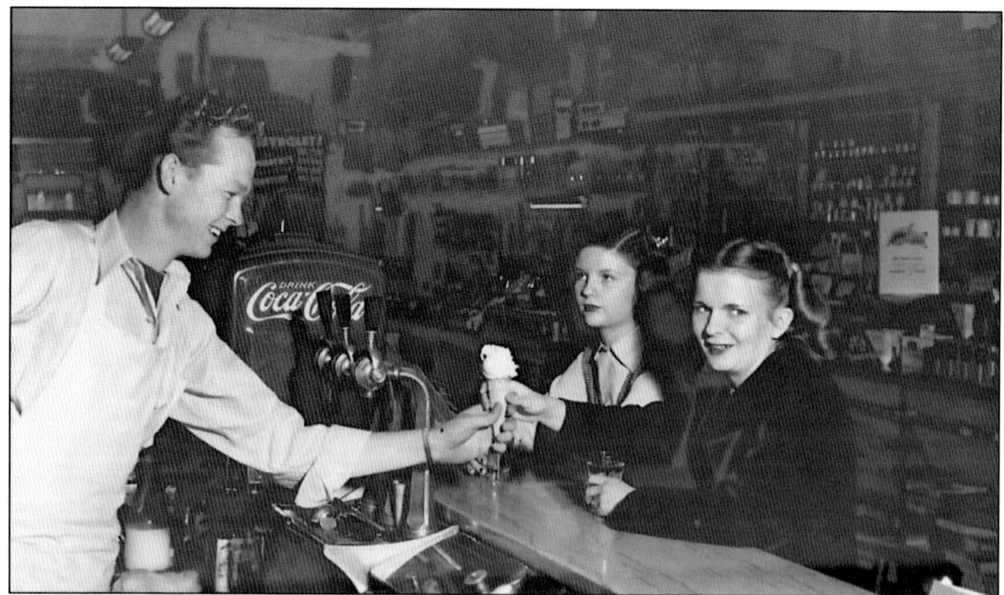

A trip to town meant a stop at the City Pharmacy for a Coke, a sandwich, and some ice cream, of course. Here, Talmadge Phillips serves ice cream and sodas to friends out for an afternoon in downtown Winder. They may have just visited the drugstore for lunch, or they may be going to one of the several dress shops and department stores located in Winder in 1948. (Courtesy of Evelyn Arnold.)

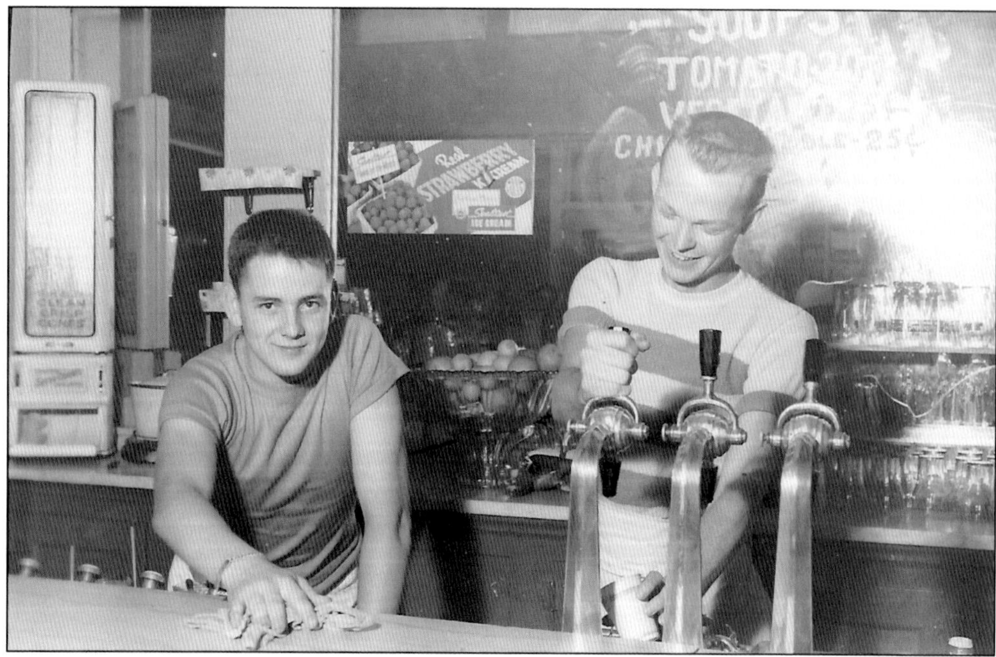

Joe Haynie (left) and Talmadge Phillips were two of the friendly faces jerking sodas at City Pharmacy in downtown Winder. The drugstore became a social center during "the war years" as neighbors gathered for news from overseas. A fixture from the beginning of City Pharmacy and Wages Drugs before it, the soda fountain had marble countertops, bentwood stools, and marble-topped pedestal tables with sweetheart chairs. (Courtesy of Evelyn Arnold.)

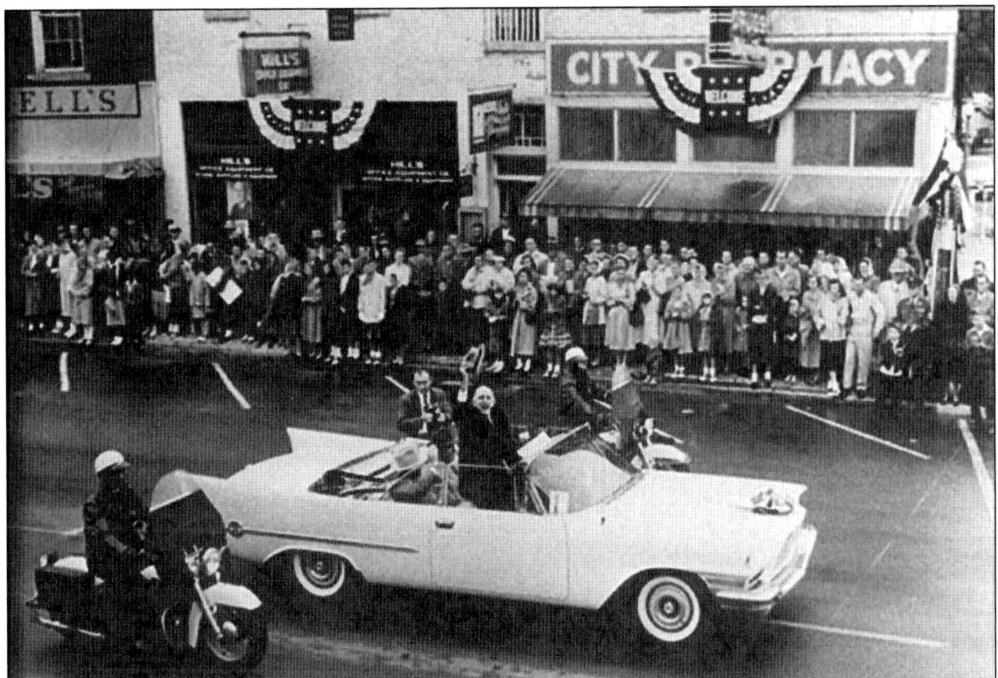

No book about Winder would be complete without mentioning its favorite son, Sen. Richard B. Russell Jr. Senator Russell's long career in public service not only benefited the state of Georgia and the entire country but the city and county. During his three decades in the Senate, Richard Russell never forgot his beloved Winder and came home often to visit family and friends until his death in 1971. Below, Fort Yargo State Park, part of the Marbury Creek Watershed Project, was the beneficiary of a recreational lake that also serves as a conservation site. When the project was dedicated in the 1960s, Richard Russell came home for the event. (Above, courtesy of Bob Hill; below, courtesy of Joe Bowen.)

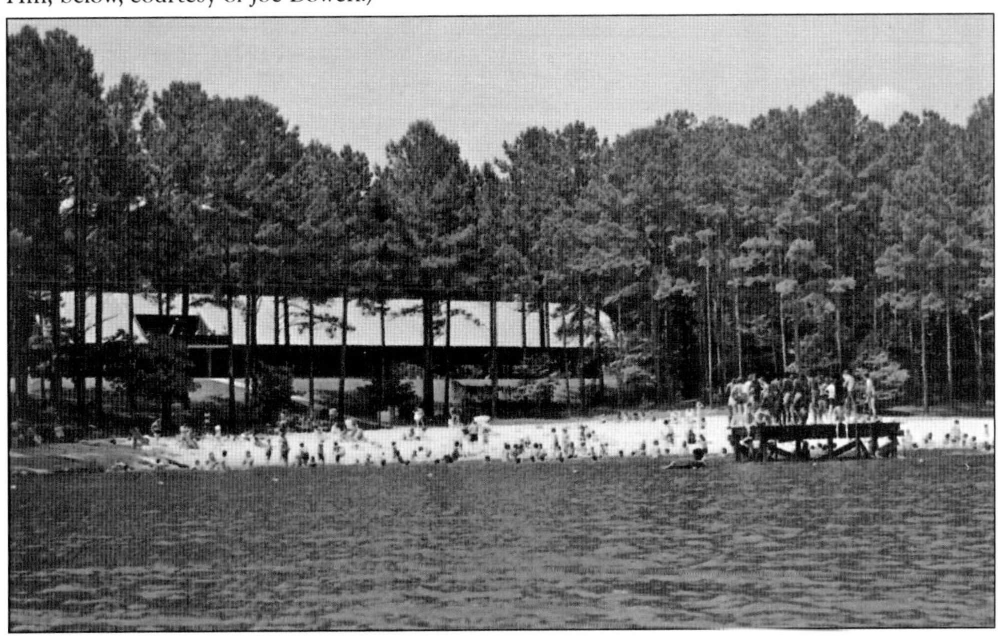

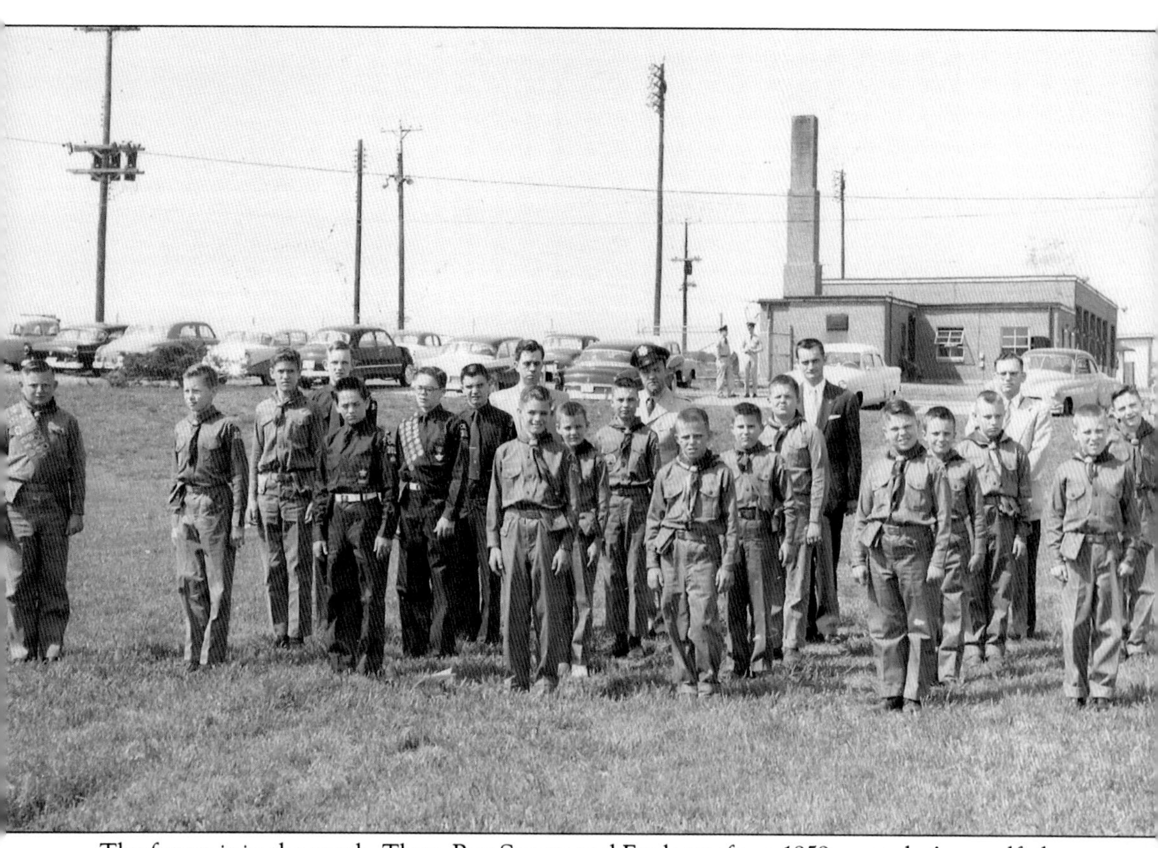

The future is in the youth. These Boy Scouts and Explorers from 1959 are today's grandfathers, civic and business leaders, and active retirees. Their future is based on experiences from their pasts; the people who made their hometown what it was, is, and will be; and how they perpetuate their heritage to be embraced by the leaders of tomorrow. Demonstrating the interdependence of the people of a community with the organizations and facilities contained therein, this troop met at the local National Guard Armory. The National Guard has been part of Winder's fabric since the Winder-Barrow (now Barrow County) Airport was opened shortly after World War II. The airport was established after the military used the site for touch-and-go exercises during the war. (Courtesy of Evelyn Arnold.)

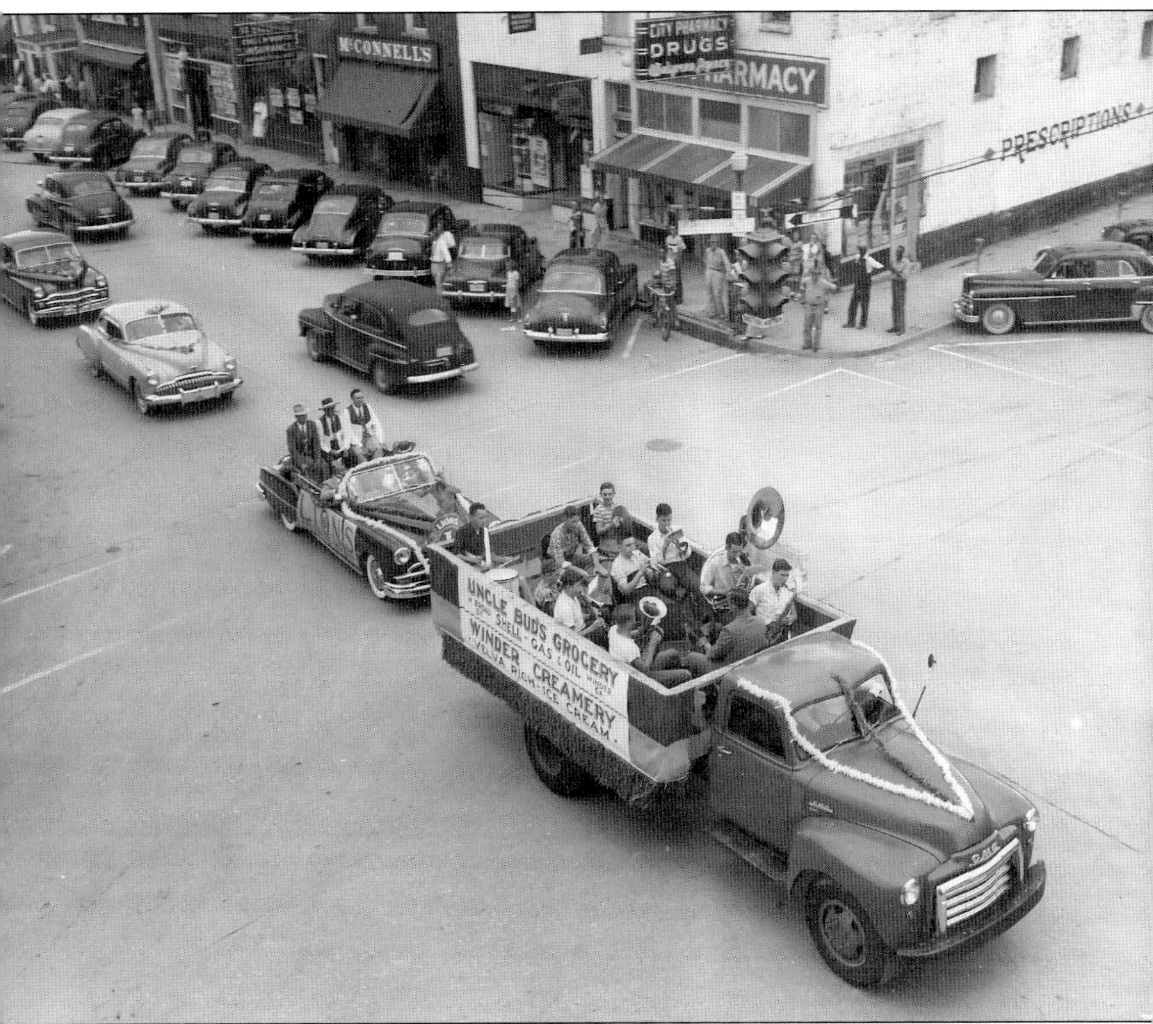

Celebrations have always been a big part of life in Winder. Whether paying homage to a favorite son like Sen. Richard Russell or recognizing youth organizations, businesses, or civic groups, special events play a critical role in supporting the community. Parades and festivals allow the town to encourage and confirm—and commemorative events unite the town for—the common goal of celebrating identity, achievements, the past, and the present. Community events help townspeople recognize and remember interconnectedness and how the path into the future is the key to creating and continuing a vibrant community. As people and parades fade from view, Winder's built heritage serves to remind residents and visitors of the people and events that brought the town to where it is today and inspires visions of the future. (Courtesy of Evelyn Arnold.)

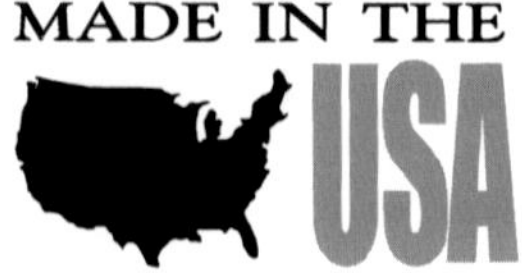
MADE IN THE
USA